DESMOND FENNELL was born in [illegible] ty College Dublin and Bonn [illegible] from the National University [illegible] ked abroad; he taught English in [illegible] rked as a newsreader for German Overse[illegible] an theatre critic for *The Times*. From 1961 to 19[illegible], where he worked as an exhibitions officer for the Arts C[illegible] as an active art critic. He has written for numerous journals and n[illegible]pers, including the *Irish Times,* the *Evening Press* and the *Sunday Press*. He has lived in the Conamara Gaeltacht, where he was involved in the Gaeltacht Civil Rights Movement. From 1976 to 1982 he lectured in Politics and Modern History at University College Galway. In 1990 the National University of Ireland awarded him a doctorate in literature for his published work. In 1993 he retired from teaching English at the Dublin Institute of Technology.

AMONG DESMOND FENNELL'S PUBLISHED WORKS ARE:

Mainly in Wonder (Hutchinson, 1959)
The Changing Face of Irish Catholicism (Chapman, 1968)
The State of the Nation: Ireland Since the 60s (Ward River, 1983)
Beyond Nationalism: The Struggle Against Provinciality in the Modern World (Ward River, 1985)
Nice People and Rednecks: Ireland in the 1980s (Gill and Macmillan, 1986)
A Connacht Journey (Gill and Macmillan, 1987)
The Revision of Irish Nationalism (Open Air, 1989)
Bloomsway: A Day in the Life of Dublin (Poolbeg, 1990)

HERESY

The Battle of Ideas in Modern Ireland

DESMOND FENNELL

THE
BLACKSTAFF
PRESS

BELFAST

First published in 1993 by
The Blackstaff Press Limited
3 Galway Park, Dundonald, Belfast BT16 0AN, Northern Ireland

Typeset by Paragon Typesetters, Queensferry, Clwyd

Printed in England by
The Cromwell Press Limited

A catalogue record for this book
is available from the British Library

ISBN 0-85640-513-2 hardback
0-85640-505-1 paperback

To Bernadette McAliskey
with respect

One loves the freedom of men because
one loves men.
There is therefore a deep humanism in every
true Nationalist.
PÁDRAIG PEARSE

CONTENTS

FOREWORD

THE RECENT ESSAYS gathered in this book represent a view of Ireland in the world garnered in thirty years of active observation and reflection. Born in Belfast, I was brought to Dublin as a child, grew up there and made it my city; but until I was eighteen I spent every Christmas and some summer holidays in Belfast. It was my other home. After various exiles, the last of them in the Conamara Gaeltacht and Galway, I returned to Dublin in 1982 and have spent the last eleven years there. In Dublin now, because of the prevailing wind, most of my ideas rank as thought-crime. They are not approved of by right-thinking people and, because these control the national media and influence or partly occupy the academic world, not publicly discussed. Hence the title, which is more fully explained in the last essay.

My central concern, obvious in this book, is the restoration of Irish humanity after its historical wounding. If I must choose an ism, it is humanism. I take particular inspiration from the humanism of Douglas Hyde, who, a hundred years ago, helped to found the Gaelic League and thereby, as Pearse said, start the Irish Revolution. More clearly than any before him, Hyde perceived and said that the restoration of Irish humanity must begin with the restoration of Irish intellect. For him the Gaelic League was 'the intellectual movement'. The revolution which it unleashed was, essentially, the reassembled Irish mind creating

ideas, lives and literature, and generating courageous action. Standing in this tradition, and conscious that it is under assault from
within, I have worked at developing it, restating it and applying
it to present circumstances. Although the fact that, at home, we
are only 4 million people makes success a very reasonable object,
we Irish are still far from being, in our modern incarnation, a
successful human collective – economically, demographically,
intellectually or, for the past quarter-century, politically. This
merits thought. But thought, and particularly humanistic thought,
depends for its efficacy on realism. Consequently, the secondary
concern of these essays is for realistic vision – for naming things
by their names, dispelling murk and illusion, exposing propagated
lies.

The first two pieces were written in 1981–82, when I was near-
ing the end of my fourteen-year sojourn in the West, the others
in Dublin between 1984 and the beginning of 1993. Presented
in chronological order, they constitute a progressive reflection
that culminates in the long concluding essay.

Some of them might not have seen the light if they had not
been commissioned; hence a special word of gratitude to Dr
Declan Kiberd and Professor Richard Kearney. Dr Kiberd, first
as editor of a special issue of the *Crane Bag*, later as Director of
the Yeats Summer School, inspired, respectively, 'The Last Years
of the Gaeltacht' and 'The Humanism of James Connolly and
George Russell'. Professor Kearney, as editor of *The Irish Mind*
and *Across the Frontiers: Ireland in the 1990s*, prompted 'Irish Socialist
Thought' and 'The Independence of Ireland in the 1990s'. For
the hard work of 'Getting to Know Dublin 4' I am grateful to
Austen Morgan for inviting me to read a paper to the Fourteenth
Lipman Seminar at Ruskin College, Oxford, in 1992.

My monograph on the reputation and poetry of Seamus Heaney
raised the questions of what makes poetry great and how to charac-
terise the poetry of consumer capitalism, which succeeded that
of modernism. In contemporary Irish literary criticism, such large

themes are seldom addressed, and my own views on both topics still remain unanswered in Ireland. On these, as on every other topic I have dealt with, it was neither my aim nor my hope to have the last word. It just happened that way, and the silence frustrated me. Indeed, the Heaney essay was a conscious breaking both of the virtual critical silence on Heaney in the Republic – apart from reviews, there had been only three or four short pieces while nine books appeared elsewhere – and of the total critical silence, in the Republic, on the overblown reputation his poetry had acquired abroad. Inasmuch as my aim was to correct this hyperbolic reputation, level the playing field for contemporary Irish poets, and reclaim sovereignty for Irish criticism in the assessment of Irish literature, I believe my essay accomplished, in Ireland and Britain, what it set out to do.

The last two essays, 'Getting to Know Dublin 4' and 'Intellect and National Welfare', are published for the first time in this book. I am very grateful to Dr Brian Arkins for his helpful comments while I was working on them.

MINSK, JUNE 1993

1

THE LAST YEARS
OF THE
GAELTACHT

LONG BEFORE THE GAELTACHT was christened it had begun to die. *Exister c'est mourir un peu* was always its motto. It began its anonymous dying in places like north County Dublin, south Wexford and east Down in the early seventeenth century. More than two centuries later, when it was finally named the Gaeltacht – after its Scottish counterpart – it existed only west of the Shannon, in Donegal and Kerry, and in poor, geographically isolated pockets in most of the other counties.

The Gaeltacht Commission, appointed by the Free State government, reported in 1926 that the 'Irish-speaking Areas' (groups of district electoral divisions where more than 80 per cent of the people were able to speak Irish) had a population of 165,000. The commission also noted 'partly Irish-speaking Areas' with a total population of 295,000. In 1956 the government drew a line on the map to define the Gaeltacht. This official Gaeltacht, which everyone knew to be considerably larger than the real Gaeltacht, had a population of 86,000. By 1971 that had shrunk to 71,000. Four years later I investigated the extent of the real Gaeltacht – the districts and pockets where Gaelic was the usual language spoken – and found that it had a population of 29,000, located in two districts in Donegal, one in Conamara and one in Kerry,

From the *Crane Bag*, Vol. 5, No. 2, 1981

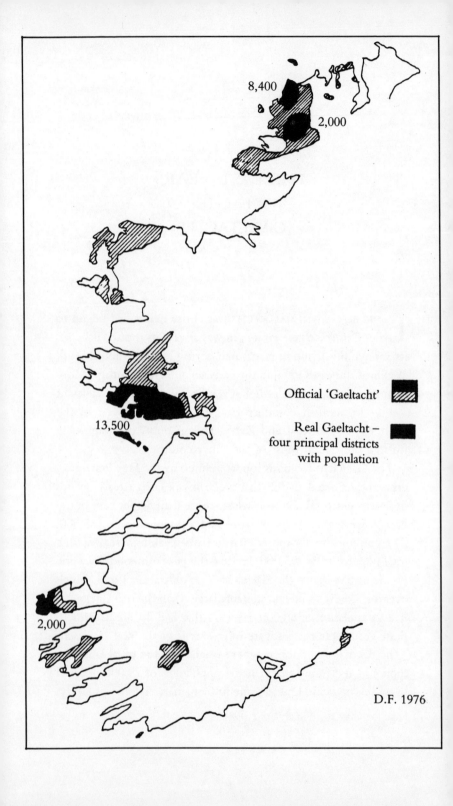

8,400

2,000

Official 'Gaeltacht'

Real Gaeltacht –
four principal districts
with population

13,500

2,000

D.F. 1976

and eight pockets of 200–800 inhabitants. The district comprising most of South Conamara with the Aran Islands was the largest: it had a population of 13,500.

In the course of the 1970s, in most parts of the (real) Gaeltacht, most parents of young children began to rear them in English. Families rearing their children in Gaelic became a matter for comment. Both on this account and because families with English-speaking children were returning from Britain to share in the Gaeltacht's growing prosperity, the language of several large Gaeltacht primary schools changed from Gaelic to English. It seems, therefore, that the end of the Gaeltacht is now in sight.

When I settled, with my wife and two sons, aged five and three, in Maoinis, near Cárna, Conamara, in 1968, Maoinis was entirely Gaelic-speaking. It is an island, joined to the mainland by a bridge, and has a population of about 180 people. Almost everyone here still speaks Gaelic, but English is making inroads. My two sons, under the influence of their school and playmates, changed their usual language from English to Gaelic. Their three sisters have grown up Gaelic-speaking but, like everyone else in the Gaeltacht, able to speak English too. Judging by the way things are going, we will have been among the last immigrants into the Gaeltacht to become Gaelic-speaking. Previously, of course, this was a common phenomenon. The Gaelic-speakers of the Conamara Gaeltacht are by no means all pure Gaels – as the family names Welby, Dundass, Maude, Cooke (Ó Cuaig), de Búrca, Bairéad, Breathnach, etcetera testify.

Brian Friel's play *Translations* dramatises the alienating effect on Gaelic-speaking people of the Gaelic place names being translated into English, or anglicised, by the Ordnance Survey in the nineteenth century. In fact this was only a superficially alienating experience because the Gaelic-speakers continued to use the original Gaelic names, at least for the places in their own immediate localities. Something much more alienating happens when the spoken language changes to English, for then a whole network of local place names dissolves in a collective amnesia.

Since I got to know the land and sea names in and around Maoinis, I have often thought of this. Every large rock on sea or land, every cove and field, every rise or turn on the road, has a name. Consequently, as one looks out across a scene, it is not a mere scene but a dense web of names, a minutely intelligible grid in which one can fix the position of a man or a thing precisely. This detailed naming of the land and sea over centuries is the basic activity by which people domesticate raw nature. By imposing meaning, in this manner, on a section of the earth's surface, they make it mentally manageable and transform it into a place where they can feel at home.

I know from visiting places that have lost Gaelic recently, say, in the previous generation, that most of this toponomic network here in Maoinis will get lost in the translation to English. Crompán na gCapall will be 'that cove over there', Carraig an Iarainn 'that rock', Ard na gCadhan 'that hump there on the road beyant'. Meaning and homeliness will vanish, largely, from the environment. There will be a sort of silence as things and places cease to answer with names to the looking eye. Places where Gaelic has been lost recently are palpably sad – as I am sure are those places that have recently lost Welsh, Breton or Sardinian. It takes a long time for all that naming to be done again in the new language.

The Gaelic that is spoken today in the Gaeltacht, and which is gradually being abandoned, is a very thin language compared with the spoken Gaelic of three hundred, a hundred, or fifty years ago. While the Gaeltacht has been shrinking, territorially, its language has been shrinking in vocabulary. Among the first sets of words to go, I suppose, were those connected with Brehon law, the aristocracy and the Gaelic political structure. These were replaced to some extent, but not in the same abundance, by new terms referring to the corresponding English realities.

Much nearer our own time, a huge loss of vocabulary occurred

when the craft industries largely disappeared from the countryside in face of competition from factory products. In Maoinis today
you see people working in the fields, fishing, gathering seaweed,
building houses and making boats. Eighty years ago there were
coopers, nail-makers, sail-makers, weavers, tailors, cobblers and
so on. There were two grain mills within a few miles. People
burned limestone in kilns, made kelp from seaweed. The technical
vocabularies connected with all of these and other crafts are completely gone, and nothing equivalent has replaced them. Most
of the new technical terms are the raw English words, not even
phonetically gaelicised. Similarly, with the disappearance of herbal
medicine and its practitioners, a huge wealth of medical and
botanical terms has gone.

More recently still, when the arrival of television put an end
to evenings listening to the *seanchaí,* another great impoverish-
ment took place. It was not that the language of the old tales
or of the *seanchaí*'s historical anecdotes had ever become part of
the everyday speech of his listeners – no more than stylish literary
language or the vocabulary of history enters into everyday speech
in any tongue. It was rather that the *seanchaí*'s language of imagination and of past realities lodged, to a greater or lesser degree, in
people's minds, expanded the known frontiers of their worka-
day Gaelic, and gave them a non-utilitarian verbal resource on
which they could draw, occasionally, in thought or speech.

Obviously, what sets a language on the road to death is, in
the first instance, a complex of political events and circumstances
and the impact of these on the speakers' feelings and consciousness.
But once the ball has been set rolling, so to speak, the central
and decisive factor that keeps it rolling is the language as a
representation of the speakers' actual world. As one linguistic
register after another is lost or torn to shreds, the language becomes
a wounded thing, a less and less efficient instrument for that
representation of experienced reality that is a language's basic function. And all the time, the winning language is beckoning with

its superior capability for just such a representation.

Of course, the language revival movement has been well aware of the need to make Gaelic, once again, an adequate instrument for representing the world. It has made it capable of rendering the Treaty of Rome, teaching chemistry, and discussing aesthetics in a contemporary manner. There is probably a Department of Education manual that supplies Gaelic names for all the parts of a car. But virtually none of this has impinged on the Gaeltacht. The language movement has been largely an urban – and principally a Dublin – phenomenon, and it has not concerned itself with supplying the Gaeltacht's needs. Thus, the 'new Gaelic' of the language revival has seemed for Gaeltacht people, by and large, a strangers' language. For this reason, most Gaeltacht schoolteachers shy away from it in the classroom. Just as they would be embarrassed to speak it at home or to their neighbours, they would be embarrassed to teach it to the children with whom they share a common *native* language of impoverished Gaelic mixed with English.

If I seem to be saying that the Gaelic now ordinarily spoken in the Gaeltacht is not much loss, I am not quite saying that, but something near to it. There is still rich Gaelic speech, and even the most commonplace phrases of the spoken language have such a poignancy, resonance and rightness in their environment that the thought of this language not being spoken here is very painful. At the same time, living in the Gaeltacht and sending children to its schools, I cannot help being horrified, both on educational and on moral grounds, by the linguistic mishmash of Gaelic and English in which the schooling is now delivered – partly due to the lack of adequate textbooks in Gaelic, partly because the Department of Education includes pockets of complete English-speakers in the catchment areas of Gaeltacht schools, and partly because most of the native Gaeltacht teachers do not take Gaelic seriously as a *subject*. One sees that; one knows the language is lost; one thinks of that dreadful, impending silence of the much-named landscape; and one wishes – whether rationally or not – that, for the people's sake and the children's sake, the decision to change to English could be taken *now,* by decree, and carried through by all sorts of intelligent, skilful committees in a planned and merciful fashion.

I have discussed elsewhere why the attempt by the Irish state to 'save the Gaeltacht' has failed[1] and I will not rehearse it all again here. Suffice to say that, basically, it is because, when the effort started, the Gaeltacht was shrinking as it had been shrinking for three hundred years, and no one, then or later, aroused in the people of the Gaeltacht the will to stop that shrinkage, or even tried seriously to do this. Consequently, the shrinking went on as before, while all the state's efforts – the language movement had more important things to do! – resulted, from the 1960s onwards, merely in reducing emigration from the diminishing Gaeltacht and in making what remained of it materially prosperous. (The latter was achieved, initially, by imported factories which were managed, by and large, by English-speakers.)

During the past twelve years, in the four main Gaeltacht districts with a total population of 25,500, we have had a tantalising glimpse of what might have been. Powered by the rising prosperity, and by the imaginative leadership of a few groups and individuals comprising essentially about thirty persons, the Gaelic-speaking communities have put together a structure of life and activity that, if the will to stop the language erosion were there, could have launched them, Gaelic-speaking and expanding, into the twenty-first century.

In Iarchonnacht – that is, the South Conamara Gaeltacht with the Aran Islands – this lurch towards collective self-possession has been on the biggest scale and most pervasive. A dense network

1. See pp. 339–43 of 'Organising Connacht for Economic and Social Growth', *Administration,* Autumn 1976; 'The Last Days of the Gaeltacht' and 'Why the Gaeltacht Wasn't Saved', *Irish Times,* 3 and 4 June, 1980; and 'Can a Shrinking Linguistic Minority Be Saved?', in E. Haugen, J.D. McClure and D.S. Thomson (eds.), *Minority Languages Today* (Edinburgh: Edinburgh University Press, 1981)

of elected half-parish councils and of cooperatives made this the most highly organised district of 14,000 inhabitants in all of Ireland. Agitation brought about a local radio station with sub-studios in Kerry and Donegal and struck back against the *Translations* process by getting the barbarities removed from the bilingual signposts and the Gaelic names displayed alone. Locally written journals were distributed, sold and read. One of the largest and most modern fleets of trawlers in Ireland was assembled and manned. New literary and musical festivals and new football tournaments were organised. The old sailing boats, no longer used – or hardly used – for fishing or transport, were refurbished and crewed for annual regatta seasons. And virtually all of this was done in Gaelic. But far from being a linguistic takeoff, it was the last wingflap of the wounded eagle.

Three years after we settled in Maoinis, my six-year-old son came back to the house one day and told me that he had been on the beach with a neighbour's child and they had been talking to a Frenchman. The Frenchman had asked questions, in English, about the Gaelic language which he had heard being spoken. The neighbour's child informed him, 'Gaelic is no good.' 'Nach raibh sé sin an-droch-bhéasach?' – 'Wasn't that very ill-mannered?' – my son said to me. He was shocked, in his innocence, that anyone should speak thus of the language they spoke and could find no more appropriate word to describe the indecency than 'ill-mannered'. For myself, as I reflected on the child's words – 'Gaelic is no good' – it was more than a shocking lapse of taste. Translated back into the thought it sprang from – 'Níl aon mhaith leis an nGaeilge' – it was the poisoned pin inserted into the eagle's body four centuries ago, in places like north County Dublin, south Wexford and east Down, and never removed.

2

IRISH SOCIALIST
THOUGHT

IN HIS HISTORICAL PREFACE to the English translation of Anton Menger's *Right to the Whole Produce of Labour* (1899), Professor H.S. Foxwell of University College London wrote that 'Socialist propaganda has been mainly carried on by men of Celtic or Semitic blood.' When he used the word Celtic, he was thinking primarily of the Welshman Robert Owen and Irishmen such as William Thompson, John Doherty, Feargus O'Connor and James Bronterre O'Brien.

The leading thinker of that group, and the first Irish socialist, was William Thompson, born in Cork in 1775. His father, Alderman John Thompson, a prosperous Cork merchant and member of the Protestant Ascendancy, had a 1,500-acre estate at Roscarbery, forty miles west of the city. As a young man, William Thompson travelled on the Continent and spent some time in France and the Netherlands. He read Saint-Simon, Sismondi and similar French thinkers who believed (as he later wrote) that the 'tendency of civilisation and of manufacturing improvements was to deteriorate the situation of the industrious classes as compared with that of the idle classes'. Back in Ireland he was a supporter of Catholic emancipation. When he inherited the family property in 1814, he went to live in Roscarbery and became an improving

From Richard Kearney (ed.), *The Irish Mind* (Dublin: Wolfhound, 1985)

landlord. Besides giving leases on generous terms and seeing that his tenants were well housed and properly equipped, he instructed them in the latest agricultural methods and put his knowledge of chemistry and medicine at their disposal. His personal kindness made them tolerant of his atheism and anticlericalism, and of his utilitarian carping about the number of Church holidays.

Thompson was a humorous, idealistic man of penetrating mind and frugal habits: he neither smoked nor drank and, in the latter part of his life, he was a vegetarian. As a member of the local Philosophical, Scientific and Literary Society, and as one of the proprietors of the Cork Institution – founded to provide education cheaply for middle-class children – he took a prominent part in the intellectual life of Cork. Obsessed by a sense of guilt about living on rent, 'the produce of the effort of others', he sought redemption by devoting himself to the welfare of others. He hoped thereby to 'raise himself to an equality of usefulness with the productive classes'. As the word 'usefulness' there might indicate, and as I have already suggested, he was a utilitarian and a follower of Jeremy Bentham. Finding that the Cork Institution was not fulfilling its functions properly, and that he was making no headway with his co-proprietors, he addressed himself to the public in a pamphlet called *Practical Education for the South of Ireland*. While working on this he had some correspondence with Bentham. They became friends and Bentham invited him to London.

Essentially, Thompson was a humanist. His basic concern was that men and women might live together contentedly, free from anxiety, and as human beings ought to live – morally, generously, and in relationships of mutual trust, respect and help. Believing that the 'excessively unequal' distribution of wealth prevented this, he wanted to work out a science of society that would show the wrongness of this inequality and of the production relationships based on it, and justify the creation of a different system favourable to man. This was the purpose he had in mind when, in 1822, he accepted Bentham's invitation and went to study the problem in the capital of modern capitalism.

In London, first in Bentham's house and later living near him, he got to know the leading English utilitarians. He also met Robert Owen and studied his ideas on cooperative communities. From the first, he disagreed with Owen's belief that such communities could be brought into being by the enlightened action of the rich or with funds supplied by capitalists. He wrote:

> The rich, as a class, like all other classes in every community, must obey the influences of the peculiar circumstances in which they are placed, must acquire the inclinations and the characters, good or bad, which spring out of the state of things surrounding them from their birth.

Only 'a few individuals' may rise above the impulses of their class and view impartially matters closely related to them. Thompson became convinced that cooperative communities, created by the 'industrious classes' themselves, were the right way to organise society.

In 1824 he published his first major work, *An Inquiry into the Principles of Distribution of Wealth Most Conducive to Human Happiness; Applied to the Newly-Proposed System of Voluntary Equality of Wealth*. That last phrase referred to the Owenite communitarian programme. The central argument of this book is that the distribution of wealth should be reorganised on the principles of equality and of the labourer retaining the full product of his labour. The existing, unequal distribution of wealth stood condemned because it was conducive not to the greatest happiness of the greatest number and to virtuous living but to their opposites, and because it involved the robbery and exploitation of the majority who possessed no capital by the minority who did.

Building on Ricardo's thesis that the value of a commodity was equal to the value of the labour that produced it, Thompson argued that labour was the source of value. Capital was 'that portion of the product of labour which, whether of a permanent nature or not, is capable of being made the instrument of profit'. In natural justice the labourer was entitled to the full value that his labour had provided, less depreciation of the capital employed. However, 'as long as the accumulated capital of society remains in one set of hands, and the productive power of creating wealth in another, the accumulated capital will be made use of to counteract the natural laws of distribution and to deprive the producers of the use of what their labour has produced'. The 'surplus value', that is, the product value over and above the lowest wage payable, will be appropriated by the capitalists. They had the power to do this, not only because they possessed, in their capital, the available means of production, but also because they controlled directly or indirectly the state power, the judiciary and priesthood. 'As long as a class of mere capitalists exists . . .' they 'must be always law-makers'. 'The whole system of human regulations' was 'little more than a tissue of restraints of one class over another'.

Distribution of Wealth had much to say about the 'competitive' nature of modern capitalism (Thompson was the first to use this word to describe it, as he was the first to use 'industrial' in its modern sense). In measured, passionate language, he described how the enforced competition between individuals, rich and poor, corrupted human relationships and caused widespread apathy, fury, and spiritual suffering.

Cooperative communities, Thompson argued, would eliminate competitiveness and allow both the equal distribution of wealth and the retention by the labourers of the full product of their labour. Productivity, far from decreasing (as some suggested) because the whiplash of fear and insecurity had been removed, would increase greatly through the release of the creative forces of the individual workers. The resulting, more widespread affluence would not, as Malthus argued, lead inevitably to an excessive increase in population. On the one hand, the tendency to improvident multiplication decreased with affluence; on the other hand, people could be educated in methods of birth control. Then, with sexual intercourse made independent of childbearing, women equal with men, and divorce easily available, each community could make rational regulations for sexual intercourse and pursue a prudent population policy. Thompson predicted that under communism the state and religion would wither away. 'Almost all the occasions for the exercise of the ordinary functions of government would have ceased.' Public opinion would replace coercive laws. With spreading enlightenment and growing affluence, 'the trade of religion, like the trade of law' would gradually cease.

With the publication of *Distribution of Wealth,* Thompson became at one and the same time the founder of 'scientific' socialism and the leading theoretician of Owenite 'utopian' socialism. At home again in Cork, he worked on a book entitled *Labour Rewarded – the Claims of Labour and Capital Conciliated; or, How to Secure to Labour the Whole Products of Its Exertions.* This appeared in 1827 and contained more of Thompson's theory of the state as well as his recommendations for labour politics and trade unionism. No positive furtherance of cooperation, he argued, was to be expected from the existing state, which was merely 'the aristocratic law-making committee of the idle classes'. He criticised its overcentralisation as both tyrannous and inefficient. The most important immediate reform that labour should seek was the democratisation of parliament, because a parliament representing the workers would be certain to facilitate the building of a cooperative commonwealth. At the same time, the people should create a decentralised political system based on self-governing communes and provinces. Trade unions had an important role to play. They could not, under the existing system, secure just wages for the workers, but they could prevent individual competition among workers. To do this effectively, they must establish a 'central union of all the general unions of all the trades of the country'. They should also establish producer cooperatives which would develop into cooperative communities.

In Bentham's circle in London, Thompson had met Anna Wheeler, daughter of a Church of Ireland archbishop, who had fled from an unhappy marriage in County Limerick. An intellectual and a socialist, she was well acquainted with contemporary French socialism, had encouraged Charles Fourier during his early years in Paris, and was active in the English cooperative movement. She and Thompson became close friends and, in collaboration with her, he wrote *An Appeal of One Half of the Human Race, Women, Against the Pretensions of the Other Half, Men, to Restrain Them in Political and Thence in Civil and Domestic Slavery*. The immediate occasion of the book was an article by the utilitarian James Mill, which argued that it was unnecessary for women to take part in public life or politics. The *Appeal* criticised the legal 'rightlessness' of women and argued for their full participation in politics and law-making. It was a more comprehensive statement of the feminist case than Mary Wollstonecraft's *Vindication of the Rights of Women* (1792) and the first book to deal directly with female suffrage. In the dedication, to Anna Wheeler, Thompson summed up most of his programme:

You look forward, as I do, to a state of society very different from that which now exists, in which the effort of all is to outwit, supplant and snatch from each other; where interest is systematically opposed to duty, where the so-called system of morals is little more than a mass of hypocrisy preached by knaves but unpractised by them, to keep their slaves, male as well as female, in blind uninquiring obedience; and where the whole motley fabric is kept together by fear and blood. You look forward to a better state of society, where the principle of benevolence shall supersede that of fear; where restless and anxious individual competition shall give place to mutual cooperation and joint possession; where individuals, in large numbers male and female, forming voluntary associations, shall become a mutual guarantee to each other for the supply of all useful wants, and form an unsalaried insurance company where perfect freedom of opinion and perfect equality will reign, and where the children of all will be equally educated and provided for by the whole.

In 1830 Thompson published his last book, *Practical Directions for the Speedy and Economic Establishment of Communities, on the Principles of Mutual Cooperation, United Possessions, Equality of Exertions and of the Means of Enjoyment*. This was a minutely detailed guide to the establishment and running of cooperative communities, more or less on the lines of the early Israeli kibbutz or the Maoist commune. Thompson argued against any notion of a return to the social or technological conditions preceding the Industrial Revolution, and for the full use of the new technology. The communities he envisaged, whether agricultural or industrial or mixed, would replace both the village and the town, combining elements of rural and urban life in a new synthesis.

Thompson played an active part in the first three cooperative congresses in England in 1831–32. *Practical Directions* was adopted as the guiding model of the Owenite cooperative movement in preference to Owen's own ideas. Thompson visited the cooperative community in Ralahine, County Clare, and presented a copy of the book to its manager, Edward Thomas Craig. He had drawn up plans for a community on his own estate, and had some of the buildings erected. But his poor health, which had dogged him throughout his life, culminated in a fatal illness and he died in Roscarbery in May 1833. He bequeathed his body to science and most of his property to the cooperative movement. But the latter bequest was contested in the courts and frittered away there.

The Ralahine commune, established by the landlord John Scott Vandeleur, was one of the few Owenite communities that actually got off the ground. Vandeleur had heard Owen lecturing in Dublin in 1823 and was converted to his ideas. After visits to Owen in England and correspondence with him, he decided to establish a cooperative village on his untenanted 600-acre estate at Ralahine, near Bunratty, peopling it with tenants from his other estate. He built comfortable stone cottages, dormitories for single men and single women, a store, a school, a large dining room and a meeting room. In 1831, having persuaded Craig, the editor of the *Lancashire Cooperator,* to be the manager – if his tenants approved – he assembled the tenants and had them elect fifty-two persons to form the Ralahine Agricultural and Manufacturing Cooperative Association. Vandeleur, the association's self-appointed president, rented the land to it and lent it livestock and farm implements, at 6 per cent annual interest, until it would have made enough money to buy them. Rules were agreed, wages and prices fixed. There was a currency of labour notes, acceptable for internal purchases and changeable into money for spending outside. Various labour-saving machines were introduced. The community prospered for two years until, in October 1833, Vandeleur lost all he owned at gambling and left suddenly for America. The Vandeleur family resumed direct possession of Ralahine and evicted the community without compensation.

William Thompson's thought had no influence or sequel in Ireland and his analysis of competitive capitalism did not become a significant part of Irish working-class ideology until the end of the century, and then by way of Marxism. Irish politics and the Irish economy differed sharply from those of England and the rest of Britain. Manufacturing industry, which had been unprotected against cheap British imports since the union with Britain, had been declining rather than expanding, except in the northeast. The main political feature of the 1820s had been O'Connell's campaign for Catholic emancipation, and the early 1830s were marked by the tithe war – the violent rebellion of the rural tenantry against the payment of tithes to the Church of Ireland. In England, however, Thompson's *Distribution of Wealth* exerted a strong influence on neo-Ricardian economic thought and on working-class ideology. His *Labour Rewarded* encouraged the growth of trade unionism and inspired the demand for the democratisation of parliament which issued, from 1838 onwards, in the Chartist movement.

Many British trade unions established consumer or producer cooperatives to gather capital for the founding of cooperative communities. John Doherty, a cotton spinner from Buncrana, County Donegal, was the outstanding trade union organiser of the time. Rather than the local unions that were the norm, he wanted unions spanning the entire state and organised on the lines of O'Connell's Catholic Association. In 1829 he founded the Grand General Union of Operative Spinners of Great Britain and Ireland, based on Manchester, and, in 1830, the National Association of United Trades for the Protection of Labour. This 'central' union, which soon embraced 150 unions and had its own, widely read newspaper, *The Voice of the People,* was an early precursor of the British Trades Union Congress (TUC). Like Thompson, with whom he worked on committees of the cooperative congresses, Doherty regarded trade unions as dual-purpose agencies: for worker protection in the short term, and for the creation of the cooperative commonwealth in the long term.

As a mass movement of the lower classes under a middle-class leader, Chartism was the British parallel of the Irish Repeal movement. Feargus O'Connor, the Chartist leader, had begun his political career as a parliamentary colleague of O'Connell; he was elected for County Cork in 1833 and 1834, but was deprived of his seat on the grounds that he lacked the necessary property qualification. He went into working-class politics in the north of England and, from the power base that he created there, hijacked Chartism from its London founders. They and many other Chartists were socialists, but O'Connor cannot be so described. He hated industrialism and what it was doing to people, and wanted to resettle the unemployed on the land in noncollectivist colonies, as peasant proprietors. He believed this would have the added beneficial effect of raising the wages of the urban workers by reducing competition for employment.

Among the socialists in the Chartist leadership was James Bronterre O'Brien from Granard, County Longford. A graduate in law of Trinity College, Dublin, he had worked under Thompson in the cooperative movement. He was the chief intellectual of Chartism – O'Connor nicknamed him 'the schoolmaster'. Most of O'Brien's ideas were drawn from French socialism, especially Babeuf, Blanqui and Saint-Simon, and his writing was mainly in periodicals. He was the first to use the term 'social democrat' in English. In the early 1850s, as a founder and leader of the National Reform League, he formulated an evolutionary socialist programme which envisaged the conquest and use of the existing state rather than its replacement. In this general respect, and in some of its particulars, the National Reform League programme foreshadowed the Independent Labour Party's policies in the 1890s.

While the Chartist movement and its successor groups ran their course, another Irish socialist, Hugh Doherty, refrained from political activity because he believed, as Owen had, that it was pointless. Doherty was the principal exponent in Britain of the doctrines of Charles Fourier about the immutability of human nature and the construction, in place of the existing state, of a system of social 'solidarity' based on communities called 'phalansteries'. In these same years Christian socialism emerged in Britain, as various socialist and social movements based on Christianity had already emerged, or were now appearing, on the Continent. Interestingly, and indicative of the ingrained secularism and individualism of modern Irish Christianity (Catholicism in particular), neither in this period nor later did any Irish Christians find inspiration in their religion for thought or action of a socialist kind.

One of the aims of O'Brien's National Reform League was the gradual nationalisation of land and the use of the resulting rent or tax on land use to cover all state expenditure. In Ireland, a

couple of years previously, Fintan Lalor had described the landlords
as usurpers of the nation's ownership of the land and advocated
the payment of all land rents to the nation 'for public purposes'.
Lalor, who was championing the cause of the tenant farmers and
plot-holders, was on the left wing of Young Ireland with Devin
Reilly and John Mitchel. They were not socialists, but they preached social revolution. Reilly had written in the *Nation* about the
French socialist Louis Blanc, and both he and Mitchel, in the *Irish
Felon,* used socialist rhetoric in writing about the workers' revolt
in Paris in 1848.

In Ireland in the second half of the nineteenth century, revolutionary fervour among the poorer classes took the forms of
republican nationalism (mainly Fenianism), or the struggle for the
land, or a combination of both. The National Land League,
founded in 1879, was the outstanding instance of both causes combined. Its founder and chief organiser, Michael Davitt, also united
both causes in himself, while at the same time being deeply committed to the industrial workers' struggle, particularly in England.
The son of an evicted Mayo tenant farmer who had moved with
his family to Lancashire, Davitt had worked in a factory as a child,
lost an arm in an industrial accident, joined the Irish Republican
Brotherhood and spent seven years in jail for his activities on their
behalf. He was released in 1877. By the time he was returned
to jail in 1881 – together with Parnell and other leaders of the
Land League – he had moved, ideologically, to a socialist position. In his book *Leaves from a Prison Journal,* which he sketched
out during his fifteen months' imprisonment, Davitt argued for
land nationalisation, cooperative production, state 'regulation and
organisation of labour', and a labour party in the House of
Commons.

His arguments for land nationalisation, and a tax on land use
which would fund state expenditure, were probably derived from
Henry George, whom he had met in America in 1878 and whom
he invited to visit Ireland. But George did not propose the

nationalisation of the land – he advocated merely the 'single tax' aspect and later called his scheme by that name – and he believed in a *laissez-faire* economy free from state interference.

Davitt began by arguing that the real relations between labour and land, and between land monopoly and poverty, could best be discerned in Ireland, where there was no abundance of industry to obscure the matter. Land and labour 'are absolutely essential to one another'. 'Land is valueless without labour' and labour, which creates value, 'cannot exert itself without land'. When the ownership of land is monopolised by a special class, they can and do determine access to land, and consequently, both the amount of wealth produced and its distribution. They exclude many people from access to land, and when they permit access it is on terms that deprive their tenants of most of the value they produce and allow them mere subsistence. Moreover, the land monopolists receive, as an extra bonus, the unearned increment that accrues to land by virtue of the growth of population and the spread of towns and industry. This unjust state of affairs can be righted, and the productive capacity of land and labour fully realised, only by taking all land, including mines and minerals, into public ownership and 'taxing it, exclusive of improvements, up to its full value'. 'By the term improvements,' Davitt continued, 'I mean such erections or qualities as can be clearly shown to be the results of the labour of those now in the occupation or enjoyment of the land or their predecessors.' Thus land would be available to all, 'and every individual worker would be in a position to command exactly that share of the wealth produced which he had by his labour created; while the community at large would be put in possession of that part of the wealth produced of which it was the sole creator'.

Davitt was strongly opposed to peasant proprietorship as a remedy for the land problem. 'Increasing the number of those holding private property in land' would not remedy 'the evils of land monopoly'. Peasant proprietorship is 'simply landlordism in another form'. 'A million proprietors, or petty landlords, would act together as cordially as the present landlord party in the three kingdoms.' To increase that party, 'and particularly with public money' (by buying out the landlords), would be 'suicidal' for 'popular liberty'. Moreover, peasant proprietorship 'excludes the [agricultural] labourers from all hope of being able to elevate themselves from their present degraded condition'.

With regard to the industrial workers, Davitt believed that his land nationalisation scheme would benefit them both by increasing the amount of productive enterprise and by making land available to the poor. In both ways, the competition among workers for jobs would be reduced and employers would have to compete for labour. However, if the industrial workers were to receive the full value of their labour, more was needed. Industry must be cooperatively organised, 'on the basis of joint ownership of capital and absolute control on the part of the worker'. But that was 'a thing of the future'. It could be hoped for only as a result of educating the workers and creating successful examples of cooperative industry which would inspire them 'to look in this direction for their emancipation from their present state of dependence'. In the meantime, and in preparation for that eventuality, 'social reformers would do well to exert themselves to extend state regulation of the relation between labour and capital, and governmental control and ownership of enterprises similar in character to those which are already subject to such supervision or ownership'. This 'state' and 'governmental' action should occur at the local as well as the central level. In a chapter on Irish self-government – which he no longer envisaged in a republican form but on the Canadian or dominion model – he advocated elective county boards with wide powers, including control of the police; each county would be 'as far as practicable, a self-governing community'. (The thought occurs that, if the Home Rule proposal had included county self-government on these lines – or if such a measure had been implemented, say, in the 1890s

– Home Rule would not have seemed so threatening to the north-eastern capitalists.)

Leaves from a Prison Journal provides the only comprehensive statement of Davitt's socialist beliefs. In the years after his release from prison, he often spoke in favour of land nationalisation, but apart from Bishop Nulty of Meath and Archbishop Walsh of Dublin – who supported the idea in principle – few in Ireland would hear of it, least of all the tenant farmers or the growing numbers of peasant proprietors. His views on this matter got a better reception in Britain and America. In his career as a member of parliament in the Irish Home Rule party, Davitt was a Labour-Nationalist (or Lib-Lab) favouring 'state socialism' – in effect, a reforming state paternalism. He became well known and acquired considerable influence in the English and Irish labour movements. Chiefly he worked to create two unions of interest: on the one hand, between the Irish agricultural labourers, urban workers and tenant farmers, on the other (as Feargus O'Connor had attempted before him), between the Irish national movement and the British working class. In 1890–91 he initiated the process that led three years later to the foundation of the Irish Trades Union Congress (ITUC). Shortly before his death in 1906, he had the satisfaction of forging an electoral alliance between the Irish parliamentary nationalists and Keir Hardie's Independent Labour Party, and of fighting the general election on that basis.

In the second half of the nineteenth century, the cooperative movement in Britain shed its socialism. It became a movement consisting of consumer cooperative societies – engaged in retail and wholesale trading – and, to a lesser extent, producer cooperatives, with no end in view beyond the successful operation of these enterprises and the benefits, material and moral, to be derived therefrom. Its guiding principles were those of the Rochdale cooperative society in Lancashire, founded in 1844; interest was paid on share capital, and dividends were issued on members' purchases. Legislation in the 1850s and 1860s gave binding force to the societies' rules and limited the liability of members to their shares. In Ireland there were very few co-ops until the 1890s when, under the leadership of Horace Plunkett, Robin Anderson, Father Tom Finlay and others, a major cooperative movement got under way. For Plunkett, who was a wealthy, patriotic unionist and the main driving force, the overriding purpose of the movement was to rebuild the 'character' of the Irish people by encouraging self-reliance, care and enterprise.

Most of the new co-ops were engaged in agricultural business of one kind or another, especially dairying. The Irish Agricultural Organisation Society was founded to provide overall servicing and direction, and by 1913 it had 985 affiliated societies. To a considerable degree, the movement was inspired by the advanced state of agricultural cooperation in Denmark – Ireland's principal competitor on the British market – but organisational models were derived from other Continental countries also, notably France and Germany. Looking back to the Ralahine venture, Plunkett praised E.T. Craig as 'the author of the most advanced experiment in the realisation of cooperative ideals', but doubted whether joint ownership of land, except for common grazing, was practicable.

In 1913, Father Finlay expressed tentative hopes that the cooperative movement would lead to a 'cooperative commonwealth' which would remove the exploitative element from capitalism. The notion of a cooperative commonwealth had become separated from the notion of socialism, largely because the latter term was now associated primarily with the urban context, industrial workers, and state or municipal ownership or control. However, this did not prevent cooperativist thinking from assuming *de facto* socialist or near-socialist forms, and this was the case with George Russell (AE), particularly in his book *The National Being* (1917). Russell, who was primarily a poet and mystical philosopher, had been brought into the cooperative movement by Plunkett in 1897 and trained as an organiser. Later he became the editor of the movement's journal, the *Irish Homestead*, and both there and in other writings such as *Cooperation and Nationality* (1912) he moved towards the notion of a cooperatively organised Ireland. He regarded Ralahine as an inspiring forerunner and a pointer towards the Ireland of the future.

In *The National Being*, Russell writes:

> It is not enough to organise farmers in a district for one purpose only – in a credit society, a dairying society, a fruit society, a bacon factory, or in a cooperative store. All these may be and must be beginnings; but if they do not develop and absorb all rural business into their organisation, they will have little effect on character. The specialised society only develops economic efficiency. The evolution of humanity beyond its present level depends absolutely on its power to unite and create true social organisms.

Moreover, cooperation must extend into towns and factories. 'I desire to unite countrymen and townsmen in one movement, and to make the cooperative principle the basis of a national civilisation.' The industrial workers should begin by acquiring cooperative control of the distributive trade. Then, working from that base, their trade unions could gradually 'transform themselves into cooperative guilds of producers'. At the same time, scope must always remain both for individual business enterprise and for other kinds of collective ownership. 'By degrees it will be discovered what enterprises are best directed by the state, by municipalities, by groups, by individuals.' But the cooperative economy would be the 'spinal column' of the national body, setting the tone for every other form of economic activity. Voluntary initiative and effort was the way to bring it into being.

Russell was as sceptical as Thompson before him of any really transforming action by the capitalist state. 'Governments in great nation-states, even representative governments, are not malleable by the general will.' They are controlled and manipulated by 'the

holders of economic power'. Similarly with the press, which does
not reflect public opinion but, rather, 'capitalistically controlled
creates public opinion'. Russell noted that, in the institutions of
self-government proposed for Irish Home Rule, 'the signature
of the Irish mind is not apparent anywhere'. It seemed that the
English system of self-government, with all its inefficient, oppressive and antiquated features, was to be imported into Ireland. 'I
fear the importers of this machinery will desire to make it do
things it can only do badly, and will set to work with the ferocity
of the new broom, and make it an obstruction' which will prevent
the genius of the Irish people from expressing itself and 'enchain
us for centuries to come'. If Irish self-government were really
to be government by and for the Irish people, then the 'national
assembly concerned with general interests' must be accompanied
by 'councils, representative of classes and special interests, controlling the policy and administration of the state departments
concerned with their work'. Speaking with the cooperative movement's experience of the Irish Department of Agriculture in mind,
Russell says that 'the continuous efficiency of state departments
can only be maintained when they are controlled in respect of
policy . . . by the class or industry which the state institution was
created to serve'.

While the land had been the main social issue in the late nineteenth century, urban trade unions had been slowly growing and
in some cities there were groups of socialists. The First International, based in London and under the virtual leadership of Karl
Marx, had a substantial Irish membership. James Stephens, John
O'Mahoney, John Devoy and other leading Fenians belonged
to it, and it had branches in Dublin and Cork and among the
Irish in England. A manifesto of the Irish section in 1871 stated
that the establishment of these branches had helped to end 'the
national antagonism between English and Irish working men in
England' which had been 'one of the main impediments in the

way of every attempted movement for the emancipation of the working class, and therefore one of the mainstays of class domination in England as well as in Ireland'. After the disintegration of the International the small groups of socialists in Dublin and Cork attached themselves, like the Irish trade union movement of the time, to British organisations. Then in 1894, with the foundation of the ITUC, this situation began to change. Two years later it changed further when the Dublin Socialist Club, learning that James Connolly in Edinburgh was in dire need of work, offered him a job as organiser at one pound a week. Connolly, who was then twenty-eight years old, came to Dublin and within a couple of weeks had persuaded his new comrades to found the Irish Socialist Republican Party, with himself as secretary.

The importance of this event lay not so much in itself as in what it signified, namely, Connolly's determination to create a socialist theory and practice that would be rooted in Irish history, persuasively related to Irish circumstances, and grafted onto both the revolutionary nationalist movement and the broader movement of national humanism of which it was the core and concentrating force. This humanist movement, in its various manifestations, sought to heal the broken humanity of the Irish people – to restore them to personal integrity, self-possession and self-reliance. Already by 1896 it included enterprises as diverse as the nationalist Gaelic Athletic Association (GAA), the non-political Gaelic language movement, the rural cooperative movement, and the nascent literary revival. To these would be added, in the following few years, Arthur Griffith's Sinn Féin, D.P. Moran's *Leader* and Yeats's Abbey Theatre, and finally, after another few years, the 'redemption by blood' project of Pearse and the other poets of the Easter Rising. From all of these, successively and collectively, the nationalist revolution drew its force.

Connolly was a humanist by instinct who believed 'there is nothing on earth more sacred than humanity'. The Irish nationalism he had imbibed as a boy in the slums of Edinburgh, and the

Marxist socialism he had learned in the same city in the 1890s, combined to focus his humanist zeal on the Irish working class, and to convince him that the only way it could recover its lost humanity was through a national and social revolution that would liberate its nation and put it in control of the nation's material resources. In the meantime its struggle towards that goal was a humanising process. 'Every victory for labour', he wrote, 'helps to straighten the cramped soul of the Irish labourer.' Jim Larkin's new, militant industrial union, the Irish Transport and General Workers' Union (ITGWU), was to be praised because 'it found the workers of Ireland on their knees, and has striven to raise them to the erect position of manhood; it found them with all the vices of slavery in their souls, and it strove to eradicate these vices and replace them with some of the virtues of free men'. Moreover, like Thompson, Connolly made clear that the humanity he was concerned about was equally female as male. 'The worker', he wrote, 'is the slave of capitalist society, the female worker is the slave of that slave. . . . Down from the landlord to the tenant and peasant proprietor, from the monopolist to the small businessman eager to be a monopolist, and from all above to all below, filtered the beliefs, customs, ideas, establishing a slave morality which enforces the subjection of women as the standard morality of the country.' But 'in Ireland the women's cause is felt by all labour men and women as their cause; the labour cause has no more earnest and wholehearted supporters than the militant women'.

The necessity in Ireland for national liberation and social emancipation was the core of Connolly's doctrine. Many of its other points arose either from his effort to present this core persuasively to Irish workers, socialists and revolutionaries, or from his defence of one or other aspect of the resulting corpus against criticisms by other socialists.

From the start he maintained that primitive communism had existed in Ireland under the Gaelic clan system until the seventeenth century, and that an Irish socialist republic would therefore be a restoration in contemporary terms of this native Irish principle. Searching for a forerunner in the Irish revolutionary tradition, he fastened at first on Fintan Lalor – his social revolutionary zeal, his hatred of landlordism, and his clear contention that the ownership of the land was vested by right in the nation. Later, in *Labour in Irish History* (1910), Connolly rewrote Irish history since the seventeenth century from a labour standpoint, dwelling on Thompson, Ralahine, the Irish socialists in England, and the social and labour dimensions of Young Ireland and Fenianism. With regard to Ralahine he said that an independent Ireland 'must seek the happiness of her people in the extension on a national basis of the social arrangements of Ralahine'.

Facing the Ireland of his day, he maintained that the workers' republic would be 'the application to agriculture and industry . . . of the republican ideal' to which the Irish Revolution had committed itself. At the same time it would be a 'cooperative commonwealth', and therefore a goal that the rural cooperative movement and urban labour could collaborate to achieve. (Connolly noted with praise and appreciation George Russell's progress towards a junction with the urban labour movement.) Labour was the 'natural ally' of the language revival movement: both had in capitalism a common enemy and both were aiming to restore self-respect in Irish people. Repeatedly Connolly attacked the 'middle-class' and 'gombeen' nationalists who hoped to achieve, through Home Rule, a self-governing, capitalist Ireland. That, he argued, would mean continued economic subservience to London and no real change in circumstance for the majority of Irish people. He described the northern Protestant workers as 'slaves in spirit' who accepted enslavement by their 'pastors and masters' because they had beneath them, in the Catholics, people who were even more oppressed. Socialism demanded, he told them, that the people of Ireland should rule and own Ireland, but on the day that Home Rule went through, the socialists would 'go into opposition'.

While seldom referring to Marx and never calling himself a Marxist, Connolly used Marxism, selectively, as a method of social and historical analysis, modifying it or adding to it as he saw fit. His belief in the socialist necessity of Irish national liberation was in accordance with Marx's express teaching, but he went further than Marx in denouncing the subjection of any nation by another nation and in defining socialist internationalism as 'a free federation of free peoples'. This definition occurred in the course of his controversy with William Walker, the Belfast 'gas and water' socialist, who maintained that the aim of Irish independence ran counter to the internationalism required of workers within the United Kingdom. For Walker, as for many socialists of the time, internationalism meant collaboration between the workers of different nations regardless of whether some of these nations were subject to others. Connolly remarked that such 'internationalism' was 'scarcely distinguishable from imperialism'. (Lenin, several years later, developed a doctrine on the rights of nations that was close to Connolly's without going quite so far.)

Again, Connolly differed from Marx and many other socialists in maintaining that socialism was not an all-encompassing philosophy with views on everything. The socialist movement, he wrote, had been 'hampered by the presence in its ranks of faddists and cranks, who were in the movement, not for the cause of socialism, but because they thought they saw in it a means of airing their theories on such questions as sex, religion, vaccination, vegetarianism, etc.', whereas socialists 'as a body were concerned only with the question of political and economic freedom for our class' and 'were not repositories of all truth'. In particular, socialism had been harmed by those socialists who mixed anticlericalism and hostility to religion with their socialist propaganda. Anticlericalism was a survival from the eighteenth-century freethinkers, and a product of capitalist individualism that had no place in socialism. Nor was religion part of socialism's concern: the socialist creed had to do with secular and human matters only, and could therefore coexist with any religion, and particularly with Christianity. In *Labour, Nationality and Religion* (1910), written in reply to criticisms of socialism by an Irish Catholic priest, Connolly corrected the critic's misinterpretations of socialism, cited passages in the scriptures, Church fathers and Christian philosophers that seemed to point to socialist principles, and predicted that the Church would adapt, ultimately, to socialism as it had adapted to a variety of social systems in the past. This was typical of Connolly's relationships with Christian clergy, whether hostile or friendly: unyielding on principles and insistent on clarifying the facts, he persistently claimed identity of purpose and welcomed collaboration when it occurred.

As to the means of social emancipation – given national independence – Connolly wrote in 1899 that it would be achieved through the 'ownership by the state of all the land and materials for labour, combined with the cooperative control by the workers of such land and materials'. Resources and enterprises should be made 'the property of the government' only 'in proportion as the workers are ready to make the government their property'. At this stage, Connolly envisaged the workers' political party as playing the leading role by winning control of the government. But already, as can be seen from the above, he was aware of the simultaneous need for the growth of direct control of production by the workers as distinct from the state, bureaucracy or party. Later, this awareness crystallised in the synthetic syndicalism he adopted from the American socialist Daniel De Leon – a combination of Marxist analysis with a syndicalist praxis deriving ultimately from Marx's opponent Proudhon. Craft unions must give way to 'industrial unions' spanning each entire industry; and these, combined in one big union, would build up the 'working-class administration' – the 'industrial republic' – to the point where, with the help of direct political assault through the ballot box, and possibly with armed force, it could take over and replace the bureaucratic, capitalist state. Connolly gave his fullest exposition of this sydicalist programme in *Socialism Made Easy,* published in Chicago (1908) during his period in the United States. Later, in *The Reconquest of Ireland* (Dublin, 1915), he reaffirmed it, in combination with cooperativism, in a manner reminiscent of Thompson in *Labour Rewarded* and close to Russell in *The National Being:* the industrial unions were to be the means of establishing, in place of the existing state, a cooperative commonwealth administered by the unions.

In the years 1912–14 Connolly played a leading part in persuading the ITUC to establish a labour party which would serve as its political agent. But his main work in these final years was with the ITGWU founded by Jim Larkin, which had become the largest affiliate of the ITUC. Larkin, the son of Irish emigrants to Liverpool, had come to Ireland in 1907 as an organiser for a British union. He was a syndicalist and an Irish republican; his great gifts as a labour leader lay in his oratory, personal magnetism and fighting spirit. He founded a very successful paper, the *Irish Worker,* as the organ of the ITGWU. In the great lockout of 1913, Larkin, seconded by Connolly, led the union against the Dublin employers. When he left for America in 1914, Connolly took over as acting general secretary of the union, editor of the *Irish Worker,* and commander of the Irish Citizen Army. This small workers' army – the world's first Red Guard – had been set up to protect workers during the great lockout, and then reconstituted 'to enforce and defend' the principle that 'the ownership of Ireland, moral and material, is vested in the people of Ireland'.

In the period leading up to the Easter Rising Connolly wrote about guerrilla warfare and drew close to Pearse. It was in this context that he made his final theoretical adaptation to the national revolution. Over twenty years previously he had stopped practising his religion, and he subsequently ceased to be a Christian believer. Pearse, on the other hand, was a deeply religious man who saw the coming rising as an act that would redeem the Irish people, morally, in a manner analogous to Christ's self-sacrificing death. Connolly, responding to this notion, remembered the words of a French socialist he had known in Edinburgh and made them his own in the *Workers' Republic* (5 February 1916): 'Without the slightest trace of irreverence, but in all due humility and awe, we recognise that for us, as of mankind before Calvary, it may be truly said "Without the shedding of blood there is no redemption."' In prison after the Rising, he received the sacraments again, and his last words, spoken to the chaplain as he faced the firing squad, were 'Father, forgive them for they know not what they do.'

Pearse, in his turn, was influenced by Connolly. Already Lalor and the 1913 lockout had been radicalising his views on property; Connolly, in those last months, made him a socialist. In Pearse's final political essay, 'The Sovereign People' (March 1916), he wrote that 'the nation's sovereignty extends . . . to all the material possessions of the nation, the nation's soil and all its resources, all wealth and all wealth-producing processes within the nation'. 'No right to property is good against the public right of the nation.' Furthermore, 'right to the control of the material resources of a nation . . . resides in the whole people and can be lawfully exercised only by those to whom it is delegated by the whole people, and in the manner in which the whole people ordain'. It was against the background of this basic agreement on the social question between Pearse and Connolly that the Proclamation of the Irish Republic declared 'the right of the people of Ireland to the ownership of Ireland'.

When the First Dáil met in January 1919, one of the fundamental texts read and assented to was the famous Democratic Programme. It began by restating that phrase from the Proclamation and some of the key passages on sovereignty and property from Pearse's 'The Sovereign People'. Then it committed the Republic to policies of social welfare, declared 'the right of every citizen to an adequate share of the produce of the nation's labour', and stated that the Republic would ensure that industries were 'developed on . . . progressive cooperative industrial lines'. This broadly socialist declaration had been drafted at the Dáil's request, by Thomas Johnson, treasurer of the ITUC and Labour Party (which had not participated in the general election which led to the establishment of the Dáil). The more extreme and explicit socialism of Johnson's original draft was modified before the document was put to the Dáil and passed in a mood of thoughtless euphoria. Both the new Irish Republic and the labour movement were sympathetic to the new soviet regime in Russia. The government of the Soviet Union recognised the Republic, and the Dáil authorised the establishment of diplomatic relations.

After Connolly's death, and with Larkin still in America, the labour movement was left under the leadership of cautious functionaries. The most talented of the Irish Citizen Army died in the 1916 Rising or shortly afterwards, and the army, under ineffective leadership and virtually disowned by the ITUC/Labour Party, went on to play a passive and undistinguished role in the War of Independence. The new acting secretary of the ITGWU, William O'Brien, was a syndicalist who regarded the achievement of national freedom as a matter for Sinn Féin and the Irish Republican Army. O'Brien and Johnson – an Englishman who had come to Ireland in 1892 and lived for many years in Belfast – were the leading figures in the ITUC/Labour Party during the revolutionary years and afterwards. Both were dedicated trade unionists who believed that the winning of economic power through the growing trade union movement was the direct road to the socialist society. They called that society the 'cooperative commonwealth' or 'workers' republic', and Johnson said that the Labour Party's constitution (1918) was based on the teachings of James Connolly and George Russell. While the urban trade unionists and unemployed, the small farmers and landless labourers became increasingly involved in the republican struggle, the

ITUC/Labour Party held to the neutral line on Irish nationalism that it had pursued since before the 1916 Rising. A practical reason for this was the fact that many ITUC members were northern unionists. At the same time, in indirect and informal ways the labour movement helped the nationalist cause, most notably by the general strike against conscription into the British army, by winning recognition for Ireland at international labour conferences, and by local or transport strikes directed against the British during the War of Independence.

These were years of great growth for the trade unions, and particularly for the ITGWU. The labour leadership seems to have believed that this growth would lead, inevitably and without violence, to the cooperative commonwealth. Nominally, the ITUC/Labour Party executive was committed to promoting cooperative societies, but it took no steps to do so, and the only cooperatives sponsored by trade unions were long-established ones in Belfast and a clothing factory set up in Dublin by the ITGWU. Moreover, on those occasions during the War of Independence, Truce and Civil War when groups of country people seized land, or groups of workers seized factories and set up 'soviets', the ITUC/Labour Party leadership gave no encouragement and evaded the issue.

When in 1922 Labour at last contested a general election to the Dáil (winning 17 seats out of 128), it did so on a purely reformist programme. This set the tone for Labour thenceforth. It became, in the Dáil, a reformist, economist party, advocating state paternalism on the British model (including a degree of public ownership and state industrial enterprise). Just as the Bolshevik leadership in Russia stopped short at the state despotism which, in its own theory, was to be the prelude to the communist society, so the Irish labour leadership confined itself to advocating and supporting a state paternalism which, in its own theory, was at best a holding position on the way to the cooperative commonwealth. In effect, therefore, the cooperative commonwealth was tacitly shelved. Nor was this state of affairs altered by the various socialist flurries of the 1920s: Larkin's return, his splitting of the ITGWU and founding of the Irish Workers' League as the Irish affiliate of the Comintern; Roddy Connolly's Communist Party of Ireland; the socialist rhetoric of Liam Mellows, Peadar O'Donnell and others on the left wing of the outlawed IRA. All of these were impotent in face of the double-edged fact that the mass of the labour movement and its formal leadership were committed to state paternalism and that Fianna Fáil was on the way to making this the socio-economic orthodoxy of the state.

Labour described itself as the party of Connolly and called for the implementation of the Democratic Programme. De Valera, speaking for Fianna Fáil, proclaimed his allegiance to the Democratic Programme and his adherence to Connolly's social vision. Both parties in practice offered state paternalism, but Fianna Fáil, as the left wing of the national revolution – as that which Connolly had wanted the Labour Party to be – was uniquely able to offer it in combination with militant nationalism. By doing this Fianna Fáil came to power, ruled the country for sixteen years, and outdid contemporary social democratic governments in the degree of state paternalism it practised – particularly in its expansion of the state sector of the economy. After that – whether governed by Fianna Fáil or by coalitions of Fine Gael, Labour and others – the Republic was set in the pattern of state paternalism that has characterised all liberal democracies in the twentieth century. The trade union organisation, now called the Irish Congress of Trade Unions and devoted primarily to wage bargaining, became a leading institution of the state, and its officials wielded considerable influence. The Labour Party struggled on, fell under the sway of middle-class liberals, and survived on the electoral crumbs left over by the two big parties.

In these circumstances, socialism, whether as a fervour or a theme, has become as marginal to Irish life as it has been, say, to life in the USA since the First World War. It has been an issue, sporadically, in the trade union movement, and it has rumbled, occasionally, in the Labour Party and the republican movement, giving rise to splits or splinterings. In the late 1940s, the ITGWU, in a bout of power politics, alleged communist infiltration of the Labour Party, and for a time set up a rival organisation. In the last twenty years, 'socialist trouble' in the Labour Party has arisen from left-wing caucuses rebelling against the party's lack of socialism. On one occasion, in the late 1960s, the party took the bull by the horns, declared that the 'seventies will be socialist', presented an election programme with some socialist features – and fell back from 21 to 17 seats in a Dáil of 144 seats.

In the republican movement, veerings towards socialism have occurred as reactions to the failure, or poor prospects, of physical force. In 1933, with de Valera triumphant, the left wing of the IRA, led by Peadar O'Donnell and George Gilmore, split from the IRA to form the Republican Congress with the Communist Party and other left-wing groups. This lasted until 1936, when the chief militants went off to fight on the republican side in the Spanish Civil War. Again, in the 1960s, after the failure of the IRA's campaign in Northern Ireland, Sinn Féin under Tomás Mac Giolla turned to social issues and cooperative-building. Roy Johnston and Cathal Goulding tried to remodel the movement on Marxist principles. This contributed to the spilt in 1970, when the Provisional Irish Republican Army emerged. During the 1970s the Provisionals redefined republicanism as a military movement fighting for British withdrawal from Northern Ireland, and a political movement aiming at a democratic, socialist; federal Ireland. Their programme, which envisaged four federated provinces based on self-governing districts, cooperative production and distribution, and national ownership of the chief resources, was the most explicit revolutionary programme published in Ireland for decades. But the movement's commitment to federalism and to radical decentralisation was never more than nominal, and the federalism was effectively rejected at the Sinn Féin Ardfheis of 1981.

While socialist activism has been confined to the margins of recent Irish life, socialist thought has been virtually nonexistent. Connolly, whether nominally or really, is still the chief reference source of Irish socialism, with no other Irish thinker intervening in the past sixty years. Notable socialist writing has been confined to historical works such as Rayner Lysaght's *The Republic of Ireland* (1970), Michael Farrell's *The Orange State* (1976) and the historical essays published by the Irish Communist Organisation.

However, this cessation of creative socialist thought must be seen in context. From the end of the 1930s until the late 1960s, there was hardly any Irish theoretical writing about society or the state, apart from Jeremiah Newman's erudite books on political morality. Only in the last fifteen years has a slight revival occurred with Charles McCarthy's *The Distasteful Challenge* (1968), which argued for decentralised government, participatory democracy and worker-management, and Tom Barrington's profound critique of Irish governmental structures in *From Big Government to Local Government* (1975) and *The Irish Administrative System* (1980).

3

THE HUMANISM
OF JAMES CONNOLLY
AND GEORGE RUSSELL

I USE THE WORD 'HUMANISM' in the sense in which Desmond
Ryan uses it in his books on Pearse and Connolly, or Heidegger
in his 'Letter on Humanism'. Heidegger defines it as 'thinking
and caring so that human beings may be human, and not inhuman'. Expanding on that, I would say humanism is a combination of concern, thought and action with the aim that people,
in their social groups and individually, realise their human nature.
Clearly, then, I am not using the word to indicate something
different from, or opposed to, religion or the supernatural: a
humanism can be religious or non-religious.

Most humanists, like people generally, assume that mankind
exists as nations and within nations: that nations are representative human societies or relative human wholes. Taking that for
granted, they perceive that, in all nations or their own, people
are not living humanly and are being prevented from so doing.
Feeling concerned about this disorder, they work out a method
or programme for remedying it, or put their faith in such a programme which already exists. If they are activist types, they set
about implementing the remedial programme. Generally speaking, therefore, a humanism involves five things: a conception
of the proper or realised condition of man in nations; the

Paper to the 1984 Yeats Summer School, printed in the *Crane Bag*, Vol. 9,
No. 1, 1985

perception that he is not realised, in all nations or in one's own; concern about this; a theory of why it is so and how it can be remedied; and action directed towards remedying it.

The movement of national regeneration that took place in Ireland between the founding of the Gaelic Athletic Association (GAA) in 1884 and the election of the First Dáil in 1918 was a movement of national humanism with many contributory strands. Whether through organised sport, the establishment of co-operatives, language revival, literary creation and presentation, theosophical preaching, militant trade unionism, the symbolic re-enactment of Christ's death and resurrection, military training or armed rebellion, it was an attempt to restore man in Ireland, or the Irish people, to proper human being. According to the individual or the group concerned, stress was laid on various attributes of realised humanity: on character or intellect, authentic language, creativity, nobility or vitality, on unity of being, aesthetic sensibility, moral courage or physical fitness, on collective ruling power, political or mental autonomy, brotherliness, self-respect or self-reliance, awareness of man's divinity – and so on. This humanist movement was directed against materialism and capitalism, which were often seen as embodied by England and its industrial civilisation. It strove to elevate, instead of matter or money, man.

Two of the leading figures in this movement were James Connolly and George Russell, known as AE. I link them because, although their humanisms were very different in inspiration, they were linked in practice and in the minds of the labour movement after 1916. Russell's ideal of a cooperative commonwealth was endorsed, wholeheartedly, by Connolly at the end of his book *The Reconquest of Ireland,* where he refers to Russell's 'great genius and magnetic personality' and welcomes his idea of joint cooperative-building by farmers and urban workers. In the years after Connolly's death, the terms 'workers' republic' and 'co-operative commonwealth' were used by the labour movement

as interchangeable names for the socialist society. When the Labour
Party constitution was drawn up in 1918, Thomas Johnson, the
party's leader, stated that it was based on the principles of Connolly
and Russell.

Moreover, as is evident from Connolly's description of Russell
quoted above, he had a high personal regard for the man. When
Connolly was in jail before his execution, he told his wife to discuss
the future of the family with AE, and AE, on being approached
by her, organised a subscription. Russell, for his part, had some
reserves about Connolly's character and preferred Larkin; but he
respected Connolly, sympathised with his socialism, and recognised
his superiority over Larkin inasmuch as he had a constructive
programme.

AE and Connolly had both begun by acquiring a general
humanist theory, without special reference to Ireland; then later,
at a particular point in their lives, they began to express that theory
in specifically Irish terms and to relate it to Irish circumstances.
AE began to read theosophical literature in 1886, when he was
nineteen, and in 1889 he joined the Theosophical Society in
Dublin and devoted himself to the study and practice of its
teaching. But it was not until 1895, when he read Standish
O'Grady's *History of Ireland,* that he began to rethink the
theosophical docrines in Irish terms.

Madame Blavatsky, the leading teacher of theosophy at the
time, believed that theosophy's account of cosmic reality underlay
all the world's mythologies, but she had not illustrated this in
the case of Celtic mythology. AE proceeded to do so. He found
that Lir, the god of the sea, corresponded to the Absolute of
theosophy. The trinity that emanated from the Absolute – Logos,
World Soul, and Light of the Logos – were Manannan, Dana
and Aengus, respectively. Those were the first stages in the descent
of the Absolute through successive planes to its imprisonment
in reincarnating human beings and other material bodies. What
theosophy called the heaven-world, beneath the God-world,

was Tír na nÓg. The Tuatha Dé Danaan were the gods of ancient Ireland.

This translation of theosophy into Gaelic Irish mythology linked AE with the Gaelic intellectual movement and gave him his niche within it. He, too, became, but on his own terms, one who wanted the Gaelic past renewed and revived. Moreover, inasmuch as the Gaelic movement found inspiration in the nation's 'ancestral self' AE could identify with it in theosophical terms; for theosophy taught that the separated souls of the present world derived from the manifested Logos under the name of the Ancestral Self, and were contained in that Self.

It was in the years when he was making this adaptation – from 1897 onwards – that AE, invited by Plunkett and urged by Yeats, became active in the cooperative movement. Here too he made a translation of general doctrine to Irish circumstances. Cooperativism, as propounded principally by Kropotkin, held that cooperatives were a renewal in modern form of the self-governing village communities that had once covered Europe, Africa and Asia. AE held that in Ireland cooperativism was a renewal of the communal ownership of the Irish clans.

When Connolly came to Ireland in 1896 at the age of twenty-eight, he was already a socialist with a view of history, the world and the labour struggle that were basically, though critically, Marxist. An Irish nationalist from his early youth, he had already, during the few previous years in Edinburgh, begun to apply his socialism, in a general way, to Irish circumstances. With his arrival in Dublin and the foundation of the Irish Socialist Republican Party, he rapidly extended and completed this adaptation. In the course of doing so he reformulated his socialism not only in general Irish terms, but specifically in terms of the Irish cultural and political revolution that was then in its formative period.

Committed to an Irish republic, he argued that socialism was the full realisation of the republican democratic ideal. He explained why socialists should support the language revival, and applied the Marxist belief in primitive communism to Ireland by main-taining that communal ownership had been practised by the Gaelic clans. He also researched and wrote the history of socialist and social revolutionary thought in Ireland, and anchored his socialism in that tradition.

A humanist who devotes his mind and efforts to his nation often has, within the nation, a special 'chosen people' who repre-sent to him the essential nation and who serve either as an inspira-tion for him or as the special field of his endeavour. Yeats said, 'Connaught for me is Ireland', meaning by 'Connaught' the poor of the western countryside. Later, the Anglo-Irish were to be his special or chosen Irish people. For Connolly, Ireland was essen-tially the poorer strata of urban workers, whom he called 'the working class', 'the workers', or 'labour'. He said: 'The cause of labour is the cause of Ireland, and the cause of Ireland is the cause of labour.' He listed various categories of Irish people who did not belong to the Irish nation as he envisaged it: rack-renting landlords, profit-grinding capitalists, sleek and oily lawyers, prosti-tute pressmen. AE did not have a special Irish people in the same sense, or at least not consistently. True, his cooperative project was directed principally, though not exclusively, to the rural peo-ple, and for a while he shared Yeats's predilection for the poor peasants of the West of Ireland. But the spiritual aspect of his humanism – that which sought to make people fully human by making them aware that they were essentially members of God – addressed itself to all sorts of people, urban as well as rural.

Connolly believed that man is realised, socially, when in his various nations he is working productively, and possesses that *collective ruling power* over his social organisation and over nature which accords with his human nature. This was the goal of socialist endeavour described by Engels in *Socialism: Utopian and Scientific* in the following terms: 'Man, at last the master of his own form of social organisation, becomes at the same time lord over Nature, his own master – free.' For Connolly, therefore, man realised in Ireland meant an independent, democratic republic in which the nation, consisting of workers, would possess state power and through it all the wealth-producing resources. From about 1902 onwards, when he espoused Daniel De Leon's form of syndicalism, he saw this worker-controlled state as a federation of industrial unions and professional associations electing a ruling committee of experts. Within this context of socially realised humanity, individuals would be realised as self-possessed, self-reliant, courageous, fraternal, working persons.

The way to this humanist goal was threefold. First, Irish workers must see, with the help of socialist doctrine, how the world was organised to their detriment: as a nation, as a class, and as persons; they must see the injustice of this, the need to right it and the way to do this. They needed, in other words, *a special secular vision*. Second, they must engage in national struggle, in alliance with the other classes, to achieve liberation from British rule. Third, they must engage in class struggle against the master class in order to achieve humane working conditions and control over the nation's resources and their own labour. The organisational form for this struggle was industrial unions, which would ultimately come to form 'One Big Union' embracing the entire working class, and thus stand poised to seize state power by means of a general strike.

But this class struggle was itself a humanising process and that, apart from its political dimension, was its chief value in Connolly's eyes. The primary purpose of the workers' struggle was not material gain, but political power and humanisation. The struggle was the process by which the workers humanised themselves, individually, on the way to their social humanisation as possessors of collective ruling power in their independent nation.

AE believed that man is realised, socially, when in his various nations he is working creatively and living in *brotherhood*. He gave this primacy to brotherhood because, in theosophic doctrine, individuals are separated emanations of God, elements of the same divine substance. Thus brotherhood is a divine law and its enactment expresses and realises man's original and intrinsic oneness. Ideally, brotherhood would be expressed, in Ireland as in other countries, in the form of rural and urban cooperative societies – AE once referred to these as modern versions of the medieval city-states – which would overcome the antagonism between town and country, and form the predominant part of the economy, while leaving room for private enterprise. There would be a democratically elected parliament, and vocational councils controlling the activities of those government departments that served major branches of the national economy. That would be the ideal. But increasingly, from about 1916 onwards, AE came to believe that, if brotherhood were not achieved this way – and there were increasing signs that it would not be – then the divine will would see to its implementation through all-powerful, all-regulating states, and perhaps through a world empire.

As for the qualities of individual self-realisation, AE agreed with Connolly on the attributes 'self-possessed, self-reliant, courageous and brotherly'; 'worker', too, if it meant creator, but there was one important difference. He regarded spiritual vision, aided by the doctrines of theosophy, as a necessary attribute of the realised human being. Specifically, to be fully human, people must perceive that they are divine beings in a spiritual and divine environment. As he said on that day in 1895 when he preached on the seafront at Bray:

> The earth beneath you is as sacred as that of Judea, and the Golden Age is about you if you would but claim it. All men bear within them their own divinity, and it needs only some adventure of the spirit, some gesture against materialism, for each man to gain his inheritance.

AE's understanding of 'self-possessed' human beings contained this extra element.

For AE then, as for Connolly, the way to achieve a human-ised Ireland was threefold. First, people must learn to see divinity in themselves and their environment: they must do this by the study of theosophy, by practising meditation, and generally by liberating their vision from materialism and opening their eyes. Second, farmers and urban workers must form cooperatives and develop federations of cooperatives for large-scale enterprises. Third, and simultaneously with the first two, national self-goverment must be attained (AE favoured Home Rule and would have been content with it, but he supported the Free State vigorously when it arrived).

If we set Connolly's concept of man realised alongside AE's, we find that, while Connolly envisaged this as a self-governing nation of self-possessed, self-reliant, courageous, fraternal, working per-sons exercising collective ruling power, AE envisaged it as a self-governing nation of self-possessed, self-reliant, courageous, creative persons imbued with spiritual vision and living together in ac-tive brotherhood. Connolly, as we have seen, had a role for special vision – namely, for the socialist secular vision – but merely as a *means* to humanity, as a lever raising the workers towards that goal. He did not regard a special vision of any kind as an attribute of man realised; nor did he believe, as Marx did, that the changed production relationships would necessarily produce a particular, corresponding kind of vision or consciousness. Accepting that people will always see certain things differently, especially in the fields of religion and morality, he believed that any of those ways of seeing things – provided it did not contradict the basic socialist principle – could coexist with a socialist society; and he believed, moreover, that people of any religious persuasion, or none, could take part in the struggle for that goal. He wrote:

Socialism, as a party, bases itself upon its knowledge of facts, of economic truths, and leaves the building up of religious ideals or faiths to the outside public, or to its individual members if they so will. It is neither Freethinker nor Christian, Turk nor Jew, Buddhist nor Idolater, Mahometan nor Parsee – it is only human.

As it happens, Connolly believed and frequently said that Christianity, properly understood, was positively favourable to the socialisation of man. In particular, he said this to Irish Catholics; and when some of their clergy opposed socialism, he responded by trying to show those clerical critics how and why they should be on his side. He probably believed that other religions, properly understood, were similarly favourable to the socialist project. At all events, he rejected the antireligious, anticlerical and libertine ideology of the Enlightenment which had imbued the thought of William Thompson, and which permeated contemporary Continental, though not British, socialism. (In this respect, Connolly's socialism belonged to the British rather than the Continental school.)

Since AE, unlike Connolly, was, so to speak, in the religion business – or at least in the business of the supernatural – he was not able to share Connolly's indifference in these matters or his undiscriminating tolerance. Although he believed that the theosophical doctrines, most clearly transmitted by Hinduism, were to be found in a veiled form in all religions – in Christianity, for instance, in the Gospel of Saint John and some of Saint Paul's writings – he was in practice opposed to institutional Christianity, and particularly to that form of it that provided the main obstacle to his own mission, namely, Irish Catholicism. He saw Irish Catholicism as a religious system characterised by priestly dominance, which, though formally a religion, in practice made people materialists and even atheists. It did not, in other words, enable or help people to have that spiritual vision of themselves and their environment that, for AE, was the defining attribute of the real God-believer and religious man. He once referred to Christian ministers, pointedly, as 'the blind leading the blind'. He criticised the Church doctrine on hell for cowing manhood. Furthermore, he regarded Irish Christianity as philistine: it fostered bad art and gave rise to no good art; it neither loved beauty nor awakened creativity. This sterility, he believed, was basically the consequence of its lack of any cosmogony or psychology worth mentioning. It had produced only two spiritual thinkers: Eriugena and Berkeley. AE, like Yeats, resented the fact that Christianity in Ireland had removed holiness from the land of Ireland to Rome and Judea.

Connolly, like Thompson before him, rejected the modern state, as exemplified, say, by Britain. He regarded it as a bureaucratic tyranny extraneous to human society. Unlike Marx, who wanted it to wither away only after it had served to establish the workers' power, Thompson and Connolly wanted its removal to coincide with the workers' coming to power. Thompson had wanted it to be replaced by a society of cooperative communities; Connolly, as we have seen, wanted a political system based on the industrial and vocational principle.

AE was most ambiguous about the modern state. On the one hand, he could refer to states and empires as 'devils' and constantly decry the Irish tendency to depend on the state. On the other, he could see a greatly enhanced version of the modern state as the means by which the divine law of brotherhood would be enforced, if people failed to do so voluntarily by cooperative methods. For a time, he praised the Bolshevik state in the belief that it was encouraging cooperatives, but he changed his mind about this in 1920. Later, and more significantly, he became an ardent supporter of the American state of the New Deal period. He admired the Mosaic state of the Old Testament and decried Christianity's failure to influence the state and set the norms for economic activity. In this respect, and in this aspect of his personality, he was a religious prophet or ayatollah, longing to see God's will done at all costs, and if necessary by constraint. Ideally, however, he wanted a modified form of the modern state, providing services to a society organised cooperatively. He criticised the parliamentary state on the grounds that its representative national assembly was fitted to deal with general interests, but not particular ones – and that bureaucrats who were not experts in their particular fields controlled the administration of the particular interests. It was on these grounds that he stressed the need for vocational control of vocational interests, though not to the comprehensive degree that Connolly advocated.

There was no real clash of views between AE and Connolly with regard to whether unions or cooperatives should be the vehicle of socialisation. AE supported trade unionism, and specifically the workers' strike of 1913 on behalf of their right to be members of a union. Connolly, as we have seen, welcomed and praised the cooperative movement and saw it as a means for replacing the capitalist economy. He probably envisaged a marriage of some kind between cooperativism and the syndicalist political system based on industrial unions.

It is difficult to be precise here because the fact of the matter was that, whilst many cooperatives did exist and the movement promised well, the syndicalist political system did not exist, even in embryo, and could therefore only be theorised about. Significantly, however, both Connolly and AE regarded the cooperative community at Ralahine, County Clare, which had existed for two years in the early 1830s, as the signpost pointing the way to the future cooperative commonwealth or workers' republic.

In identifying the forces frustrating human realisation in Ireland, Connolly and AE discovered many enemies in common: British rule, individualism, capitalism, poverty, fear, the spirit of dependence, the state as constituted in Ireland. Connolly would have added 'the lack of socialist vision' and false understandings of socialism, such as economism or the socialism that trumpeted anti-clericalism. AE would have added spiritual blindness and the forces causing it: materialism, Christianity, science (because it was materialistic).

Both Connolly and AE – as Thompson before them – explicitly included women in their humanism, and were strong asserters of the equality of women. In addition to the roles women shared by right with men, AE attributed to them a special role as civilisers and beautifiers of domestic life: if it had not been for women, he said, men would still be living in cave dwellings. Connolly said that 'the women's cause is felt by all labour men and women to be their cause' and he welcomed the new breed of militant women who were taking the lead both in the labour movement and in other revolutionary bodies.

Connolly was vehemently opposed to workers participating in capitalist wars, but believed in their right to use force, if necessary, in their class struggle and to secure national liberation. He held, moreover, that the spilling of blood could help to redeem their degraded humanity. AE believed that the highest morality forbade the use of force, and he would have liked to be able to believe that it was always, in practice, wrong, but found he could not maintain this position intellectually. It was clear, he said, that the Irish had never got anything from England except by the use of force. Speaking more generally, he wrote:

> There is an absolute morality, and below that there are relative moralities. The purely spiritual man who has a superb reliance on divine law to justify and sustain him will return good for evil, will endure all things without anger, and will not take to the sword because he believes he is throwing into the scales something which will outweigh all physical powers. But if he has not this illumina-tion, then, if a man is oppressed, it is relatively better morals for him to fight than to be a slave, because that is the choice for him.

Actually, Gandhi said much the same thing.

Except in so far as most of Ireland became politically self-governing and AE and Connolly both contributed to this – Connolly more

notably than AE – their teachings cannot be said to have had enduring consequences. A limited cooperative movement survived, but more as businesses than as a new social form, and not
as the spearhead of a cooperative commonwealth. The Irish,
despite their massive religious adherence, did not abandon their
materialistic vision and acquire a spiritual vision of themselves
and their environment. Trade unionism did not develop as Connolly hoped it would. The workers did not win control over their
work, let alone over the nation. Trade unionists and, even more
noticeably, trade union leaders, did not become free men, with
that freedom from the chip on the shoulder and the whine that
characterises the free personality.

But of course the thought and action of AE and Connolly alone
could not have effected those things, or even contributed to them,
without intellectual comrades and successors to develop and apply
their thought critically. They did not have these largely because
the teaching which AE gave frequently in his later years, as editor
of the *Irish Statesman* – that the Irish must develop the intellectual faculty as well as the imaginative one – was not heeded. After
a thirty-year blossoming of thought and philosophy, with a meagre
after-bloom of ten or fifteen years, the Irish relapsed into the role
of 'imaginative, thoughtless Celts' that their Anglo-Saxon masters
had assigned to them. They became, again, parrots of the thought
of other nations and despisers or avoiders of their own.

Thus, for example, AE's teaching that each person has within
his or her outer mind an inner mind endowed with special powers
of vision – and that that vision alone is real – was not taken
seriously, and investigated, developed or refuted by psychologists
or theologians. Nor was there any serious intellectual development of cooperativist or socialist thought. Most fundamentally
of all, however, there has been no serious humanist speculation
of any kind – no original exploration in Ireland of the big questions
that AE and Connolly asked and answered: what is man? how
is man now? how can people in the contemporary world, or

specifically in Ireland, overcome the manifest dehumanising tendencies of the times and enable themselves to live humanly? Or rather, to be more precise, such speculation of that kind as was engaged in after 1918, partly by AE himself, petered out in the 1930s.

How did this come about? It has much to do with the manner in which the intellectual events and currents in nationalist Ireland in the years 1884–1918 have been seen over the past sixty years. The wood has not been seen for the trees. The trees, which *have* been seen, were distinct movements of ideas of various kinds – literary, linguistic, mystical, political – or the subdivisions of these into poetical or theatrical, Gaelic or Anglo-Irish, Rosicrucian or theosophical, republican, socialist, cooperativist, labourite and so on. The wood, which has not been seen, is the humanist movement to which all of these added up and which all of them were part of. What has not been seen, in other words, is that all those distinct currents of thought and endeavour arose out of concern about the condition of man in the contemporary world, and especially in Ireland, and were aiming in their various ways at the restoration of man in Ireland and the world. Since this central and pervasive humanist theme has hardly been perceived over the past sixty years or so, it is little wonder that it has been neither explored coherently nor developed critically, whether with relation to Connolly and AE or in any other respect.

I finish, then, with a plea that Irish intellectuals perceive and see this humanist movement that was bound together by the theme of remaking man in Ireland and the world; that they explore its content, and re-explore its leading figures in that light. There are three good reasons for doing this. First, and least important-ly, it would lead to someone among us at long last writing a book about the humanism of Yeats or, if you like, Yeats's philosophy of society and the human person.

Second, I believe that, lurking and hidden in that humanist movement of which Yeats was part, we would discover what might be called the Irish Dream, and that it could be at least as inspiring for us as the original American Dream has been for American intellectuals in the various ups and downs of their national history. They have that, always, as a basic touchstone and bedrock of American revolutionary allegiance. Our own intellectuals have no such bedrock, for they have failed to discover and articulate the humanist dream and project of the Irish Revolution. Consequently, in these recent decades, when economic, political and ideological reaction against the Revolution are rampant in this republic, they have lost themselves, by and large, in a maze of clever, disintegrating and ultimately conformist criticism which ends up in a gaping void; and that void diminishes both themselves as Irish intellectuals and the nation they should be serving. Both for their own sake, therefore, and to be of service, they need to discover the Irish Dream.

Third and finally, Pope said, and he was right, that the proper study of mankind is man, and there is a sense in which a nation that does not engage in that study, as we do not, falls short of being part of mankind. So our humanity is at stake in this matter. I believe that, as we made ourselves aware of that powerful humanist movement in our recent past, we would feel prompted and encouraged to do what our humanity requires. We would feel prompted to rebegin the study of man and the discourse about man. By means of that activity we would be resuming and continuing the reconquest of our Irish humanity that we ventured on some time back, and then drew back from. Our decolonisation would be under way again.

4

A PROJECT
TO END THE
PARALYSIS

S OME TIME AGO AT University College Galway, I attended a
gathering of about forty intellectuals from all parts of Ireland
who spent most of a weekend discussing the present crisis of Irish
identity and what, if anything, should be done about it. The occasion had been organised by Patrick Sheeran and Riana O'Dwyer,
of the English department of UCG. The principal achievement
of the weekend was not any clear decision on the question raised,
but rather a new way of talking about it which I believe could
be fruitful. Most of the time, instead of talking about the national
identity as such, we were talking about the national 'project' –
the project, if any, that the nation gives itself and seeks to fulfil.
The reasoning behind this was that, with a nation as with a person,
it is in the choice and pursuit of a life project that identity is forged.

People are wrong who say that, apart from a few intellectuals,
no one regards our national identity as a matter of importance.
These last twenty years, many journalists, politicians and businessmen have worked very hard at telling us that the Irish nation
is not Gaelic or Catholic, and is not characterised, historically,
by a centuries-long struggle for freedom against England. They
would hardly have done this unless they considered our national
identity (which means, in effect, our idea of our identity) very

From the *Irish Times*, 8 July 1985

important indeed. Clearly, all these hard-working people believed it was very important that we should not think or feel that we were a Gaelic, Catholic nation, characterised by a long struggle for freedom against England of which we could feel proud.

However, though many were prepared to show in this manner that they regarded the matter as important, it is very difficult, now that the attacked national identity has been demolished and not replaced, to get serious public discussion of the problem this leaves us. The fact that we no longer think or feel that we are a Gaelic, Catholic people characterised, historically, by a long freedom struggle, and have substituted no equivalent self-image, leaves us bereft of something that every nation needs and that most have. No wonder that everyone is talking about 'the depressed mood of the country' and of how the government and every other source of major initiative seem 'paralysed'. But, precisely in such circumstances, it is very difficult to get serious thought or discussion started about such an apparently remote, abstract and static thing as the 'national identity' or 'our concept of ourselves'.

That is why I welcome the turn that the discussion took in Galway. A 'national project' is, and appears to be, something dynamic. It suggests goals and action. To talk about it seems to meet the needs of a time when a feeling of paralysis is lying heavily on people and national purpose is palpably absent. Moreover, whereas talk about identity seems to threaten to call up old, tired arguments and adjectives, talk about a project points towards the future and suggests something new. And finally, those who are concerned about the national identity can take part in good conscience in discussion about the national project once they realise that it is in the pursuit of such a project, if it is distinctive, that a distinct national identity is forged.

Those who were chiefly responsible for giving this direction to the Galway discussion were Pat Sheeran and Nina Witoszek – an occasional Polish visitor and student of Irish affairs. Linking together the *Crane Bag,* the Field Day pamphlets and the University College Dublin lecture series on RTE last year – on the grounds that the *Crane Bag* Holy Trinity Seamus Deane, Declan Kiberd and Richard Kearney had a hand in all of them – Sheeran and Witoszek delivered a joint critique of this *'Crane Bag* intellectualism'. They faulted it for having engaged in an excess of brilliant critical analysis of the Irish identity forged in the first half of the century, while advocating no positive national project except that Ireland should catch up fully with the European Enlightenment. For their own part, they proposed an alternative project: that Ireland should 'regain and redefine its identity by using its spiritual resources to lead the New Age movement'. In their paper they expressed it thus:

> In taking our place in the vanguard of the worldwide New Age movement, we have the unique opportunity in Europe of turning our anachronisms to a virtue. Paradoxically enough, at a time when the world is starving for soul, for transcendence, for myth, we are being asked to seek a belated Enlightenment. The most belated race in Europe yet again!

For those who are not familiar with the term, the New Age movement is an alliance of all those groups and movements that, in one way or another, reject the values and methods of the modern world and propose an alternative, 'post-modern' way of living. In place of the modern world's materialism, they urge cultivation of man's spiritual nature; in place of centralisation, decentralised societies; instead of the abuse of the earth and its resources, ecological care and organic farming; instead of giant technology and debased food, human-scale technology and healthy food.

Suffice to say here that Richard Kearney and Dermot Moran defended the *Crane Bag* ably and that Sheeran and Witoszek, when they put forward their project verbally, narrowed it to the 'soul, transcendence, myth' aspect of the New Age movement, and urged that Ireland find her role in cultivating spirit for her own and the world's sake. This, predictably enough, found little favour from the meeting. Most contemporary Irish intellectuals cultivate a tough-minded aversion to the spiritual – a sort of machismo of materialism which regards the supernatural as cissy stuff and demotes consciousness below matter. In Galway the statement that 'consciousness is primary' evoked incomprehension from the audience.

Be that as it may, I think that the weekend, taken as a whole, sketched out the framework within which constructive discussion of a project for Ireland could take place. The choice is, indeed, between a 'modernising' project of some sort and one that aims at a better-than-modern life. Given that choice, I believe the Sheeran/Witoszek proposal, in its original not its narrowed form, points towards the sort of collective enterprise we need. Both to end our mournful navel-gazing and to regain a distinctive personality in the world, we need a project aiming at a better-than-modern life.

'Modern' has always meant what is in vogue, in the way of lifestyles, technology and opinions, in the power centres of the capitalist world. Secondary nations have had the choice either of aping that, provincially, and finding themselves always lagging, or of striking out on their own for a better-than-modern life. Ireland and Russia, at the beginning of this century, were two secondary nations which opted, simultaneously, for the latter course. Or rather, in both countries intellectual leaderships attempted it with varying degrees of popular support.

In Ireland, Pearse in the educational field, Yeats in theatre, Plunkett, Russell, Connolly and Larkin in economic and political organisation, Russell and Yeats by working for the restoration of myth and sacredness, the Catholic clergy by building a holy Ireland to convert the world, most of the leading revolutionaries by exalting rural civilisation, all set their faces against 'the filthy modern tide' and aimed to create a new and truly human life which would radiate from Ireland and transform the age. It was

with that in mind – envisaged variously from their different
perspectives – that they worked for or looked to the establishment of an Irish state. But in Ireland as in Russia, the project of
building the new state that would make possible the New Life
gradually replaced the New Life project. In Ireland, moreover,
some elements of that project (such as Yeats's hopes for a poetic
theatre re-educating the people's sensibility) had either petered
out before the state was founded or been excluded *ipso facto* by
its frankly capitalist nature. Nevertheless, even the remnants of
that Irish better-than-modern project, the nominal pursuit of
them, and the lingering aura of the revolutionary years sufficed
to give Ireland, through the 1920s, 1930s and 1940s, a distinct
identity that made her one of the three chief personalities of the
English-speaking world, alongside England and America.

Both in Ireland and in Russia, the failed attempt to realise the
better-than-modern project resulted in a low material living standard at a time when living standards in the capitalist world
generally were beginning to rise sharply. If the Irish state had,
like the Russian state, prohibited emigration and disposed of a
language barrier, censorship, and radio-jamming apparatus, which
excluded information about the outside world, its low standard
of living would not have mattered. But because the Republic of
Ireland was a liberal democracy and spoke English, it mattered
so much that it became urgently necessary to improve the
economy by whatever means. Hence the last national project that
we have had; one of the modernising, conforming kind. Launched
in the late 1950s, it got into trouble in the mid-1970s, chugged
on for a while on borrowed money, and then petered out. Or
rather, its economic dimension, which is what it was essentially
about, petered out, while its mental superstructure – 'Hello
London, hello New York, what are today's guidelines?' – continued, and still continues, to spancel us.

Another modernising national project? I don't think it is on
the cards and it is not what we need. What we need is a

better-than-modern national project hatched by free-thinking Irish minds and put persuasively to the nation. Was this, perhaps, what Professor Joseph Lee really meant when recently he advocated a better-than-London approach to our problems, on the grounds that London's modernity, our primary lodestar, is now so second-rate?

In the nature of things, a better-than-modern national project will be a combination of projects unified by a better-than-modern view of human nature and what is right for man. To get it off the ground, therefore, we need thinkers who tear themselves free from the parochial rut of present-day Irish thinking, and who direct their minds, critically, to the human condition in the modern world and modern Ireland. We need, in other words, inventive thinkers who look for 'what is basically wrong with Irish life today' not in the Irish past, nor in the not-quite-British elements of the present – Catholic Church, IRA, Fianna Fáil, GAA, etcetera – nor in their West British counterparts, but in Ireland's participation in a view and style of life that are destroying man piecemeal (look at man today in Dublin) and are capable of destroying him outright.

After that, it is a matter of looking at modern life and institutions as these are exemplified in Ireland, and of asking, in one domain after another: is that a fit life for man, a pro-human or anti-human arrangement, or the most intelligent way of organising things? That was precisely how the movement for a better-than-modern life got started in Ireland eighty years ago. It was with such questions in mind that Pearse looked at education, provincialism and the commercial morality; Yeats at the relationship between people and art; Russell, Connolly and Larkin at the organisation of production and the economy; Yeats, Russell and the Catholic bishops at the contemporary materialism and godlessness.

Today those same aspects of modern life, as they are manifested in Ireland, need to be looked at again with enthusiasm for man, a critical eye, and an inventive imagination; but together with them, all the other aspects of modern living that strike thinking people now need to be questioned: for example, the sprawls of chaos that our cities are becoming; the new unemployment and the very concept of 'unemployment'; the overcentralised state and its frustration of creative initiative; moribund religion which substitutes sentiment for vision; the use of the electronic communications media to sedate and isolate people; the destruction of sexual morality and its consequences for women; mental, cultural and economic colonialism; the growth of police forces and of their powers and armaments; the link between consumerism and the financing of nuclear weapons. Add others and take your pick. All are aspects of modernity which we live with and which are detrimental to us, as they are detrimental to all the other peoples who make up the modern world.

The notion of tackling and solving these problems, in an exemplary way, in Ireland makes practical sense, inasmuch as it is much easier to do so – much more likely to be done – in a fairly small country with a small population than in a large country with a population of many millions. This is indeed, pre-eminently, how a small nation can be of real use to the world and find a positive role in it.

Our first better-than-modern movement began to issue in new institutions – agricultural co-ops and the Irish Agricultural Organisation Society, St Enda's, the Abbey Theatre, the ITGWU, the Citizen Army, Dáil Éireann, even Yeats's Order of Celtic Mysteries – which were meant to embody, produce or defend the new life. A new better-than-modern project, directed at present circumstances, would have a similar result. More precisely, institutional innovation and transformation is what it would be all about. And in this instance, too, the first institution to be changed would be language: there would be a new and encouraging way of talking about our life, a language revival in that sense.

5

THE INDEPENDENCE
OF IRELAND
IN THE 1990s

THE REAL INDEPENDENCE OF IRELAND, and the means of attaining and maintaining it, must always be our first priority, and any thinking about Ireland and Europe in the years ahead that ignores these matters is of no positive use either to the Irish or to Europe. I will expand briefly on that statement, give voice to those Irish people who would pooh-pooh it, and answer them. Then I will suggest how we can work realistically through the 1990s towards a really independent Ireland.

By 'real' national independence I mean something quite modest. I mean sufficient independence for a nation to be the shaper, by and large, of its own worldview, life and international relationships. Everyone agrees that this is a fundamental human good, that it is wrong for a nation to be deprived of it, and that a nation without it is a nation only in name. It is a human good because a nation is a unit of mankind with a particular history, existing in specific circumstances, and it is only by having effective control of its life that this group and its members can realise their unique humanity, collectively and personally, and thus contribute their due share to the inherent and enriching diversity of mankind – or of Europe, if they are a European nation. By the same token, mankind, and Europe specifically, need the

From Richard Kearney (ed.), *Across the Frontiers: Ireland in the 1990s* (Dublin: Wolfhound, 1988)

real independence of their constituent nations in order to *be* mankind and to *be* Europe. But real independence is also the primary practical good of a nation, for the good reason that none but itself and its members can identify and advance its interests, and they need independence to do this. Consequently, however one views the matter, the real independence of Ireland is an imperative for the Irish and a necessity for Europe.

But standing in opposition to these truths and realities is the obvious fact that we live in a world that is unfavourable to the real independence of small nations, and particularly to that of a small nation such as Ireland which shares a common language with its two powerful neighbours, one of whom is immediately adjacent to it and its coloniser and controller for centuries. Both in our own case and in that of many nations, a proposition once believed in as dogma has proved to be untrue: namely, that for a small nation to have real national independence, it is sufficient for it – barring overwhelming armed invasion – to possess a state of its own. Since the Second World War, developments in communications and in the international organisation of industry, finance and commerce have brought about a situation in which major states or, more precisely, world power centres, can control small nation-states, or decisively limit their freedom of action, without recourse to military invasion or occupation. Empire can now be, and is, exercised at a physical remove and by indirect means.

From this obvious conflict between the present state of the world and our need in Ireland for real national independence, two things follow logically. In the first place, a vision of Ireland in the years ahead, if it is to be of any positive use, must include realistic thinking about how we can achieve and maintain real independence. Second, we share a common interest with all other small nations, and particularly with those that labour under such extreme disadvantages as we do, in reshaping the world and its power structures so that they will be less unfavourable, and, ideally, favourable, to the independence of small nations, ourselves included.

There are many in Ireland today who would demur at those two propositions. I am talking about people who are actively concerned about the independence of Nicaragua, Honduras, Cambodia, or Namibia, but who would demur at the suggestion that what we Irish most need is independence to shape our own worldview, culture, polity and external relationships. Ireland, they believe, is for one reason or another an exception to the general rule – which applies to Nicaragua, Honduras, Namibia, Zimbabwe and so on. What Ireland needs most, they say, is to be more like other countries, especially Britain and America, but selectively of course in both instances; and to be able to provide a decent living for the Irish who stay at home, and useful education for those who go abroad to take up jobs in Britain, on the Continent, in the USA or the Middle East. We are, after all, in the EEC (or the EC as it is now called), and that opens endless opportunities for our young people, and makes independence to do our own thing, shape our own life, play our own role in the world, superfluous. France, West Germany, Britain, Italy? Well, yes, but they are big countries; we are a very small, tuppence-halfpenny country on the outer edge of Europe. As for our sharing a common interest with other small nations in reshaping the world, that does sound a bit pretentious, not to say unrealistic. A common interest, perhaps, with some of them, the democratic ones, the neutral ones maybe. But rather than reshaping the world – some enterprise that! – we should be thinking of getting the most we can out of it as it is.

I think it is fair to say that opinions about Ireland in the Republic today are divided between that sort of view, which does not take Ireland seriously as a nation, and another view which does, and which I share. I reject the first view because it implies that, as an Irishman, I belong to a failed project – a nation that has given up. It treats as unimportant the fact that we have not yet in history created a state; that we feel constrained to live in a British-made state which we are afraid to reorganise to suit us; that our culture from our political institutions and language to 'For He's a Jolly Good Fellow' and horse-racing is largely derivative; that our journalists belong to a British trade union and the stock exchange in Dublin is a section of the London Stock Exchange; that our thought and hence our worldview are largely borrowed from London and that we have not contributed anything of significance to the thought of our time; that when we import ideas or practices we seldom digest and rethink them so as to transform them into something marked by ourselves; that our industrial exports are mainly those of foreign firms in Ireland which repatriate their profits; that we have failed to generate, out of our own enterprise and resources, an economy sufficient to maintain ourselves; that we collaborate with Britain in suppressing rebellion against British rule in Ireland and, in betrayal of our neutrality, have allowed the Republic to be integrated into the British military and military surveillance systems; and lastly, that we lack both an independent foreign policy and its principal fruit – foreign alliances created by ourselves to serve our interests.

All of those things, which are of no importance to the view of Ireland that I have outlined and reject, are of importance to me. They are the evidence that shows that we have no real independence and are not, therefore, living up to our nationhood or, simply, to our practical potential as 4 million well-fed, intelligent and imaginative people. Those Irish who tell us in effect to ignore this because it does not matter are, in fact and willy-nilly, collaborating spokespersons of the imperial propaganda that would have us believe just that. Moreover, in so far as they are members of our political and administrative elite – whether of the national or the Euro kind – the thwarting of Ireland's independence is, for many of them personally, a matter of practical indifference, because quite irrespective of its condition in the world the Irish nation-state provides them with jobs, careers, influence and formal status.

Patriots who cite the list of social dependencies and inertias that I have cited above often do so in order to exhort us morally: they urge us to get up off our backsides or our knees and show more spirit, pride, enterprise and the like, as citizens or as politicians. I do not join in this exhortation because I believe that, for the most part, those dependencies, inertias and servilities merely illustrate the predictable effect on us of a world so organised – around Ireland and within it – as to prevent the independence of small nations, Ireland included. And there are, to my mind, only two honourable and effective ways of dealing with this situation, mitigating its disgrace, and lessening its damage. We can call off our separate Irish project, become by acts of will and law British or American, and throw all our frustrated talents into making a splendid success of the UK or the USA. Or, recognising that we share a common interest with other small nations in reshaping the world and its power relationships to make them at least less unfavourable to our project and theirs, we can start thinking how that might be done – and gradually move from thinking about it to sustained and intermittent action. This is my choice, and consequently my hope for Ireland in the 1990s is that at least some among us will be doing such thinking, and that it will take practical effect.

The thinking will start, necessarily, by rejecting – losing faith in – the prevalent image of contemporary reality, and by identifying how things really are and how they came to be that way. The established view of the world, the world image that is presented to us and by which we largely see the world, is, needless to say, the tranquillising propaganda image disseminated by London and New York. Its purpose is to represent the Western world – both as it is and as it impinges on the rest of the world – as benign, natural, normal and inevitable. This system of power and control depends for its existence not on nuclear bombs or standing armies or accumulated wealth, but on the faith of hundreds of millions – including 4 million Irish – in that imperial world image and its message. It follows that as we rid our minds of this illusion and construct another, truer, and inevitably subversive image, the constricting system weakens a little, and we begin to get hints and glimpses of a different, possible, less unfavourable world. We can start with nation-states.

The world is made up of states that call themselves nations and purport to be nations. A few centuries ago there were very few of these nation-states, but as every nation wanted to be like Britain or France or to a lesser extent Spain – these were old nation-states offering models for others to follow – there came to be nation-states all over the world. When we look closely at those states that served as models, we notice that they are each made up of several nations and (in the case of France and Spain) parts of nations: for example, part of the Basque nation in Spain, parts of the Basque, Catalan, German and other nations in France. In each case, to begin with, an imperial core nation – English, Frankish, Castilian – hammered together into a single state a collection of national communities and ethnic groups and called them a nation. The resulting 'nation' – a sort of umbrella nation or state-nation – was originally a fiction, but through schooling and inter-state wars it was made into a sort of accepted fact which coexisted among the subject nations and ethnic communities with their own thwarted communal lives and consciousness. Not surprisingly, then, as the habit of making nation-states took on and spread, many of them were similarly multinational conglomerates, culminating ultimately in the monster nation-states of the USA, the Soviet Union and China.

If we look again at the three original models, we notice that from an early stage the chief city of the core nation – London, Paris, Madrid – came to dominate the entire nation-state, including the core nation. Drawing strength and wealth from the communities it was subjecting and destroying – as it replaced the collection of communities with a mass of uprooted and isolated individuals and nuclear families – it attained in fact an imperial status and exercised an internal imperialism. Ancient Rome did the same in Italy while building its empire abroad, and these modern European capitals also built empires abroad. It has been a convenient fiction of the modern age to speak of the British, French and Spanish empires, when in fact the empires in question, at home and abroad, were those of London, Paris and Madrid. The inhabitants of the respective nation-states worked, as empire-builders and favoured clients, to increase, in the first instance, the power of these imperial power centres. So great was their power, relatively, that, together with other centres of similar power such as Vienna, Berlin and St Petersburg in their heydays, they became world power centres. London and Paris have re-mained that even after 'losing' (a relative term these days) most of their imperial domains abroad.

The upshot of it all was that over the past two centuries as more and more new nation-states emerged, each with its imperial power centre, major or minor, the world arranged itself not in the first instance as an assembly of nation-states large and small, but in the first instance, and effectively, as *great hierarchies of power centres*. New York–Washington (or New York for short) is now the chief world power centre. Through its dependent power centres it holds dominion directly over the USA and indirectly over the rest of the American continent, Western Europe and further afield. Moscow, controlling the Soviet Union and much outside it through another hierarchy of power centres, vies with New York for the top place. Beneath New York stand Chicago, Los Angeles, Dallas, Boston, Bogotá, Rio de Janeiro, Tokyo, London, Paris, Brussels, and beneath each of these its satellite power centres – Dublin being one of London's. This is the New York empire.

An important thing to understand about the power centres, major and minor, is that they are castles as much of mutual fear as of actual or would-be domination. As they came into existence, they frightened each other into existence – each of them concentrating as much power within itself as it could so that it might withstand, and possibly overcome, its threatening rivals. And standing now, confronting each other competitively and fearfully, they maintain each other in existence. By an intricate system of interaction, London towers as high as it does over Ireland, England, Scotland, Wales, because in their various ways New York, Moscow, Beijing, Tokyo, Paris and Frankfurt compel it to tower high – as they compel each other, mutually and collectively, to tower high. Meanwhile Dublin does its best, with the resources available to it in Ireland, to be our local London.

When I use a city name to name a power centre, I am referring in the first instance not to that mass of individuals – no longer a real city community – and the radiating force that its sheer mass and its economy generate, but rather to the decision-making and controlling powers that exist there, and the accumulated resources, human and material, that they have at their disposal there. But of course the power exercised by a power centre does not all issue directly from it. It issues also through a network of attached agents and collaborators 'in the provinces', and is increased by these. When the power centre is of world status its provinces are far-flung and include many legally independent states; and in each of these is a 'national' power centre with its provinces; and in these again, in some states, are subnational power centres, each with a province of its own.

Attached, therefore, to the hierarchies of imperial power centres are hierarchies of dependent provinces which rank higher or lower roughly in accordance with the rankings of their national power centres. In short, we live in a world of empires and provinces, more precisely in a world of provinces depending on hierarchies of power centres which, within their respective dominions and collectively, rule the world. Ireland is a province of the London region of the New York empire, and is dependent also on the

Brussels confederacy which a group of major West European power centres dominate.

I have been using the word province in its qualitative sense to mean a society that is generally dependent and derivative – mentally, culturally, economically and politically. Patrick Kavanagh, describing a typical member of such a society in the mental aspect, wrote: 'The provincial has no mind of his own. He does not trust what his eye sees until he has heard what the metropolis – towards which his eyes are turned – has to say on the subject.' Imagine such a mentality multiplied by millions – or even by thousands in a provincial elite – and it is clear that the life that follows from it must be generally dependent and derivative. A province is the opposite and the negation of a community, whose hallmark is autonomy and autonomous life – springing from the distinct discourse and worldview that the members of the community have fashioned together.

Communities are the natural form of human social existence. They are made up of persons and – if they are of more than the smallest size, which comprises a number of nuclear families – of other communities also. Provinces are communities (or communities of communites) disempowered, disintegrated, and transformed into atomised, dependent 'individuals' who, in each province respectively, fall into two malleable masses, one considerably smaller than the other. This smaller mass, the 'provincial elite', provides the collective directorate in the provincial power centre. At the same time, its active provincialism collaborates with the external imperialism to transform the former community into a province or to maintain it as one. Provincialism is the disvaluation and alienation of a community by its dominant self. As the accomplice of imperialism, it is the joint agent of provincialisation and the force, which along with imperialism, maintains the provincialised world.

Latently, then, our world of power centres and provinces is a world of communities, national or subnational, old or embryonic,

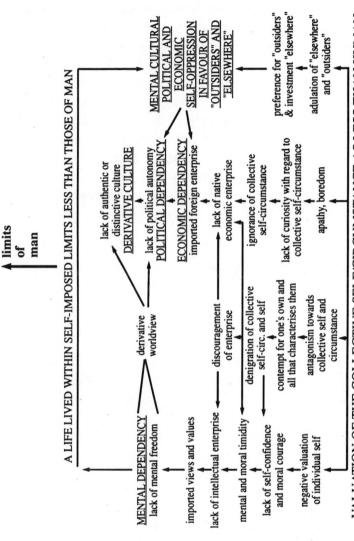

limits
of
man

A LIFE LIVED WITHIN SELF-IMPOSED LIMITS LESS THAN THOSE OF MAN

MENTAL CULTURAL
POLITICAL AND
ECONOMIC
SELF-OPPRESSION
IN FAVOUR OF
"OUTSIDERS" AND
"ELSEWHERE"

preference for "outsiders"
& investment "elsewhere"

adulation of "elsewhere"
and "outsiders"

lack of authentic or
distinctive culture
DERIVATIVE CULTURE

lack of political autonomy
POLITICAL DEPENDENCY

ECONOMIC DEPENDENCY
imported foreign enterprise

lack of native
economic enterprise

ignorance of collective
self-circumstance

lack of curiosity with regard to
collective self-circumstance

apathy, boredom

derivative
worldview

discouragement
of enterprise

denigration of collective
self-circ. and self

contempt for one's own and
all that characterises them

antagonism towards
collective self and
circumstance

MENTAL DEPENDENCY
lack of mental freedom

imported views and values

lack of intellectual enterprise

mental and moral timidity

lack of self-confidence
and moral courage

negative valuation
of individual self

VALUATION OF THE COLLECTIVE SELF/CIRCUMSTANCE AS LESS THAN HUMAN
NORM - HENCE AS INVALID, VALUELESS AND MEANINGLESS FOR HUMAN BEINGS

The Provincial Syndrome (a partial view).

which are negated and thwarted in the manner described. All of them, though maimed and muffled, are more or less conscious of themselves, perceive themselves as *wes*, but are unable to realise that communal consciousness as autonomous life. Their more conscious and spirited elements try sporadically or persistently to do so, but are continually counteracted by two forces: on the one hand, the dinned-in imperial image of the present world as the normal, humane and inevitable world; on the other, the attachment of the masses, rulers and ruled, to the goodies labelled the Good Life that the imperial system delivers and promises with the constantly reiterated assertion: 'These are to be had only in these shapes and packagings, and delivered by this system on these terms.' Which is a lie.

That, roughly, is the nature of the world which is preventing Ireland and other small nations from having the independence they need; and, as I said above, identifying this real state of affairs is the first stage in thinking about how it might be transformed into a state of affairs less unfavourable to us. The second is, by a leap of mind and without thought of ways or means, to imagine this present world changed into a world that would positively facilitate an Ireland in which we are no longer copycats, parrots and catcher-uppers living by laws, working in factories, lodging in a state, and accepting a worldview that others have prescribed or financed or made, but have become again, as we once were, a people creating our own sufficiency of wealth and our own unique worldview, life and culture.

What would that world be like that would favour this? The empires and provinces have been replaced by a world community of communities – the world in its natural human shape. Big Ben still chimes and Westminster Bridge still stands, but London's usurped powers of government and wealth production, and many of its inhabitants, have returned to Scotland, Wales, Mann, Cornwall and the regions of England. The Seine still flows through a Paris that has lost its fat, and it is still a lovely city in the spring; but Brittany, Normandy, Occitania, Corsica, Alsace and Picardy have come into their own again. California, New England, Dixie, Texas, the Sioux, Apaches and Hopis, and many other nations – one along the Hudson – whose names we do not yet know, have replaced the New York empire on its home territory. Armenia, Azerbaijan, Uzbekistan and Kurdistan, Estonia, Lithuania, Ukraine and Georgia, all in their own full right and under their own governments, contribute once again their uniqueness to the world; and Siberia is astonishing the world with its new song. Zulus, Afrikaners, Masai, Yoruba and Ndebele, the absurd colonial boundaries and the Pretorian empire cast aside, join with Ngoni and Xhosa in the assembly of African nations. In short, the world is much as the map on pages 72 and 73 shows; it was made by Peter Broberg of Malmö, Sweden, who has a similar vision.

Technology is no longer such that it compels bigness of organisation and institutions; in all its forms it is available for effective small-scale use, so that the choice between large-scale and small-scale is made pragmatically, in accordance with the individual and collective needs of communities and persons. States are no longer marshallers of people, but the pragmatic instruments and agencies with which peoples manage their common affairs and formal international relationships. Desires for wholeness, integrity, omnipotence, absolute justice are catered for by other means.

Many groups of small nations adjoining a large nation are linked as confederations balancing the weight and influence of the large nation. While the peoples of North and South America speak, for the most part, English or Spanish, most nations speak their own individual tongues and use them in their educational systems, while also using as a *lingua franca* some other suitable language – often that of a large nation adjoining them. In the British Isles what should have happened centuries ago, and would have given all these peoples a happier history, is now fact: Ireland, Scotland,

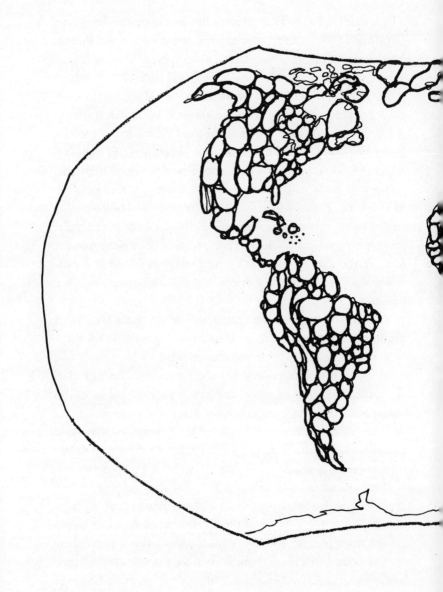

A World Community of Communities

Wales and Mann, each speaking its own language while using English as a *lingua franca,* are linked in the Confederation of Mann, balancing the weight of England.

The United Nations Organisation is in good health, its membership greatly increased and its headquarters in Mauritius. A universal upsurge against the massacring technology of modern warfare has resulted in the enactment by all nations of the Law Against Massacre, and the establishment of a United Nations police force, with worldwide detachments and unlimited inspection rights, to supervise its enforcement by national police forces. The law lays down that anyone found possessing or manufacturing a lethal or disabling device capable of killing or disabling, by its single use, more than one person, will be executed; any nation found conniving officially in a breach of the law will have its frontiers, airports and ports sealed for a period of three years.

Such a vision will serve as a guide and goal in the third and final stage of thinking about how the world and its power relationships might be made less hostile to the independence of Ireland and of other small nations. This final stage issues directly in practical action, and is consequently the kind of thinking that I hope we will be implementing in the 1990s. Aimed at the transformation of the world into a de-imperialised, de-provincialised and disarmed community of communities, it will identify the immediate courses of action that, while gradually increasing our freedom in the present, will nudge the world towards that future state. As these lines of action are identified, they are combined in an active foreign policy with political, economic and cultural dimensions.

This policy is likely to have four immediate aims.

1   Alliances that would strengthen us against London, in the first instance, against New York in the second.

2   The reconstruction of the European Community as a

grouping not of nation-states, but of national and regional communities – the national communities to include all those nations, such as Scotland, Wales, Brittany, Corsica, Euzkadi and Sardinia, which at present have no representation.

3   The encouragement by one means or another of the break-up of large states, and of automony, or greater autonomy, for nations and regions within large states.

4   The promotion by one means or another of the abolition and effective suppression of weapons of massacre.

When the Republic and the Six-County Irish, in the early part of 1988, had to endure a series of grave provocations from London such that the Irish government responded repeatedly with measured anger, the remarkable fact became apparent that Ireland had no allies. No other government, no prominent person or group in a foreign country, spoke out on Ireland's behalf. To be without allies who take its side in international disputes is an anomalous condition for a state or nation. Even before Irish independence, our nationalist struggle against London sought and found support at different times from Spain, France, Germany and the USA. Since the forging of alliances is one of the normal priorities of a foreign policy, and specifically of a department of foreign affairs, this current isolation of Ireland suggests that we are without an effective foreign policy or department of foreign affairs.

The isolation I am talking about is not of Irish people as individuals: never before have so many Irish people been in direct or indirect contact with such a wide extent of the world. It is an isolation, rather, of our nation, our collective life, our body politic, none of which reflects or exploits, in its international relationships, the far-ranging involvement of individual Irish people in the present-day world. On the contrary, our government gives the impression that, apart from our membership of the EC, it is somehow illicit for us to be closely linked with other nations.

Self-debarred on principle from being members of the British Commonwealth, it seems that we cannot be members of NATO because we are neutral, nor of the group of European neutrals because we are members of the EC, nor of the group of non-aligned nations for the same reason. But when we have a row with London, neither the other EC countries as a group nor some of them intervene on our behalf. Nor is the case any different when, quite apart from our disputes with London, matters affecting the Irish interest arise in the EC. It seems that we have no special alliance with anyone in the EC, say with the smaller countries or the agricultural ones or France or Spain. Yet we cannot, it seems, ally with Third World countries because we are developed, nor with Middle Eastern countries because they are not respectable, nor with postcolonial, anti-imperialist countries because that might seem Provo, nor with China because that would seem far-fetched, nor with Cuba though its geopolitical position *vis-à-vis* New York is very similar to ours *vis-à-vis* London. Meanwhile the only active support offered to the Irish in their dispute with London – the support from militant Irish-Americans, Libya, the PLO and the Basque ETA – is unacceptable to the Republic of Ireland because it is extended to the IRA; or, alternatively, goes to the IRA because Dublin has no use for it.

Is there some hangover in all of this from our days as 'Catholic Ireland in a pagan world'? Some notion that Ireland, that is, official Ireland, is so pure, different, noble, moral, ethereal that it is not of this world, and that therefore any conceivable alliance or special relationship that would serve the earthly interests of our national independence is not appropriate for us, would sully us? Better perish than be defiled – or judged not respectable by our superiors? Whatever the reason, this scandal of our political isolation must be looked at and discussed, its motivations rejected, and decisions taken to form relationships that will lessen our mental, political, economic and cultural dependence on London and New York, and our subjection within the EC to the collective interests of the major West European power centres.

Within Europe, to go no further, we are characterised by history and present circumstance in two ways that offer us advantageous linkages: by inheritance we are a Celtic country, and in terms of the power relationships of Western Europe we are a peripheral region. We are, moreover, the only one of the Celtic countries that has the rank of statehood, and were until this year – when Greece and Portugal became single regions of the EC – the only peripheral region of the EC with state status. On the face of it, that would seem to have fitted us to assume a leading role in both these categories. But since the end of the de Valera era – which was marked by several initiatives towards the other Celtic countries – we have largely ignored the Celtic aspect of our Europeanness; and since joining the EC we have ignored, and failed to exploit, the peripheral condition within it that we share with other regions and nations extending from Sicily and Sardinia through Andalusia and Brittany to Scotland and Jutland.

During a period when things Celtic have been in vogue throughout Europe, when traditional Irish music has been acquiring a worldwide following, and people of Celtic sentiment and culture in Brittany, Wales, Mann and Scotland have looked to independent Ireland for leadership, we have allowed the major annual Celtic cultural festival – attended by hundreds of Irish performers – to be established in Lorient, not Dublin, and we have no Irish cultural information centre, let alone a consulate, in Wales, Scotland or Brittany. In the 1970s some Bretons founded the biennial Conference of European Maritime Peripheral Regions, with its headquarters in Rennes and a membership extending from the Mediterranean through Ireland West and Mid-west to northern Norway. This, as it happened, gave me the idea of an institute, located in Ireland, for the interdisciplinary study of European peripheral regions. Assuming that EC funding might be available, I proposed it first to University College Galway, then to the Irish Council of the European Movement and the Irish Commissioner in Brussels; but none of these showed interest, and I felt, in the case of the latter two, that they regarded the notion as at best harebrained, at worst subversive. Neither then nor since have we had any Irish institute devoted to any branch of European studies. Of course, an institute for the study of European peripheral regions was only one of the ways in which Ireland, the only member state that was also a peripheral region, might have marshalled the periphery of the EC to assert its interests *vis-à-vis* the dominating centre – the Birmingham–Milan–Hamburg triangle and its supporting governments. In the event we chose no way.

What we see here under both heads, Celtic and peripheral, is a shunning by Ireland of her place and reality within the British Isles and within Europe – a place and reality that, if asserted, would be very much in her interest and would give her a leading role. And this shunning of our real location in the cultural heritage and geopolitics of Europe is symptomatic of our general refusal in today's world to be ourselves and therefore first-rate and strong, in favour of being not ourselves and therefore weak, second-rate and failing. Instead of embodying forcefully within the British Isles and Europe the Celtic idea and the peripheral interest, and gathering allies around itself under both heads, the Republic of Ireland has chosen to hover shiftily in isolation from all but London, a sort of mini-England with an interest in agricultural prices and subsidies.

In effect I am suggesting that the Republic of Ireland play as creative and self-interested a role in the restructuring of the EC as the Irish Free State did in the restructuring of the British Commonwealth; and I am arguing that, for the successful maintenance of our body politic and a lessening of our dependency, it is imperative that we do so. With the EC structured as it is, and with partial free trade among its member states, the economically stronger regions have grown stronger and the weaker ones relatively weaker, with a resulting increase in dependency and emigration in the latter. It is reasonable to assume

Professor Northcote Parkinson's suggestion of 'The Little (United) States of Europe' in *Profiles*, Brussels, 1975

that under the conditions of full free trade that will operate from 1992 onwards, this process will intensify unless effective counter-measures are taken. 'Europe' will be integrated, but it will not be Europe, because many of the autonomous social personalities – including Ireland – that have gone to make Europe will have ceased effectively to exist. The 'pro-Europeans' among us who are not concerned about this are not pro-Europeans, but enemies of Europe and of Ireland who are serving an anti-Irish, anti-European and anti-human idol – a nothing-god of geography and power economics.

Yann Foueré, a Breton who settled many years ago in Conamara, published a book in 1968 called *L'Europe aux cent drapeaux* (Europe of the Hundred Flags). The title speaks for itself. Foueré argues that the construction of a European Union on the basis of existing nation-states would – because of the operation of the centre-versus-periphery process – result in the final destruction of most of the nations, ethnic and regional communities that the larger states contain. To prevent this, and to construct a unified Europe that would both preserve Europe and revive its rich diversity, he advocates two processes: first, the transformation of the big states into federations of region-states, together with the adjustment where necessary of existing state boundaries to restore the integrity of split nations or ethnic groups such as the Basques, the Flemings or the Tyrolese; second, the establishment of a Community government based on the region-states and giving their delegates, collectively, the power to decide the norms on which the Community would operate. Under this arrangement larger nations such as the English and French would have larger representations than smaller ones. England and the French part of France, divided respectively into, say, eight regions, would each have eight times the representation of a nation possessing only one region-state.

I believe that in our own interest, and without waiting for 1992, we should adopt this programme, canvass and organise support for it throughout the EC, and demand that the assembly of the (real) nations, ethnic communities and regions of Europe have the right to look again at the Single European Act and all other EC measures, and take all future decisions about the shape and trading regulations of the EC. Naturally, it would take time to bring about this transformation but the support for it would be such that we could reasonably hope that by the mid-1990s Ireland would belong to a European Community which would not be inimical to her national and social interests.

Already three of the big West European states have begun to lay the foundations for such a Community. West Germany is a federation of eleven states which lead vigorous autonomous lives. Italy has twenty, Spain seventeen, devolved regional assemblies with considerable powers. In Eastern Europe, Yugoslavia, in one of the boldest constitutional ventures of modern times, is a federation of six very autonomous republics and two autonomous regions.

It is in our national interest to encourage throughout Europe and the world at large all decentralisation of power within large states, whether this be by way of granting autonomy (federal or devolved) to distinct nations or ethnic groups, or similar autonomy to regions within the same nation. Even more so, it is in our interest to encourage national breakaways from large multinational empires. All such developments would diminish the power of one or other of the major power centres, thereby lessening, as by a chain reaction, the felt need for power in others, so that by one means or the other -- direct or indirect – the power centres directly dominating us would become less dominating. But our interest apart, all domination of nations or regional communities, whether within states or across state boundaries, is imperialism, and it is therefore not only self-interested but in keeping with our anti-imperialist tradition – and a continuance of it – to take this line, pursue this policy, and let it be known worldwide that we are doing so.

If a small nation such as Cuba can pursue its own brand of anti-imperialism, even to the point of military involvement, in countries distant from its shores, so can we, by diplomatic means and propaganda, without going so far as to dispatch regiments. Of course we could do this with a better conscience if we decentralised ourselves: if we set about reorganising our own country as a federal state of four or five units – persuading Britain and the Ulster British to aid and abet this with regard to Ulster. But even without doing that, and simply as a small nation in whose interest it is that power be deconcentrated in the world around it, we can make this a foreign policy aim with good conscience and our heads held high.

It is in our interest that Estonia, the other Baltic nations of the USSR, Armenia, Georgia and Uzbekistan successfully assert their national rights *vis-à-vis* Moscow. It is in our interest that the native American nations of the USA, having already proven their legal right to be recognised by Washington as 'governments', go on to secure the recognition of their independence and their territorial integrity, thereby beginning the transformation of the USA into an assembly of independent nations. It is in our interest, again, that Tibet regain autonomy from China, that the Kurds divided among three countries acquire a state of their own, that the Zulus separate from South Africa, that the Vietnamese withdraw from Cambodia and Laos, and that Scotland becomes independent. Once we have got used to seeing our interest in these and similar terms, the means of encouraging such developments – by every means from the supportive telegram or delegation to the vote at the United Nations or the provision of technical assistance – will occur to us as each case arises.

Finally, there is the matter of our interest in working actively for world disarmament. It is clearly contrary to the interests of a small nation that powers that can reach it should possess weapons of massacre, whether these be bomber planes or missiles capable of delivering nuclear, chemical or biological death. It is not, in the first instance, a matter of such powers actually using these weapons against us, but of the intimidatory force that their possession of them gives to their demands on us and to all their dealings with us. But weapons of massacre are also grossly immoral, and it behoves us, as a nation so taken by morality that our public discourse is mostly moralising, to be much more active in getting rid of them than we have been hitherto. Hundreds of millions of hearts sickened by the horror of modern warfare are waiting for leadership in this matter of a kind far more radical than any that has yet been seen. We could give the world that leadership, and it would give a dignity and constructive content to our professed neutrality which at present it sadly lacks.

We could begin by ending our surreptitious integration into the British military and military surveillance systems which, apart from their application to Northern Ireland, are concerned largely with preparations for a nuclear war. We could then – and how strange and telling that this suggestion is shocking to the contemporary Irish mentality! – call a conference of small nations on disarmament, not confining the invitations to their governments. What Ireland could and should do afterwards would emerge from that.

I believe that the various elements of a foreign policy that I have sketched here would fit together coherently, and that the resulting policy, executed in political, economic and cultural terms, would not only serve our national independence – which is what a foreign policy is supposed to do – but would also make Ireland again, both in the minds of many of its inhabitants and in the world's eyes, an interesting instead of a boring country.

6
CAN HISTORY HELP
TO RECONCILE?

IT IS OFTEN SAID THAT THE HISTORY of the peoples of Ireland can be told and taught in such a way as to promote conciliation between them rather than antagonism and opposition. Not only that it *can* be so told and taught, but that it *should* be. I support both propositions, but they raise several questions, not least the question of what kind of history-writing would have that desirable effect.

The conciliation I have in mind is between the Irish people and the people whose preferred ethnic names are Ulster and British, and whom I will therefore call the Ulster British. The history of the Irish reaches back 1,500 years and has occurred throughout Ireland and abroad. That of the Ulster British goes back about 400 years and has occurred in Ulster and abroad. I am talking about both these histories in their entirety, but I am concerned particularly with the four centuries when they have been in contact – mainly in Ulster – and even more particularly with the last century and a half when the Irish found coherence and bonding in the system of values known as Irish nationalism and by the Ulster British in the system of values known as Ulster unionism.

Promoting conciliation between the Irish people and the Ulster

Amended text of a paper read to the Irish Association in Newcastle, County Down, October 1989, and printed in the *Irish Times*, 10 November 1989

British does not mean encouraging their fusion, an end to their separate existence. It means, simply, encouraging mutual respect and cooperation between them, especially in Ulster where they live together. If, having arrived at that, they should later, with the passage of time, merge into one people or ethnic nation, well and good. But that is not what reconciling them means, and it is unnecessary for peace and collaboration in Ireland. Even an Ireland united politically could contain both peoples, sharing a common citizenship but maintaining their ethnic difference with mutual respect. That, among other things, is what is meant by pluralism.

When I say that history could and should help to reconcile the two peoples, I am saying that history can and should have a social function. There are historians who might agree with the 'can', but who would not accept the 'should'. History, they believe, is purely a matter of telling and interpreting the facts; that alone is its end and purpose. But there are others, perhaps the majority, who believe that history should have a social function and purpose, and who have social aims in mind when they write and teach history.

So let me pose the question thus: how can historians who believe that history has a social function tell the history of the Irish and the Ulster British so as to encourage mutual respect and cooperation? What kind of writing and teaching of history is required for this?

Straightaway we come up against a fact that is often ignored. History can play that conciliatory social role only if it fulfils history's primary social function, which is to satisfy the history needs of the people whose history it is. That is what the telling of history has always been essentially about, and it can fulfil other social functions only if it performs that one. So the kind of history-writing that is needed for conciliation is history that, in the first place, satisfies the history needs of the Irish and the Ulster British.

People need to know their history, and they need the

history-writing that conveys it to them to have three main qualities. They need it to be truthful, so that it will put them in touch with the reality of themselves and of their place in the world. This includes giving due, proportionate weight to the various events of their history, both for what they were in themselves and for their impact on the people's consciousness. Second, people need their history to be interesting, so that it will attract and hold them, and that they will thereby get to know it. This requires it to have strong narrative form and, in particular, a continuous thread or pattern of meaning, especially in the recent centuries.

Lastly, people need their history to be critically respectful of the system of values that bonds them. This value system includes cherished beliefs and aims, revered places, revered leaders and heroes, celebrated events, loved and respected institutions, songs, words and other symbols. But its central and most bonding value is the people themselves, perceived as a people who have endured through time and who on the whole and despite their faults and mistakes, have been, at least in their best and most representative elements, right-minded and right-acting, and occasionally morally splendid.

For three good reasons, whether they be Irish, English, Swedes, French or Ulster British, people need the telling of their history to be critically respectful of their value system, and particularly of their central value, themselves in history. First, their history so told will sustain their bonding, their mutual cooperation and the self-esteem they need to inspire and energise them. Second, it will help them to assess their value system critically and to amend it where collective self-interest or moral insight requires. (The respect underlying the criticism will promote this inasmuch as peoples, like persons, can take and benefit by critical assessment only if it is conveyed in a manner that does not violate their essential cohesion, self-esteem and good name.) Third, their history told in this manner will make it easy for neighbouring peoples, who see them as represented in their history, both to appreciate their value system and to respect them.

That, then, is how history-telling fulfils its primary social function of satisfying a people's history needs. I have stressed the third requirement, critical respect for the listening or reading people and their value system, because in Ireland in recent years there has been a considerable amount of history-writing that has lacked that respect, and that has offered its opposite. I must deal with it because it has achieved a certain currency and prominence, and because it has been put forward by its practitioners and others as the kind of history-writing that will help to reconcile the Irish people of the Tricolour and the Ulster people of the Union Jack.

Written for the most part by Irish historians originating in the Republic, this history is antagonistic to the bonding value system, Irish nationalism, that the Irish people constructed in the course of the nineteenth and the first half of the twentieth centuries. This kind of history-writing is referred to commonly as 'historical revisionism', or 'revisionism' for short. However, it is more accurately called 'anti-nationalist revisionism' – *Irish* nationalism being the target, not English, Estonian or French.

It is important to be precise, because of course revision, if well founded, is part of all good history-writing, part of any living ideology, and part of life itself. Moreover, I have a vested interest in revision for, as the title of my book *The Revision of Irish Nationalism* suggests, I am a revising Irish nationalist.

The anti-nationalist revision of modern Irish history began as journalism in the 1960s. With the switch in that decade from the failed nationalist economics of self-sufficiency to reliance on foreign capital, and with the simultaneous rise of consumerist economics, a new elite came to power in Dublin. These businessmen, advertising agents, civil servants, experts, journalists and politicians, who were rising with the new tide and believed in it, regarded the Revolution, the decades since Independence, and their still-surviving value system with sceptical disdain. The media, led by the *Irish Times* and the new television station, RTE, reflected the views of these people and promoted them. What was said or suggested on television is difficult to come by now, but we can get the flavour of this journalism from *Irish Times* leading articles of 1965–66. For example:

> Young people of today are, in their own phrase, tough-minded. . . . Young people coming up, no matter what allegiance their fathers had, can look at the evolution of other countries from the British Commonwealth and wonder honestly if 1916 was absolutely necessary. They can ask if, with Home Rule on the statute books, we would not today have a united Ireland, with or without some tenuous links to the British Commonwealth. (21 October 1965)

Or again:

> Young people want things in a hurry, and want to forget the past. . . . The young man sees himself appearing in the pages of *Paris Match* or *Life* magazines. . . . Without any trammel of the past, whether Protestant/Catholic or Separatist/ex-Unionist, the differentials are disappearing in our country. Our young people want to forget. Boys in Dublin gravitate to coffee-skinned girls. . . . The past is not only being forgotten by the young; it is being buried with great relish, and even with disdain. (13 January 1966)

The details are unimportant: it is the gist and tendency that count.

In the early seventies academic historians took up where the journalists had left off. The anti-nationalist view of history, from having been suggestive and inchoate, began now to be formally expressed and argued. This coincided with an increasing withdrawal from nationalism by the government, and by the Dublin establishment generally, under the influence of the developing Northern crisis. So the revisionist history-writing won favour in high places, and the kind of history that was respectful of the nation's values was pushed to one side and frowned upon.

In his essay ' "The Great Enchantment": Uses and Abuses of Modern Irish History', Professor Ronan Fanning of University College Dublin looks back on this convergence of history-writing and politics:

> Bernard Lewis says that 'those who are in power control to a very large extent the presentation of the past and seek to make sure that it is presented in such a way as to buttress and legitimise their own authority . . . ' One could scarcely find a more succinct statement of what motivated the Irish political establishment after 1969 to adopt that interpretation of modern Irish history commonly described as 'revisionist'.[1]

The new moral interpretation of Irish history by professional historians was to the effect that the Irish, inspired by their nationalism, had been wrong-minded and wrong-acting, their own worst enemies, and that their opponents were often right. It began in a low-key, suggestive and almost mannerly fashion. Later, as it progressed, became a fashion and felt it was riding high, it became increasingly bold, unsparing and aggressive in its assaults on our inherited value system – the only one we had. It was much the same as happened with the so-called sexual revolution that got under way in many countries in the sixties. Beginning by lifting a few veils, including some that could do with lifting, it progressed, as it won acclaim and needed stronger effects to shock, to stripping the veils off everything with increasing irreverence and aggression.

An example of the tentative beginnings of anti-nationalist revisionism was a radio talk given by Professor F.S.L. Lyons in December 1971. It was part of a series of lectures on the Anglo-Irish Treaty, and the first sentence of the quotation indicates how contemporary events, principally in the North, were being used as a booster rocket for the new view. Professor Lyons had

1. In James Dooge (ed.), *Ireland in the Contemporary World: Essays in Honour of Garret FitzGerald* (Dublin: Gill and Macmillan, 1986)

this to say:

> In the present situation, with the dire past still overhanging the dire present, the need to go back to fundamentals and consider once more the meaning of independence asserts itself with almost intolerable urgency. The theories of revolution, the theories of nationality, the theories of history, which have brought Ireland to its present pass, cry out for re-examination, and the time is ripe to break with the great enchantment which for too long has made myth so much more congenial than reality.[2]

The language is restrained, but its message is radically offensive and subversive. Leave aside the call 'to break with the great enchantment', meaning presumably the Irish Revolution's dream of Ireland becoming a normal European nation. That dream had, in Professor Lyons's view, made us hostages to irrationality. Note, rather, his theory of historical causation, his moralising interpretation of cause and effect.

Ireland had been brought to its present pass (in the North), not by Britain's conniving with the Ulster unionist rebellion of 1912 and its ignoring of the will of most of the people of Ireland, particularly of the Northern nationalists; nor by the scandalous fifty years of British rule in the North; nor again by the continuing refusal of Britain to recognise the Irish nation and its rights there. No, Ireland had been brought to its present pass by theories of revolution, of nationality, and of history that we Irish had entertained; the present dire situation had been caused, in other words, by *ourselves,* by our nationalism. The cause of the present evil was not the wrong ideas and action of British imperialist nationalism but the wrong ideas and action of our liberationist nationalism.

As a late example, I take Clare O'Halloran's book *Partition and the Limits of Irish Nationalism,* published in Dublin in 1987. This is an account of Irish attitudes and practice in relation to the Northern question, principally in the Free State in the 1920s

2. RTE radio lecture on the Anglo-Irish Treaty, 1971

and 1930s. There is a final chapter on the subsequent period, including a lengthy treatment of the New Ireland Forum deliberations and report. Here, as it happens, I am described along with others as 'lunatic'. Such is the language. But when you have reached that stage in the book, that does not rumple a feather, because the general tendency of the work has been to point a finger of ridicule and scorn at many Irish individuals and institutions, at the views and behaviour of Free Staters and nationalists generally in relation to the national aim of reunification, and at that aim itself. Lest my readers might think I exaggerate, I quote from the blurb.

> This book strips away the rhetoric of Irish nationalism and reveals the emptiness of much nationalist posturing. Far from regarding Irish unionists as separated brethren, the overwhelming reaction of nationalists was to regard them as enemies and aliens, and to attack and challenge them at every opportunity. Moreover, nationalism in practice was predicated on a whole series of Catholic assumptions, which are relentlessly delineated in this book. The net effect was to alienate an already embittered Ulster Protestant population and to reinforce the siege mentality that lay behind the Northern Ireland state. Far from longing for unity, nationalism in practice worked to reinforce partition by emphasising all those features of Southern life most disliked and feared by Ulster Protestants.

Now, I am not suggesting that this kind of history book should not be written or published. Polemical books, wounding books, eccentric or radically questioning books, can all have their use if they are broadly factual and interestingly written. We are discussing whether that kind of history-writing tends to encourage mutual respect and cooperation between the two peoples of Ireland. To complete the picture, imagine that a stream of books of that kind, about the history of the Ulster British, were appearing in Belfast or London. If we take the Clare O'Halloran blurb, substitute 'unionism' for 'nationalism', and make a few other small changes, you will see what I mean:

> This book strips away the rhetoric of unionism and reveals the
> emptiness of much unionist posturing. Far from treating Northern
> nationalists as fellow British citizens, the overwhelming tendency
> of unionists was to regard them as enemies and aliens, and to attack
> and persecute them at every opportunity. Moreover, unionism
> in practice was predicated on a whole series of Protestant assump-
> tions, which are relentlessly delineated in this book. The net effect
> was to alienate an already embittered nationalist Ireland and to
> reinforce the siege mentality that lay behind the Northern Ireland
> state. Unionism, moreover, far from practising its professed loyalty
> to the British constitution, used the British connection and protec-
> tion to construct a society that most British people found
> abhorrent.

The notion that this offensive kind of history-writing encourages
mutual respect and cooperation between the two peoples of
Ireland is patently false. On the contrary, if it became the norm
it would have the opposite effect. In the first place, such history
will be disowned by the two peoples. Most of them will not find
such hostile diatribes about themselves even interesting – not only
because of their offensive quality, but because revisionism, having
rejected the pattern of continuous meaning in the traditional
narrative, has substituted no equally gripping story pattern. Consequently, this sort of writing and teaching will float somewhere
in the academic air, the actual history of neither people, encouraging neither of them to anything.

Second, the peoples deprived thus of history that satisfies their
history needs, and sustains their bonding and their will to be, will
either disintegrate, wilt and lose all positive collective will to
anything – including cooperation among themselves internally
or with another people – or they will seek a satisfying, animating
history from other sources, regardless of whether it is truthful
or not, and preferably if it denigrates their neighbours; no matter, so long as it nourishes their self-esteem and their will to be.

And the final reason why the kind of history I have been talk-ing about cannot encourage mutual respect and cooperation must be very obvious: how could anyone respect a people who are shown to have been, and who presumably still are, such a mess of wrong-mindedness, malevolence, duplicity and bad behaviour?

No, the history-telling that will encourage mutual respect and cooperation between our two peoples will be of a different kind. It will of course be truthful and interesting; and interesting, by the way, means appealing to the hearts as well as the minds of the learners or readers. Above all, however, it will be critically respectful of the evolving value systems that have bonded and animated both peoples in modern times; and it will be particularly respectful of their central value in each case, namely, themselves as a generally OK people in the past and present. (There is a well-known pop-psychology book on human relationships entitled *I'm OK, You're OK*. You will recognise the importance of those two linked sentiments in establishing or maintaining good relation-ships.) Notice that I said 'evolving' value systems. Irish nationalism and Ulster unionism were what they were in the past; are, in each case, something rather different now; and will in the future be different again or will be replaced by new, bonding value systems that will require different names. But for the present, even if in disarray, they are, in fact and potentially, the only bonding value systems that these peoples possess, and as such require the critical respect of historians who aim to conciliate.

Ulster British historians, writing Ulster British history, can make a special contribution by doing something that has not been their wont. I mean, when telling the history of their own people, to deal to a substantial degree with Irish history generally, and pre-sent the value system of the Free State and the Republic with critical respect. And incidentally, is it not about time that we had even one book, but better several, on the history of Ulster, including the history of both Ulster peoples since the Reformation? Written with all-round critical respect, that history could have a very directly reconciling effect because it would be dealing with the Irish and British peoples in their field of contact in Ireland. Why has no one done this, or any of the many 'reconciling' organisations sponsored it or offered a prize for it?[3]

In addition to having the basic characteristics I have outlined – truthfulness, interest, critical respect for communal values – the history that will help to conciliate will, within its various historical frameworks, make the following three things clear to readers in both peoples.

1   How the central principles of both nationalism and unionism are natural and just. For example, how it is natural and just that Irish people living in any part of Ireland up to this present day have required that Britain and the Ulster British recognise, in formal political terms, their non-British nationality; and how natural and just it is that people whose ancestors came from Britain to Ireland, and who have not identified with the Irish people, should continue to feel themselves British and want to be linked with the British Crown.

2   How with the passage of time, Irish and Ulster British, especially in Ulster, came to share to some degree a common culture and local loyalties and heroes, and how both peoples have, to some degree, shared common experiences and causes: such as religious discrimination, the United Irishmen and 1798, emigration to North America, resistance to tithes, the struggles against landlords and for better factory wages, hostility to England and the English, and membership of the British forces in both world wars.

3   How Irish nationalism and Ulster unionism are at bottom not as antagonistic or threatening to each other as they might seem. For example, how Irish nationalism has from the start, and into the present, extended the hand of friendship – at

3. Since this was written, Jonathan Bardon's *A History of Ulster* (Belfast: Blackstaff Press, 1992) has appeared.

least formally and in its doctrine, words, and flag – to the descendants of the colonists in so far as they give their allegiance to Ireland; and how unusual it is for national movements based on the natives to take this attitude, even formally and in theory, to the descendants of colonists. Or again, how the profession of Protestant religion has never of itself been a barrier to entrance into the Irish mainstream, or to prominence and celebration within it. Or finally, how in the history of unionism up to the present day, the determination to maintain the Union has sprung not so much from affection for Britain, let alone for England, as from a desire to maintain the Ulster British peoplehood and ethos in a beloved Ulster, within an Irish environment that was perceived as threatening.

History of that kind would encourage mutual respect and cooperation between the peoples of Ireland. History of itself can do no more.

7
PEACE IN THE NORTH

AFTER THE PARTITION OF IRELAND in 1921–22, Irish political nationalism adapted to the new circumstances by maintaining:

- that Northern Ireland was part of the Irish national territory;
- that the entire population of Northern Ireland was part of the Irish nation;
- that the injustice perpetrated by Britain was the partition of Ireland – because this prevented a united, self-governing nation;
- that the division in the North was between two religious-political communities or traditions: Catholics or nationalists, who wanted a united Ireland, and Protestants or unionists, who wanted union with Britain and who mistakenly believed they were British – an illusion that would disappear if Britain withdrew;
- that it was Britain's duty to withdraw from the North so that Orange and Green could come together as a united, self-governing Ireland.

A united, self-governing Ireland remained, as before, the primary aim.

From *The Revision of Irish Nationalism* (Dublin: Open Air, 1989)

When, as we say, the North erupted, in August 1969, I was living in the South Conamara Gaeltacht, and my social and political activity there had taught me certain principles of procedure in such matters which I then began to apply to the Northern question. I believed that, if you are faced with a disordered social situation in which the humanity of people is being oppressed or frustrated, then the first prerequisite – if your intention is to order the situation in a humane way – is to reject and criticise the misrepresentations and confusions that are obscuring its communal realities, and to represent those realities faithfully in words. In situations of the kind referred to, such misrepresentations and confusions will always be found to exist. You discover the communal realities by identifying the groups – the naturally formed groups as distinct from organisations or associations – that respectively share a common 'we', and by noting from their public and colloquial speech how these groups describe and define themselves. Then you represent these realities faithfully in words by discussing the situation, publicly, in terms of them – using language that reflects as nearly as possible the groups' self-consciousness. The next step is to work to bring about political institutions or structures that, in so far as possible, give practical, political representation to those communal realities. Your ultimate aim is a situation in which the conventional verbal structures and the institutional structures are representing or imaging the felt communal realities, and thus telling truth about them rather than lies.

When I looked at the way in which our traditional nationalism, and the neo-liberal views that became fashionable in the 1960s, represented the Northern situation, I found them seriously lacking in realism, to the extent of including lies. Not surprisingly, then, my first article for the *Irish Times* that August – an article that contained *in nucleo* all that was to come – was entitled 'A Plea for Realism' (19 August). It began by saying that it was up to us in the Republic, and to the Northern Catholics, to make a realistic proposal for a lasting settlement; but that we could not do this on the basis of the existing descriptions of the situation and must first of all recognise the basic realities. The first of these, which I spelt out – the first of four – constituted a rejection of the notion that the two communities in the North formed part of the same nation or 'historic people'. I wrote:

> The first basic fact that needs to be recognised is that Northern Ireland contains two historic peoples, or rather, one such people (the Ulster Protestants) and part of another. Only the accident that both of them speak English obscures the fact that they are peoples as real and distinct as, say, the Austrians and the Czechs. But for an accident of history, they would differ in language, as do the Flemings and Walloons in Belgium.
>
>   They did so differ less than six generations ago, that is to say, for a considerable time after the plantation of Ulster.[1] But language apart, they have different origins, histories and historical mythologies. They are, moreover, very conscious of their respective histories; they honour different and opposed heroes. Their social and cultural lives differ considerably. They have different understandings of Irish and British history. They also differ in religion. If the language difference had persisted, they would be known today, quite simply, as 'the Irish' and 'the Ulster Scots' (or 'na Gaeil' and 'na hAlbanaigh').
>
>   When the language difference went, religious adherence became the most obvious principle of distinction between them. As we have seen, however, the actual distinctiveness is far wider in scope. Captain O'Neill, as Prime Minister of Northern Ireland, was well aware of the nature of this distinctiveness and often referred to it in speeches and lectures. His way of putting it was that people of the Irish Catholic tradition and of the British Protestant tradition had been thrown together by history in Northern Ireland. This was fair enough, though greater accuracy would require us to speak of 'people of the Gaelic and Irish Catholic tradition' and 'a people of the Scotto-British and Protestant tradition'.

---

1. I later learned that this is an exaggeration: some Protestant communities spoke Gaelic.

In other words, to say that the inhabitants of Northern Ireland are 'all Irishmen' gets us nowhere. It sounds good to most Irishmen; it expresses generous intentions; it is even true in a sense; but it stops short of throwing light on the real situation. The inhabitants of Europe are 'all Europeans', but there are many peoples in Europe, differing greatly in their history, culture and self-consciousness. The inhabitants of the neighbouring island are 'all British', but the Scots, the English and the Welsh are distinct historic peoples. Even accepting that all the inhabitants of Northern Ireland are 'Irish' in a general sense, we are still faced with the fact that there are two different peoples there: the Irish (or Northern) Catholics and the Ulster Protestants.

Those were the pretty conventional names that at that time I gave the 'two historic peoples', but it can readily be deduced from my description of them that I would soon become unhappy with those imprecise and misleading names. I had not as yet visited the North in conflict, and listened to how the two communities really saw themselves.

I then went on to say: 'The second basic fact about Northern Ireland is that the struggle there is between the Catholics and the Protestants, but that it is not *about religion,* but about the relative status and power of these two historic peoples.' Arising out of this, I criticised the terms 'sectarianism' and 'religious war' as used in the Northern context, and pointed out that the flag flying over the Bogside was not the Vatican flag but the Irish Tricolour. Following from those two basic realities and two others that I spelt out, I proposed a political reconstruction of the North based on a western and an eastern region, which would contain, respectively, a Catholic and a Protestant majority, and the restructuring of local government to correspond to local Catholic and Protestant majorities – in other words, something like the successful cantonal solution that the Swiss found for their religious antagonisms. (The Swiss were agreed on their nationality.)

In Belfast, Major Ronald Bunting, who was both an enthusiast for local government reform and Ian Paisley's right-hand man, found this article very interesting and praised much of it in a press conference. I went to Belfast, met him, and we agreed on five 'principles of settlement' which I published in the *Irish Times* on 26 August. At the time they were completely ignored, but in the light of all that followed and where we have arrived at now they are interesting. They were:

1   The issue is not about religion. It is a political issue, to be solved politically.
2   The two peoples are basically willing to coexist alongside each other, provided that they can each exist in their own way and on their own terms – as far as possible.
3   Threats to the security, status and cultural autonomy of either people should be removed.
4   The security, status and cultural autonomy of each people should be guaranteed by an adequate share in political power.
5   Neither people should be expected or forced to abandon any of its traditional loyalties, provided that it recognises the constitution of Northern Ireland.

The 'constitution of Northern Ireland' would, of course, be based on the sort of regional and local restructuring I have referred to.

In the meantime, in a follow-up article published in the *Irish Times* on 23 August, I had elaborated on the kind of settlement I believed it was incumbent on the Republic to propose. It would be a settlement which would (I quote):

1   increase Catholic security by removing threats to it and by underpinning it both with 'Catholic' local government in Catholic areas and a Catholic share in central (Stormont) government;
2   balance a decrease in Protestant power and pseudo-security by an increase in real security (recognition of Northern Ireland's constitution by the Northern Catholics and the Republic);

3   extend the national pluralism already inherent in the word
      'British' by making it include Northern Catholics who
      honour 1916, fly Tricolours, and educate their children as
      Irishmen;
4   extend the connotation of 'Irish' (in our eyes) by making it,
      like 'British', a word which can include more than one
      national tradition: in this case, an Ulster Protestant people
      of the Orange tradition who do not honour 1916 and who
      wave Union Jacks.

I continued:

> It is in view of such a settlement, and of making proposals which
> will achieve it, that I emphasise the two-people situation in
> Northern Ireland. Unionist bulldozing of Northern Catholics into
> their narrow concept of 'British' must stop; so must the Republican
> bulldozing of Ulster Protestants into a monolithic Irish nationality
> in the tradition of 1916.

In retrospect I can see in those formulations, with their emphasis
on communal 'security', 'autonomy', and 'guarantees', the emergence of another line of thinking, based on the notion of
'recognition', which was ultimately to predominate over my
'representation' approach, though without contradicting it.
Recognising a community means calling it by its proper name
and, in practical, political terms, letting it be what it is –
guaranteeing it a secure autonomy.

Starting from the elementary new analysis in these articles, in
my column in the Sunday Press I spent the next two years refin-
ing and modifying its pattern and vocabulary; arguing for it and
criticising the traditional approach; and – since the two governments and all parties had ignored the cantonal proposal – casting
around for some other structure that might reflect the communal
realities.

In April and July 1970 I was criticising our refusal to take the
unionists at their word when they described themselves as 'British',
and pointing out the 'imperialism' of this. Such imperialism would

make sense if, as in the internal imperialism of other nation-states, we were prepared to impose our nationality on the dissident ethnic group by force and re-education; but since we, the Republic that is, rejected the use of force, it made no sense and was counter-productive. While offering the provocation of imperialist rhetoric, it lacked imperialism's teeth.

Usually, while recognising their Britishness, I continued to refer to the unionists as 'the Ulster Protestants'; but as I took account of the fact that there were some Catholic unionists, as well as Northern Protestants who were Irish nationalists, I became in-creasingly dissatisfied with the religious naming of the com-munities. At the same time, I wanted names that would describe them not merely as political groups, but as communities or peoples – names therefore that were independent of political allegiances or circumstances. For the unionists, I occasionally tried 'West British', but was unhappy with its derogatory connotations and the fact that its established usage made it not specific to them alone. I think it was not until 1975 that I hit on 'Ulster British', or perhaps adopted it from an Englishman, T.J. Pickvance of Birmingham University, who in a pamphlet published the previous year, *The Northern Ireland Problem: Peace with Equity,* used that term. Since there were 'Ulster Irish' on both sides of the border, I called the Northern nationalists 'the Six-County Irish'.

Long before that I had abandoned as unrealistic the notion that the connotations of 'Irish' and 'British' might be expanded in the manner suggested in my second article of August 1969. On the one hand, 'British' could never be a viable or acceptable descrip-tion of a community that rejected British nationality. On the other hand, 'Irish', as the name of a historic nation, corresponded to 'English' and 'Scottish', or 'Castilian' and 'Catalan', and could not feasibly serve also as an umbrella nationality like 'British' or 'Spanish'. However, given our aspiration to establish a nation-state embracing both Irish and British people, our lack of a usable national umbrella term was a disadvantage. On the analogy of

'British' and 'Spanish', the term would be 'Hibernian' – still usable, perhaps, in the eighteenth century, but not feasible now. The best substitute I could think of, and which I advocated as the 1970s progressed, would be to declare our willingness to separate citizenship and nationality legally, as is done in the Soviet Union and Yugoslavia, and have an all-Ireland Irish citizenship that allowed free choice of Irish or British *nationality*. But it took time for me to sort that out.

In February 1971 I was calling the Northern communities 'two ethnic groups' and saying that their respective demands were really 'to live as Irish not British citizens' on the one hand, and 'to live as British not Irish citizens' on the other. I was making the point that the real issue was not religion, but those civil and political requirements; and further that those requirements were not necessarily tantamount to a united Ireland or union with Britain. In September 1971, writing in my column of 'The New Six-County Nationalism', I attacked the notion that the Northern nationalists were really struggling for a united Ireland: they were struggling for the right 'to be Irish in their part of Ireland' – 'to be free Irishmen in their own country' – and a united Ireland was merely their conventional way of proposing how that aspiration might be implemented. There were other ways. I was coming to see a 'united Ireland' as instrumental towards the desired end, and as the ideal way of achieving it; but not as the end itself, or as the only way of attaining it. Peace with justice was the first requirement. Full justice for nationalists and unionists together was certainly a united Ireland that would treat the unionists justly. But peace could be had with less than full justice for the nationalists, and was, I believed, worth having on such terms. If need be, full justice could wait.

As the state in the North was rent asunder by the nationalist rebellion, I had ceased to believe in the possibility of a solution within the UK. Consequently, from July 1971 onwards I was proposing an Irish–British condominium of Northern Ireland as the immediate way of satisfying the basic nationalist demand, while doing justice also to the unionists. In September 1972, the Social Democratic and Labour Party (SDLP), in consultation with me, adopted condominium, renaming it joint sovereignty, and recommended it in a policy document, *Towards a New Ireland*. From correspondence I received, I found that the principal support for condominium in the Republic came from Protestants. (As it happened, the SDLP man who had initially contacted me was their only leading Protestant member, Ivan Cooper.) The idea was not popular in the Dublin establishment, partly for reasons I will come to later, partly because the notion of an Irish initiative was alien to Dublin thinking.

While campaigning for condominium, I had begun to write of the ethnic 'identities' of the two Northern communities; of the need to 'respect' and recognise both identities (see 'Open Letter to Desmond Boal', *Irish Press*, 21 September 1971); and of the assertion of Irish identity being the principal force motivating the nationalist rebellion. During a visit to the North I had seen (*Sunday Press,* 19 March 1972) young nationalist men and women 'daily risking their lives and freedom to assert – not an abstract claim to an all-Ireland state – but the identity, and the right to honourable recognition, of their own nationality and people'. The IRA, I wrote, were 'misrepresenting the struggle' – more precisely, by their dogmatic united-Irelandism allowing it to be misrepresented – 'as a mindless attempt "to bomb a million Protestants into a united Ireland"'. (That expression was Cardinal Conway's.)

My predominant concern was to make attractive, and to further, *any* constitutional arrangement which, by recognising the national identities of the two Northern communities, would bring peace to the North and thereby allow normal life and politics to take their course, both there and in the Republic. Consequently, from autumn 1971, I was helping to put flesh on the Sinn Féin proposals for a four-province federation; insisting that such a federation must provide for explicit – as well as implicit or political – recognition of the Ulster British identity; writing occasional articles about it; and speaking for it at public meetings in Connacht. (I have given an account of my involvement in this project, and of related matters, in my book *Beyond Nationalism*.) The four-province federal scheme, as it evolved, seemed to me the best proposal, not only for the North but for Ireland as a whole, to emerge in these years. However, I regarded condominium as having a better chance of winning acceptance in the short term. Later, in 1975, when the Ulster Defence Association and a few others in the North began to favour an independent Northern Ireland, I wrote two articles in the *Irish Times* (29–30 July) outlining – with some help from the Belgian way of dealing with Flemings and Walloons – how an independent North might be organised so as to give recognition to the bi-national nature of the population. Although I regarded this project as far from ideal from an Irish national viewpoint, I believed that it could be implemented in a manner that would advance the national interest and bring peace. Once again, the only significant public support came from a Protestant, Senator Trevor West (*Irish Times*, 2 September).

From the start, the Dublin ideological and political establishment, and most ordinary citizens, had been hostile to any verbal breaching of the dogma that made the Ulster unionists an intrinsic part of the Irish nation; this hostility extended, logically, to any political arrangement that would recognise ethnic plurality in Ireland as a whole or in the North specifically. It was a conservatism springing partly from genuine adherence to the traditional nationalist view, partly from support for that view by the consumerist liberals who had risen to power in the 1960s, particularly in the media. These, for their own ends as auxiliaries of commerce, wanted to promote homogeneity as idea and reality, not only in the North but throughout Ireland. Both for that purpose, and for their related aim of secularising the Republic, they found the 'one-nation theory' useful. Of course, no one denied that the Northern nationalists were Irish; so what it boiled down to in practice was a general unwillingness to recognise the Britishness of the unionists.

In the *Irish Times,* commentators and letter-writers called my line of argument 'sectarian', and 'divisive'.[2] I also heard myself criticised as 'West British' and 'unrepublican'. Official Sinn Féin and its leader Tomás Mac Giolla coupled me with Conor Cruise O'Brien as a disreputable 'two-nation theorist'. Indeed the party organ, the *United Irishman,* of March 1971, writing about O'Brien at the Labour Party Conference, mistakenly credited me with 'spawning' that heresy.[3] If, the paper said, O'Brien's line on the North represented Labour Party policy, 'then the Irish Labour Party finds itself allied with the Irish Communist Organisation and their new convert Conor Cruise O'Brien in accepting the two-nation theory spawned by Desmond Fennell and Major Ronald Bunting'.

Apart from myself, the Irish Communist Organisation (ICO) was then the only voice in the Republic publicly rejecting the one-nation theory. It openly espoused the view that there were two complete nations in Ireland. An article by Jack Lane in its journal the *Irish Communist,* April 1971, depicted me as in this respect a fellow-traveller, but one whose lack of Marxist vision had led him into a distorted understanding of the matter. Although

2. As if recognising an existing division were tantamount to creating it! But verbal absurdity apart, there is a sinister, highly illiberal side to the frequent use of this pejorative term by neo-liberals to describe aspects or operations of political pluralism (referenda, regional government, etcetera) that they dislike for other, unstated reasons. The implication is that the recognition of social or cultural diversity, and even the existence and clash of different ideological views, are illegitimate political phenomena, and that a society should be as commerce or the bureaucatic state would ideally have it: uniform, monominded, undifferentiated, malleable.

3. The term 'two-nation theory' had been used at least as far back as 1914, by John Redmond in criticism of Britain's support for the Ulster Protestant secession from Home Rule.

I had never written of 'two nations' in Ireland, I was content
for a time to accept that this did not misrepresent my position
– that there was an 'Ulster Protestant nation forming part of the
British nation'. But I sharply rejected the deduction from this
made by the ICO – that we should cease pressing for a reunited
Ireland – and the similar line taken by O'Brien. I regarded it as
entirely legitimate that the Irish nation, existing throughout
Ireland, though not comprising all the inhabitants, should aim
at political unification. 'If the all-British state [in Britain] contains three nations, why shouldn't there be an all-Ireland state
containing two?' (letter to the *Irish Press,* 6 November 1971). Later,
however, I would reject the two-nation theory outright, maintaining that Ireland did not contain two nations but only one
nation, 'the people of the Tricolour', and part of another (namely,
the British) nation.[4]

The secularists (and these included traditional nationalists who
were also secularists) were attached to the one-nation theory
because it made the Northern Protestants part of the nation, and
usable therefore in that capacity as a very cogent argument, given
the national aim of reunification, for de-Catholicising public life
in the Republic. If the Northern Protestants were to be seen as
a British community, not part of the nation but merely sharing
Ulster with it, they would represent a much weaker argument
for this purpose. It followed that any scheme of reunification
which envisaged regional self-government for the Northern Protestants, or any reorganisation of Northern Ireland – whether by

4. More precisely, this was my view 'for practical purposes'. In a subtler, more
philosophical vein, I put forward – in the pamphlet *A New Nationalism for the
New Ireland* (1972); 'To Have a Nation Once Again', *Atlantis* (April 1973); and
'The No-Nation Theory', *Irish Times* (16 May 1973) – a no-nation theory
which depicted Irish nationalism as an unfinished project to reconstitute a new
Irish nation in place of the Irish nation which had disintegrated in early
modern times. This line of thinking brought me close to the thinking of John
Robb (see 'Breaking the Old Moulds', *Irish Times,* 18 November 1972),
particularly in his pamphlet *Sell-Out or Opportunity?* (Belfast: New Ireland
Movement, 1972), but also subsequently.

cantonisation, condominium or whatever – which suggested or recognised the ethnic distinctiveness of the Protestants (more precisely, of the great majority of them), would be opposed by the secularisers.

For one reason or another, then, Dublin's view of Ireland and its project for it were passionately unitarian and anti-pluralist. I had more than the Northern question to teach me this, because I was at this time, in South Conamara, battling along with others for Gaeltacht self-government, that is to say, for the practical political recognition by Dublin of the distinct identity, needs and interest of the Irish-speaking minority. Much of the rhetoric that was used against a pluralist view of the North was used also against our Gaeltacht demand. *La République une et indivisible!* We came to feel sympathy and a sort of kinship with the *dílseoirí,* the Northern loyalists, in their attitude to Dublin.

Towards the end of 1972 my column in the *Sunday Press,* which had been my weekly workshop, ceased. In three pamphlets I applied my new nationalism, combining proposals for the general reform of Irish government with my rethinking of the Northern question.[5] Through the rest of the 1970s, my occasional articles bearing on the North added nothing significant, apart from terms such as 'Ulster British' which helped to concretise the new land-scape. My basic position was that peace required mutual recognition by the groups concerned (including Britain), and a constitution that would express this: condominium, a federal Ireland of at least four units (I rejected as unviable the notion of a two-unit federation based on the Six Counties and the Twenty-Six), or even an independent Northern Ireland with ap-propriate arrangements. For my own part, I espoused the federal

5. Two of these pamphlets were, apart from their prefaces, collections of newspaper articles and letters: *Build the Third Republic* (Cárna: Foilseacháin Mhaoinse, 1972) and *Towards a Great Ulster (1969–72)* (Indreabhán: Comharchumann Chois Fharraige, 1973). The third, *A New Nationalism for the New Ireland* (Muineachán: Comhairle Uladh, 1972), was the text of a lecture given to a Sinn Féin audience.

solution and argued for it where I could, even in the *Church of Ireland Gazette* (9 February, 1979).

In 1979 Fine Gael published a policy document, *Ireland – Our Future Together,* which proposed a confederation of the North with the Republic. In paragraph 40, headed 'Northern Ireland's Sense of Identity', the party sidled towards a more realistic description of the unionist community. It was stated that 'those who favour the political connection with Great Britain for emotional or practical reasons usually feel a sense of Northern Irish or, as they sometimes express it, an "Ulster" identity, within their broader sense of being British'.

In 1980 I began to write frequently on the North again, first in the *Irish Times,* then in my resumed column in the *Sunday Press.* Impatient and angry that the agony was being let drag on, I decided that the only hope of forcing action lay in a sharper approach than hitherto. While continuing to represent the North in terms of a British and an Irish community, I would emphasise the Irish presence and identity there, and the great injustice that was being perpetrated – we had heard too little of injustice for a long time – by the refusal of Britain and the Ulster British to recognise it, verbally or constitutionally. That was causing the armed rebellion, and therefore peace meant ending that injustice by whatever means.[6]

Instrumental to this approach was a verbal tactic. By reiteration, I tried to make the phrase 'Irish identity (community, nation) in the North' and the attached argument for its recognition replace the anodyne phrase 'Irish dimension to Northern Ireland' and the accompanying talk about Britain recognising this. 'The Irish dimension' had been introduced by the British Secretary of State for the North, William Whitelaw, and his civil servants, during the run-up to the Sunningdale Agreement of 1973, and it was

6. See, for example, *Irish Times,* 18–19 February, and *Sunday Press,* 22 June, 3 August, 28 December 1980. I continued this emphasis through the early 80s.

generally taken to mean a 'cross-border dimension' – the implication being that the 'Irishness' in question lay outside Northern Ireland, in the Republic. Like most of the British rhetoric of the time it was taken up in Dublin, and it dragged its weary, impotent way through the public discourse of the 1970s. By hammering away at the Irish identity *within* the North, I hoped to replace it with a concept which, once accepted, would impel really useful action.

I had, moreover, come to realise that it was not only realistic but also good tactics *vis-à-vis* Britain to describe the Northern situation in terms of an Irish and a British community, and to make the recognition of the Irish community the prime demand. As a description of the situation and as a statement of the national demand, it was better tactics than the assertion that everyone in the North belonged to the Irish nation and that the Irish nation had a right to be united and independent. Mrs Thatcher or any British politician could shoot this down easily by pointing to the superficial fact that a majority of the people in Northern Ireland did not want a united Ireland and that Britain must uphold democracy. This had the effect of seeming to put our side in the wrong, by suggesting that we were the aggressors, making an assault on democratic equity. The new description of the situation, and the demand arising from it, could not be easily countered – could not really be countered at all, for they were so obviously true and just.

In the early 1980s I began to use the figures 600,000 and 900,000 to indicate the respective sizes of the two communities. My motive was partly to provide clear images, partly irritation with Northern Ireland's being the only instance of intercommunal dispute in the world where, apart from percentages – a mathematical abstraction – no numbers were given to quantify the communities. This was one way among many of keeping it vague, baffling, not of this world, outside the range of human experience! But I also wanted to counter the inaccurate, rhetorical and over-impressive phrase 'a million Protestants' which had slipped into the public discourse, and to show that the two communities were not all that different in size. Moreover, both because they were not, and on tactical grounds which seemed obvious, I criticised those Northern nationalist politicians who called their community 'the minority' – handing their opponents an argument on a plate. The Walloons are a minority in Belgium, but who speaks of them as that?

In 1980 Brigid Wilkinson asked me to write a background paper on a conference entitled 'Models of Political Cooperation' to be held in Queen's University Belfast under the auspices of the Glencree and Corrymeela reconciliation groups. The paper I wrote, which brought together my new analysis in some detail, proved unacceptable to the Northern organisers, but I decided to attend the conference nevertheless and to distribute photocopies of the paper. That was in March 1981. A civil servant from the Northern Ireland Office, who had seen a copy, came and asked me for two more. It may well be that there was a connection between this and certain unprecedented analysis and language in the British White Paper on Northern Ireland – the so-called 'Prior initiative' – which was published in April 1982. I refer to Part 3 entitled 'The Two Identities', and particularly to paragraphs 14 and 16.

14. The majority of the population in Northern Ireland think of themselves as British. They regard themselves as part of the social and cultural fabric of the United Kingdom and their loyalty lies to the Crown. They favour continuance of the union with the rest of the United Kingdom.

16. There is also a substantial minority within Northern Ireland who think of themselves as Irish, whether in terms of their identity, their social and cultural traditions, or their political aspirations. Many of them support political parties which would like to see a united Ireland in some form.

Paragraph 17 begins: 'This difference in identity and aspiration

is at the heart of the "problem" of Northern Ireland; it cannot
be ignored or wished away.' And paragraph 19 begins: 'Given
the importance of these two identities and traditions in Northern
Ireland . . . '. This White Paper was the first occasion on which
Britain gave verbal recognition to the Irish identity in Northern
Ireland.

In Belfast, Bishop Cahal Daly had already, for a couple of years
previously, been referring in his speeches to the two identities
defined in a similarly ethnic sense. A month after the publication of the White Paper, Garret FitzGerald, in his Dimbleby lecture 'Irish Identities' on the BBC, continued the theme, but with
a predominantly religious definition. In the genealogy of language
usage and communal definition that issued in the Report of the
New Ireland Forum (1984), it was that British White Paper which
set the *official* precedent.

The New Ireland Forum, convened in May 1983, brought
together the Dáil parties and the SDLP for a year-long study of
the Northern question and a reformulation of the nationalist
approach to it. A few months after it had started, I sent a written
submission and appended the paper from the Queen's University
conference, reworked now as chapter 4 of *The State of the Nation*.
(In the interim the text had appeared, somewhat reworked, in
Études irlandaises, December 1982.) I argued that the kernel of
the Northern Ireland problem was that Britain and the Ulster
British did not adequately recognise the Irish nation in the Six
Counties; that the Irish nationalist demand was, basically, that
this recognition be given, verbally and politically; that nationalists,
and the Forum specifically, must recognise the Britishness of the
Ulster British; and that the Forum should propose a federally
united Ireland as the means of 'formalising this mutual recognition'. I believed that the Forum, as a representative assembly of
Irish nationalism, owed it to itself to propose a united Ireland,
and at last to spell out concretely what nationalism meant by this.

But I wanted it to propose a united Ireland *in the terms I suggested* so that the recognition of the Six-County Irish as a priority, and of the Ulster British by Irish nationalists, would formally enter the discourse of Irish nationalism. Then, in the likely event that a united Ireland would not immediately materialise, those terms would provide a strong basis for flexible manoeuvre. Naturally, when I was called by the Forum to an oral hearing, I did not express that ulterior motive except by a very slight hint.

Let us glance now at the Report of the New Ireland Forum. In chapter 4, 'Assessment of the Present Problem', we read under the heading 'Nationalist Identity and Attitudes' (paragraph 4.6):

> For nationalists, a central aim has been the survival and develop-
> ment of an Irish identity, an objective that continues in Northern
> Ireland today as nationalists seek effective recognition of their Irish
> identity and pursue their rights and aspirations through political
> means.... The aim of nationalists in seeking Irish unity is to
> develop and promote an Irishness that demonstrates convincingly
> to unionists that the concerns of the unionist and Protestant
> heritage can be accommodated in a credible way and that institu-
> tions can be created which would protect such concerns and
> provide fully for their legitimate self-expression.

Under 'Unionist Identity and Attitudes', we read (paragraph 4.9):

> In public sessions of the Forum, contributors who put forward
> the unionist point of view were asked 'what is it that the unionists
> wish to preserve?' Three elements were identified in their replies:
> (1) Britishness
> (2) Protestantism
> (3) The economic advantages of the British link.

And in paragraph 4.9.1:

> Unionists generally regard themselves as being British, the
> inheritors of a specific communal loyalty to the British Crown....
> Unionists generally also regard themselves as being Irish even if
> this does not include a willingness to live under all-Ireland political
> institutions.

Further on, paragraph 4.15 states definitively:

> The solution to both the historic problem and the current crisis
> of Northern Ireland, and the continuing problem of relations
> between Ireland and Britain, necessarily requires new structures
> that will accommodate together two sets of legitimate rights:
> – the right of nationalists to effective political, symbolic and
> administrative expression of their identity; and
> – the right of unionists to effective political, symbolic and
> administrative expression of their identity, their ethos and their
> way of life.

Chapter 5 of the Forum Report, 'Framework for a New Ireland:
Present Realities and Future Requirements', sums up the report's
analysis of the problem and states, in general terms, the requirements arising from this analysis. This is the core of the report,
for it lays down the parameters to which any solution or remedial
action must conform. Among the 'Realities' listed are (8 and 9)
the nationalist and unionist identities, defined in terms similar
to those I have cited. Realities 10 and 11 are as follows:

> (10) Irish nationalist attitudes have hitherto in their public expres-
> sion tended to underestimate the full dimension of the unionist
> identity and ethos. On the other hand, unionist attitudes and prac-
> tices have denied the right of nationalists to meaningful political
> expression of their identity and ethos.
> (11) The basic approach of British policy has created negative con-
> sequences. It has shown a disregard of the identity and ethos of
> nationalists. In effect, it has underwritten the supremacy in
> Northern Ireland of the unionist identity. Before there can be
> fundamental progress Britain must reassess its position and respon-
> sibility.

The 'Requirements' section of the chapter proposes certain principles as 'necessary elements of a framework within which a new
Ireland could emerge'. These include:

> (4) The validity of both the nationalist and unionist identities in

Ireland and the democratic rights of every citizen on this island must be accepted; both of these identities must have equally satisfactory, secure and durable, political, administrative and symbolic expression and protection.

(5) Lasting stability can be found only in the context of new structures in which no tradition will be allowed to dominate the other, in which there will be equal rights and opportunities for all, and in which there will be provision for formal and effective guarantees for the protection of individual human rights and of the communal and cultural rights of both nationalists and unionists.

Clearly the 'new structures' which would meet these realities and requirements could be of different constitutional kinds, and could be erected within a variety of state frameworks: all-Ireland, UK, British-Irish, even an independent Northern Ireland. Accordingly, they could meet the nationalists' right to recognition of their national identity maximally or minimally, with varying degrees of justice: with full justice, if the framework is some kind of reunited Ireland which gives due recognition to the unionists; with justice sufficient to bring about peace and cooperation in the North, if the framework is other than a united-Ireland one. In these respects, it is obviously the intention of this new nationalism to be open-ended and flexible – aiming at full satisfaction, but open to adequate half-measures for the sake of peace.

Later, in the same chapter (paragraph 5.4), the report identifies as a further reality 'the desire of nationalists for a united Ireland in the form of a sovereign, independent Irish state' that would 'accommodate the fundamental elements in both traditions', and adds (paragraph 5.5) that 'the Parties in the Forum are convinced that such unity in agreement would offer the best and most durable basis for peace and stability'. Furthermore in paragraph 5.7 the preferred form of political unity is specified as a unitary state. But in its two final chapters the report outlines two other political structures – a 'federal/confederal state' and 'joint authority' – which had been proposed to the Forum as ways of meeting the 'Realities and Requirements'; these, we are told, the Forum had 'examined in some detail'.

The report was published in May 1984. In November of that year the Taoiseach, Dr Garret FitzGerald, met the British Prime Minister, Margaret Thatcher. She rejected a unitary all-Ireland state, and the two other structures put forward by the Forum, but the two leaders agreed to negotiate towards some other kind of arrangement that would improve the situation, and issued a joint communiqué setting out the principles to be followed. Peter Barry, Minister for Foreign Affairs, was later (23 February 1985) to describe this communiqué as both 'a fairly good summary of the Realities and Requirements set out by the New Ireland Forum' and 'a good general description' of the structures based on them which he hoped would emerge from the negotiations then proceeding. The communiqué stated that:

> the identities of both the majority and the minority communities in Northern Ireland should be recognised and respected, and reflected in the structures and processes of Northern Ireland in ways acceptable to both communities; the process of government in Northern Ireland should be such as to provide the people of both communities with the confidence that their rights will be safeguarded.

In the months leading up to the Anglo-Irish Agreement of November 1985, Mr Barry, in his comments on the negotiations and their aim, was the principal exponent of the reformulated nationalism of the Forum Report, and in particular of its key chapter on 'Realities and Requirements'. In the speech quoted above – which was to members of the SDLP in Belfast – he said, 'I have often said that what is needed here is a major transformation of the condition of the nationalist minority. That is what we are striving for.' And further on: 'We have seen the acceptance by the British of the principle that the two major Irish traditions are equal and must be put on an equal footing and we await the implementation by them of that accceptance.'

On 3 April 1985, speaking to a meeting of his political party, in Dublin, he had this to say:

The fact that constitutional Irish nationalism has not persuaded the British government that the British should now begin to work formally to establish a unitary Irish state . . . does not mean that the Irish government have abandoned that objective . . . Neither does it mean that we can arrogate to ourselves the brutally selfish 'right' to stand aside and abandon the nationalist people of Northern Ireland to their nightmare until the day . . . when a British government would bring itself to support our preference. Should the British and Irish governments come to agreement on measures which would improve the condition of the nationalists of Northern Ireland, measures which would fully accommodate their identity and their rights in new political structures, but which did not take the form of a unitary state, who in the South would have the moral right to say to the nationalists of Northern Ireland: 'We are sorry, but our desires are more important than your needs; we cannot support any improvement in your situation short of Irish unity in the form of a unitary state, even if that takes one or two or twenty more generations . . . ' On behalf of the government, I want to make two very fundamental points clear to all Irish nationalists North and South and everywhere else in the world. First, the Irish government is committed to Irish unity and will continue to work to achieve it. . . . Second, our priority commitment is to transform the condition of the Northern nationalists, to end their 'nightmare', and to do so now. . . . These two commitments are, to my mind, perfectly compatible with each other and perfectly consistent with the Report of the New Ireland Forum. They are, moreover, perfectly complementary.

Notice that in this speech Barry assumes, and I believe correctly, that the prime need and requirement of the Northern nationalists, as distinct from 'us' in the Republic – and by implication the principal motive fuelling the Northern nationalists' rebellion – is not a united Ireland, but the practical recognition of their identity and rights as Irish people in Ireland.

On 4 June 1985 Barry told the National Press Club in Canberra, Australia:

> In essence the conflict in Northern Ireland arises from a failed attempt to accommodate both the Irish and British identities in the island of Ireland. The British government's attempt to do so in the early 1920s through the political division of Ireland merely served to intensify the already existing tensions between these two identities and to concentrate them in the northeastern part of our country – in Northern Ireland. In that small area live most of those Irish people whose British and Protestant heritage is important to them, and whose roots in Ireland go back to the seventeenth century – about 900,000 people in all. . . . Another 600,000 men and women who see themselves as Irish and as part of an older nation in the whole island of Ireland also live in Northern Ireland. . . . For sixty-five years they have felt trapped and discriminated against within its boundaries and cut off from the 3.5 million people of the Republic whom they consider to be their fellow nationals.

Again, on 4 July 1985, in his Estimates Speech in the Dáil, Barry said:

> The fact is that the structures and processes of Northern Ireland have hitherto failed to recognise, respect or reflect the identity of the nationalist section of the community in Northern Ireland. For my part, and quite apart from the current Anglo-Irish negotia-tions, I have used every opportunity open to me to protect and foster the interests and the identity of the Northern nationalists. Whether our negotiations succeed or fail, I shall continue to do this.

I could cite many other passages from Barry's speeches similarly articulating the new nationalism, but one more example will suf-fice. On 24 August 1985, on the occasion of his visit to the Between Holiday House at Doughcloyne, Togher, County Cork, he said:

I believe that the point of departure in any dialogue that can take place between unionists and nationalists must be mutual respect. Respect: not sentimental affection. By respect I mean acceptance by nationalists that unionists are who they say they are, and I mean acceptance by us that unionists have a right to be what they say they are.... In practice it means acceptance of the Britishness of unionists, the very Britishness that nationalists have for hundreds of years struggled to extirpate from this island.... In practice it means that all nationalists must accept that the 900,000 people that make up the unionist community are not going to go away and that they are not going to become nationalists just because we would like them to do so. [And, addressing the unionists:] You for your part must accept the reality of nationalism. We the nationalists are not going to go away either; Southern nationalists and Northern nationalists are not going to stop being national-ists.... Unionists would be mistaken to pretend that 600,000 nationalists in Northern Ireland and over 3 million in the South are not what we say we are.

The Anglo-Irish Agreement seems to have issued, not surpris-ingly, from two different, preponderant negotiating aims on the Irish and British sides respectively. On the Irish side, the chief aim was to obtain British agreement to engage in a minimalist course of action in Northern Ireland on the lines of the 'Realities and Requirements' chapter of the Forum Report: that is, political reforms and structures which, while not doing full justice to Irish national rights in Ireland, would be sufficiently just to bring about 'peace, stability and reconciliation' – to use Margaret Thatcher's phrase, which became current in Ireland. The British, for their part, sought mainly to obtain Irish agreement to closer collabora-tion in matters of police and military action against the IRA – what is loosely termed 'security'.

Behind these different aims were two different views of how peace and stability might be obtained in the North: on the Irish side, the view that considerable legal and institutional changes

were required; on the British side, the view that security measures
to end the armed rebellion were the most effective course, though
these could usefully be accompanied by minor reforms. Both sides
wanted to end the armed rebellion, but they differed in their views
on how best to bring that about; on whether simply bringing
that about in a military sense would really amount to peace and
stability; and on whether, indeed, it was possible to overcome
the IRA by military and police methods. (The British army has
consistently been of the view that it is impossible, but the British
government often seems to take a contrary view.) Moreover, the
Irish side, probably more keenly than the British, also wanted
'reconciliation' to result – conciliation between the two Northern communities and in Ireland as a whole – and this strengthened their conviction that political measures, rather than security
action, were to be relied on.

Probably during the course of the negotiations there was some
interchange of perspectives, and both sides came to the view that
something of both approaches was required. However, it is clear
from Peter Barry's speeches in the period leading up to the signing of the agreement that the Irish side continued to see the sought
agreement primarily as a mechanism for ending 'the nightmare
of the nationalists' through political measures that would recognise
their Irish identity and legitimise – in so far as was practicable
within the framework of the UK – all that followed from this
identity. It was in these terms, while also emphasising the necessity
for nationalist Ireland to recognise the Britishness of the unionists,
that Barry's speeches heralded the agreement and sold it to
nationalist opinion. It is therefore important to read the agreement itself, and to deduce the Irish government's expectations
of it, in the context of those speeches, which I have quoted from
at length above.

Looking in the light of these at article 5a of the Anglo-Irish
Agreement, it is easy to see how the Irish side envisaged that the

agreement would work. In that article the British had agreed that
the Intergovernmental Conference established by the agreement
would 'concern itself with measures to recognise and accommodate the rights and identities of the two traditions in Northern
Ireland'. Such measures must of necessity be of a political nature.
Consequently (it was assumed), since the nationalist or Irish community was the one in immediate need of having its rights and
identity recognised and accommodated, the British government
would take the necessary political measures. Then, since British
failure to do this previously was the basic injustice fuelling the
armed rebellion, the rebellion would wither away as the remedial
measures took effect. Two beneficial results would ensue. On
the one hand, the Six-County Irish, having lost their heavy sense
of grievance, and feeling themselves recognised as Irish people
in their own country and equal in status to their British fellow
countrymen, would be willing to discuss and agree with the latter
how Northern Ireland might best be governed within the UK.
On the other hand, with the ending of the continual and often
lethal provocation of the armed rebellion, the Ulster British would
be more willing to be reasonable and accommodating towards
their Irish fellow countrymen. As an additional factor motivating
them in that direction – a sort of 'sweetener' for their having
to accept the legitimation of the Irish nationalist community in
the North – the agreement offered them (article 1) a guarantee
by the Irish government, together with the British government,
that the status of Northern Ireland would not be changed while
a majority of its population did not want it changed. In short,
the expectation on the Irish side was that, as the British government proceeded to remedy, in a minimalist manner but effectively, the basic injustice in the North, the situation would move
towards peace, stability and conciliation.

On the assumption that the British government would proceed in the manner indicated, this seems to me to have been an
entirely reasonable expectation. However, the British government

did not proceed in that manner, and there was no movement towards peace or stability. Consequently, a finger is pointed at the initial Irish assumption, and the question is raised of whether it was naïve.

Clearly it was, and not only in retrospect. On the one hand, the history of Anglo-Irish relations argued forcefully against it; on the other hand, it could be foreseen that the expected hostile reaction of the unionists to the agreement would make the British government very reluctant to provoke them further by measures in favour of the nationalists. At the very least, therefore, the Irish government should not have signed the agreement until it contained, not an undertaking by the British government to 'concern' itself with measures to end the basic injustice in the North, but an undertaking by that government to *implement* the necessary (specified) measures within a stated time. I do not believe that, in that event, the unionist opposition to the agreement would have been significantly fiercer than it was; but even if it were, it would have been a matter of facing up to it resolutely, in the knowledge that no real harm was being done to the unionists, only minimal justice to their Irish nationalist neighbours. The great gain which made that worth the risking was that the boil would have been finally lanced and the healing process set in motion. In the event, of course, the boil was not lanced; the foreseeable happened, and the uncommitted British government shrank from taking the necessary measures under article 5a.

In other words, to put it bluntly, because the Anglo-Irish Agreement lacked concrete undertakings by the British to do what was required to end the root injustice in Northern Ireland within a stated time, it was a flawed agreement. Any critical assessment of it would have perceived this straight away; and indeed, within a month of its signing, I wrote an article in the *Irish Times* (25 November 1985) criticising it precisely as I have done here. But such was the dragooning of the public mind in Dublin and the world at large into an uncritical and mindless enthusiasm for the agreement that many who might have had doubts, if they had applied their critical intelligences, joined instead in the cheering, and many who had doubts were afraid to express them. Unfortunately, this had precedents. It was a repeat, on an enlarged scale, of a far too frequent occurrence in the Dublin establishment with regard to the North over the past twenty years: uncritical, righteous and intolerant faith in the final, all-solving power of the latest British-sponsored 'initiative' – or IRA atrocity, or liberal-minded amendment to the Irish Constitution. And indeed, how could it be otherwise, when Dublin's normal, fashionable attitude to the North is 'can't bear to think about it'?

Nevertheless, even the agreement as it stood could have been used much more fruitfully than it has been, and it could still so be used. The failure of the British government hitherto to take decisive measures to 'recognise and accommodate' the rights and identity of the Six-County Irish has been due not only to British dilatoriness or bad faith, but also to the failure of two successive Irish governments to demand such measures, to secure them to some degree, and to make Britain's refusal to go the whole way into a critical political issue. This Irish failure was in effect a failure to follow through on the new nationalism of the Forum Report and Peter Barry's speeches.

Most of the effort of the Irish government hitherto has been directed, not to the crucial article 5a – 'measures to recognise and accommodate the rights and identities of the two traditions' – but to peripheral matters; particularly to such as fall under article 7a (ii), 'relations between the security forces and community'; 8, 'legal matters, including administration of justice'; and 6, dealing with fair employment, etcetera. The question of how many judges should sit in the Diplock courts became a ludicrous *cause célèbre*. Such matters are peripheral because they are concerned not with ending the rebellion, but, for the most part, with ensuring that the rebels are combated by well-behaved police and soldiers, and tried by fairer courts; and, for the rest, with righting an injustice

– discrimination in employment – which is not the injustice that the rebellion is about.

If the Anglo-Irish Agreement is really to serve as a mechanism for ending the rebellion, and bringing peace, stability and conciliation, then the Irish government, for its part, would need to return to its initial position and pursue a course inspired by the new nationalism. Specifically, it would need to direct its efforts primarily to article 5a of the agreement and to do so in the spirit of the Forum Report, paragraph 4.15, which states in effect that 'the solution . . . requires new structures that will accommodate . . . the right of nationalists to effective political, symbolic and administrative expression of their identity'. That was the basic identification of the solution to the Northern problem by the constitutional nationalist parties of Ireland after a year's deliberation. They believed, as we have seen, that the necessary structures could best be provided in a unitary all-Ireland state which would recognise the Ulster British effectively, but they were willing also to consider a federal Ireland, or a British-Irish 'joint authority', as suitable frameworks. Britain's quick rejection of all three suggested frameworks for implementing it took nothing from the fact that the Forum's diagnosis of the disorder, and its identification of the remedy, still held and holds. It meant simply that, the Forum's frameworks having been rejected, Northern Ireland within the UK became and remains the framework for implementing the 'new structures' required to accommodate and recognise the Six-County Irish.

What I have just been saying is the nub of the matter. Either the Forum's diagnosis of the North's disorder, and its related identification of the remedy, are right or they are wrong. If they are right, as I believe they are, then it follows that the Irish government should be demanding from Britain, under the terms of the Anglo-Irish Agreement, political structures that recognise the Irish ethnic community in Northern Ireland. It also follows that the treadmill of 'improving security measures' (for another twenty years?) is not the way to the solution; that neither is a devolved government in Belfast, with SDLP participation, that ignores the bi-national composition of Ulster; and that therefore the Irish government should not in any way support, or seem to support, these illusions. Incidentally, with regard to the currently fashionable notion that a power-sharing Belfast parliament is the panacea, one would have expected that the experiment on these lines in 1973–4 would have amply demonstrated its inadequacy as a pacifying agent.

If it is accepted, then, as I argue it must be, that peace in the North requires the effective recognition of the two communities, and specifically of the unrecognised Irish community, the question becomes how to do this; and that is the sole matter on which debate should centre. What follows is my own view.

There are many instances in the world of two or more conflicting ethnic or cultural communities sharing the same territory. Experience shows that the most successful and reconciling solution is to guarantee autonomy, in so far as practicable, to each of the communities, and equal status and treatment to their individual members wherever in the society they may happen to be. *Ipso facto* the measures that do this recognise that the communities exist, call them by their names, and create structures that allow them political, symbolic and administrative self-expression. The net effect is to reassure them, to accord their members personal dignity, and to enable their members to feel at home in the society – if not absolutely, then at least sufficiently. Thus accommodated, the communities are likely to be willing to work together in shared institutions for the common good.

The basic requirement is to guarantee them autonomy in so far as practicable, and the commonest way of doing this is to allow them to preponderate, in the running of affairs, in those areas where they preponderate numerically. In other words, political and administrative regionalisation based on overwhelming or substantial local majorities. If we apply this to Northern Ireland, Belgium suggests itself – not for the first time – as a rough model. There, the acute cultural conflicts between Flemings and Walloons have been defused by institutional measures that allot Flanders clearly to the Flemings, Wallonia to the Walloons, and treat Brussels as a special, mixed area.

The west and south of the Six Counties have a substantial nationalist majority. This region, which I shall call Mid-Ulster, comprises the counties of Fermanagh, Tyrone and Derry (except the northeast), along with south Armagh and south Down. Belfast, extended to include some surrounding areas, would include, along with a considerable unionist majority, a large nationalist enclave in the west. The remainder, forming East Ulster, would have a large unionist majority. Assuming that some special arrangements are made for Belfast, let these three regions elect regional councils which would be in charge of most public services and have legislative powers in certain matters. Each region would have its own regionally recruited police force, with the extended west Belfast being policed by a unit of the Mid-Ulster Constabulary. The three regional councils would combine, as an electoral college, to elect the government of the North by proportional representation. In short, and to relate it to the current political terminology, I am talking about a scheme of *territorial power-sharing* and *two-tier devolution*.

The first step should be the election of three police councils, with statutory powers, in the three regions. These would appoint chief constables who would select their teams, and recruit the forces, along lines laid down by the respective councils. (East Ulster and Belfast might well decide to adapt existing RUC structures and retain most of the personnel.) An amnesty for political prisoners would be announced, to become effective within a year. Persons charged with criminal offences could opt for trial in the Republic. Then, as the new Mid-Ulster Constabulary went on duty, the Mid-Ulster Police Council would require the British army in the region and in west Belfast to withdraw to barracks, and would discontinue service duties for the UDR. Thus throughout a large part of the North – the parts in which they have been most active – the IRA would virtually cease to have targets that any nationalists would regard as legitimate.

This process would continue as, over a period of six months or so, the police councils were transformed, by devolution, into full regional councils with all the appertaining administrative functions in health, housing, education, industry, agriculture and so on. A Six-Counties-wide anti-discrimination agency would help to ensure that members of regional minorities were treated equitably. I say 'help to ensure' because, quite apart from such supervision, a code of 'we'll treat yours right if you treat ours right' would soon evolve, inter-regionally. Finally, in an atmosphere of growing stability and peace, the regional councillors would meet to establish a provincial assembly and executive charged with general legislation and the administration of those public services best dealt with in an overall manner.

The main point in what I am suggesting is the general idea; it might well be improved on in detail. But I am convinced that nothing less than institutional changes of this degree and kind would be required to 'bite' effectively, in an assuaging manner, into the consciousness of the Six-County nationalist community. Nothing less than such measures would cause them to feel that their distinct communal identity was being recognised, that they were enjoying equal status, and that things had really changed. But I also believe that under such arrangements they would find their situation significantly changed, and that this change would register with them in the following manner. As they exercised their new-found powers and responsibilities, and shared in the government of Ulster, they would feel that further change towards fuller national recognition, while desirable, was not so imperative as to be worth risking death, or life imprisonment, for it.

A settlement of the kind suggested would constitute a gain, not only for the Six-County Irish, but for the nation as a whole. From end to end of Ireland (though in differing degrees on each side of the border) the Irish nation would be recognised; and that is one way of describing the overriding aim of our 200-year-old political nationalism. Peace, too, ending the many-sided damage to the nation from the present conflict, would be an important national gain. The nation would have a chance to heal the serious wounds it has received in the past twenty years, and to devote itself, across the border, to constructing its future.

I believe, therefore, that the Irish government should urge this settlement on the British government, both in the Inter-governmental Conference and by every other means at its disposal. If it were urged forcefully, and supported by the Six-County Irish, it could be obtained. Or rather, it would be the very least that would be obtained. If the British objected that it was too much, was too disruptive of their state, too fraught with difficulties, the Irish side would find in the nationalist philosophy of the Forum Report a ready reply: namely, that if it was too onerous for the UK to accommodate, in this adequate manner, the identity of the Six-County Irish, then the Republic of Ireland would undertake, with temporary financial assistance from Britain, to accommodate the identity of the Ulster British in an equivalent manner. In short, a reunited Ireland, accommodating the Ulster British, could be proposed as the alternative. Thus either way the matter at issue would be clarified, brought to issue, and resolved. And either way there would be national gain.

I am not hopeful, however, that the Irish government will follow such a course, for the good reason that it seems to have forgotten, or to reject, the new nationalist analysis of the Northern problem which, as the Fianna Fáil Party, it subscribed to in the Forum Report. Worse, it seems to have replaced that analysis with nothing worthy of the name, and to be stumbling from crisis to crisis unsure what to do. Nor is the case any different with that co-signatory of the Forum Report, the SDLP. What does the SDLP believe, what is its aim: who can answer that? Certainly, the party never speaks now of recognition for the Irish nation in the North; and with good reason, for it seems to have abandoned the new realism about the extent and membership of the Irish nation that was achieved, if only implicitly, in the Forum Report.[7]

For the present, only two of the actors involved in the North's agony know what they want: the IRA and the British government. The IRA wants to force Britain out of Ulster; the British government wants to destroy the IRA. Between them these two forces who know what they want, and are pursuing it passionately, are crucifying Northern Ireland and Ireland as a whole. But there is nothing to stop them, and they will continue to do so while the new nationalism of the Forum Report remains inoperative.[8]

7. See, for example, the paper that the SDLP sent to Sinn Féin in the course of discussions with the latter (*Irish Times*, 19 September 1988), in which the SDLP agrees with Sinn Féin that 'the Irish people should be defined as those people domiciled on the island of Ireland'. By backtracking in this manner, the SDLP precludes itself from using the Forum approach of demanding recognition by Britain of the Irish community or identity in the North, as distinct from the British community or identity there – though this is the nub of the matter.

8. Though this was written in 1989 I would have nothing to add now, except that the peace arrangements must include formal recognition by Britain of the Irish nation in Northern Ireland.

8

WHATEVER YOU SAY,
SAY NOTHING

I

Eliot is, in my opinion, a greater poet because his poems, finally,
say more about the human condition than Owen's do.
                              Alan Bold in *Marxism Today*, 1971

FROM CALIFORNIA TO ENGLAND the poetry of Seamus Heaney
has been acclaimed by Eng. Lit. academics more than that
of any other Irish poet since Yeats. His Irish predecessors of the
top rank, Patrick Kavanagh and Austin Clarke, came nowhere
near such approbation, nor has any of the other outstanding Irish
poets of the past twenty years approached it. Moreover, by
academic and critical acclaim – the two are almost identical –
and by popular favour in Britain and Ireland, Heaney ranks above
all other living English-language poets. Appointed Boylston
Professor of Oratory and Rhetoric at Harvard in 1984, he has
since been elected Professor of Poetry at Oxford. On both sides
of the Atlantic he has won innumerable prizes and been awarded
honorary degrees. The London editions of his most successful
books have sold 15,000–30,000 copies; not large perhaps by
comparison with Kipling or Betjeman, but very large compared
with the poets who have emerged in Britain since the fifties
(only Wendy Cope has equalled it). Already in 1984, Edward
Lucie-Smith, editing the Penguin anthology *British Poetry since*

Monograph published in 1991 by ELO Publications, Dublin, and *Stand* (Autumn 1991)

1945, could write that Heaney 'now occupies the central position in British verse which was once accorded to Ted Hughes. He is the yardstick against which other poets, of the same generation or younger, must measure their own success.' On the American East Coast, he has nudged aside John Ashbery to succeed Robert Lowell as the poet laureate of the academy. For his Harvard colleague Helen Vendler, Professor of English and American Literature, he is 'as much the legitimate heir of Keats or Frost as of Kavanagh or Yeats'. A couple of years ago it was rumoured that he was to receive the Nobel Prize.

What is it about Heaney's lyrics that makes them so attractive to academics and other poetry readers that they are in effect being presented and regarded as the exemplar of what poetry should be? That he is a good poet there can be no doubt, but the reasons for his exceptional degree of transatlantic elevation are not immediately obvious. In the mass of writing about his work and person, this question has hardly been addressed, and understandably; for once a reputation is under construction, those who raise the walls and add the storeys take the building itself for granted. But the answer is, I think, worth seeking, not only in order to explain the phenomenon itself, but because the explanation must cast light on the present state of the poetry business, the ruling criteria of poetic excellence, and the reasons why these criteria now rule. Clearly, Heaney's poetry meets certain cultural, ideological and political requirements pretty well.

Poetry is a combination of language craft and public speech. Heaney's knowledge and love of language are very evident. His frequent use of unusual and archaic words must please the academics, while causing some distress to the ordinary reader, who often does not understand, and cannot even find the word in his English dictionary. The poems that made his reputation are knit together by carefully ordered assonances, internal rhymes and half-rhymes, which, together with the crisp, clean diction, give them a cool, chiselled beauty. Their subjects apart, the pleasure they yield is of a mental, chastely sensuous kind, arising from the rightness of correspondence between words and things, and of sounds to each other. In the frequent, striking onomatopoeia of the earlier work the language is made to materialise things, so that it not merely depicts but, mesmerically, almost reproduces the material realities in question – as in these lines from 'Churning Day':

> My mother took first turn, set up rhythms
> that slugged and thumped for hours. Arms ached,
> Hands blistered. Cheeks and clothes were spattered
> with flabby milk.

Later, beginning in *Wintering Out,* the language is often not so much materialising things as being itself material, moving and acting like paint in expressionist or abstract painting, sometimes to the neglect of syntax and clear meaning.

> The tawny, guttural water
> spells itself: Moyola
> is its own score and consort,
>
> bedding the locale
> in the utterance,
> reed music, an old chanter
>
> breathing its mists
> through vowels and history.
>   (from 'Gifts of Rain')

These poems are definitely not what Keats had in mind when he said: 'Poetry should be great and unobtrusive, a thing which enters into one's soul, and does not startle or amaze with itself, but with its subject.' Again and again, the reader is stopped, pleasurably or with irritation, by meticulously chosen metaphorical adjectives and verbs, and by abstruse if apt similes, whose linguistic

pregnancy distracts him from the subject. As a result, even when
the subject is concrete, no overall visual image of it – only sharp
glimpses – comes through.

> There was a sunlit absence.
> The helmeted pump in the yard
> heated its iron,
> water honeyed
>
> in the slung bucket
> and the sun stood
> like a griddle cooling
> against the wall
>
> of each long afternoon.
> (from 'Sunlight')

However, since *Station Island* the language has quietened and
become less mellifluous; the predominant style is fluently prosaic
and austere, and communication with the reader is frequently
hazy or absent.

> Our unspoken assumptions have the force
> of revelation. How else could we know
> that whoever is the first of us to seek
> assent and votes in a rich democracy
> will be the last of us and have killed our language?
> Meanwhile, if we miss the sight of a fish
> we heard jumping and then see its ripples,
> that means one more of us is dying somewhere.
> (from 'From the Land of the Unspoken')

Throughout, except in occasional rapturous phrases, in some
poems in *Field Work,* and in the Sweeney translation, Heaney's
poetry is not musical, in the ordinary sense of having the melody
and rhythm that make a verse, or verses, clamber into the memory,
or impel the reader to recite them for a companion. (Significantly,
apart from a few well-turned and apt phrases, Heaney is not

quoted.) The sound patterns are either just that and nothing more, falling flatly on the ear, or else they are pleasing in the manner of shingle sounding when a wave breaks, or water lapping against a boat.

> Cut from the green hedge a forked hazel stick
> That he held tight by the arms of the V:
> Circling the terrain, hunting the pluck
> Of water, nervous, but professionally
> Unfussed. The pluck came sharp as a sting.
> The rod jerked down with precise convulsions,
> Spring water suddenly broadcasting
> Through a green aerial its secret stations.
>
> (from 'The Diviner')

Alternatively, these sound patterns recall the 'concrete music' of some modern composers, in which metallic and mechanical things, with their clankings, hisses, thuds and gratings, sound off against each other. I suspect that a recurrent, almost philosophical motive behind Heaney's use of language is 'the music of what happens' – to quote that line of his that Helen Vendler found so ideologically pregnant that she used it as the title of the recent collection of her critical writings. The astringency of Heaney's language craft often holds the reader at a distance; but this probably pleases academics who like a text to lie coolly, for analysis, on the page.

Poetry as public speech includes several closely linked elements, two of which are theme and tone. Heaney's tone is serious, sometimes lugubriously so, less often with a light touch, but he is almost never humorous; so his work lacks the easy access to popularity that humour gives to, say, Wendy Cope. Nor, despite two of his poems appearing (absurdly) in the *Faber Book of Blue Verse,* has his work the saleability of salaciousness *à la* Fiona Pitt-Kethley.

Saying and representing things is the main part of public speech. Measured by its saying quality, the most striking feature of Heaney's poetry is what is generally called its 'reticence', which means 'saying little, and with reluctance'. It has been called reticent mainly because that is the word used to describe a marked characteristic of mainstream English poetry since the fifties, and because Heaney, along with other Northern Ireland poets, was inducted into this tradition by the English poet Philip Hobsbaum, when Hobsbaum was a lecturer in English at Queen's University Belfast. This is the poetry of the Movement and the Group, which turned its back on the poetry of broad discourse about the human condition, contemporary history, and human passions, practised by Yeats, Eliot, Pound, and the Auden of the thirties. But Heaney, too, has encouraged the use of the term by referring, in his self-commentaries, to the 'reticence' of Ulster speech. In fact, however, the reason why this feature of his poetry is so striking is that it is not mere reticence but a kind of silence, and operates according to a strict rule rigidly adhered to.

A recent study of Heaney's poetry by Professor Thomas C. Foster of the University of Michigan-Flint adverts more than once to the recurrence of silence and inarticulateness as themes, and to Heaney's view of speech as a dangerous activity. Towards the end of the book (*Seamus Heaney*, 1989), when Foster is discussing the poems of *The Haw Lantern,* he touches on both these matters in a single paragraph:

> The movement from common experience to allegory informs several of the parable poems, notably 'From the Land of the Unspoken' and 'Parable Island'. The former of these plays off the many earlier poems in which silence and inarticulateness form the core of the action. Often they involve Heaney's father, or the neighboring farmers of his childhood, or those common laborers like the fisherman Louis O'Neill, or the poet himself: people wary of speech, mistrustful of language, conscious of how easily one may say the wrong thing. Indeed, in conversation, although he is a congenial and at times talkative man, Heaney often gives the impression of holding back, of choosing with great care not only his words but which elements of himself he wishes

to reveal. He is, after all, the writer of that anthem for the Land of the Unspoken, 'Whatever You Say Say Nothing'. The poem reminds readers of the curious paradox of a writer who, while on the one hand celebrating language throughout his career, has maintained a lifelong wariness about the damage language can do.

More precisely, Heaney is wary of the damage that language as speech, and specifically as public speech, can do. He is fascinated by and loves language as words, while viewing its *parole* aspect, (public) speech, as fraught with danger, as potentially harmful. So the poet fears what he loves. A paradox, if you like; but more importantly, it indicates a tense opposition between two aspects of Heaney's poetic work, and that opposition arose from his sharing his people's view of public speech as dangerous.

As compared with other Irish people, Northerners, but particularly Northern Catholics, have been traditionally distinguished by caution: carefulness of speech and behaviour, watchful eyes. It was not in their accepted character to produce the men and women of the IRA whom we have seen in action these past twenty years; in terms of character alone, that was a revolution. The ingrained Northern Catholic caution derives from a belief that the social environment outside what might be called the home sphere – the domestic milieu or the community, as the case may be – is dangerous. It follows that communication with that environment, public speech in this sense, is also dangerous and potentially harmful; but it is necessary, hence the folk maxim for such speech: 'Whatever you say, say nothing.'

Heaney, sharing his people's anxious belief about public speech, found in this maxim, which he grew up with, a strategy for managing the opposition between saying and silence, and transforming it into a creative discipline. The belief and the maxim together, operating as second nature, have provided him with the mindset that rules his poetic utterance: 'Because public speech can do damage – whatever you say, say nothing.' By identifying this mindset we are enabled to trace the pattern in his poetic speech – the system that determines its range and relates its parts coherently.

Poetry is often moulded by beliefs about speech, and rules of speech behaviour, that are current in the poet's native culture. The 'reticence' of English poetry after the Second World War drew on the beliefs about speech and the speech behaviour of the English officer class. When these practical guides of everyday life are applied to poetic speech, their meaning is somewhat modified by the different context. But their effect remains as in everyday life: to enable, disable, or prescribe certain manners of speaking and certain themes.

When the belief of County Derry Catholics that public speech is potentially harmful is applied to poetry that is to be published in London and New York, 'public speech' modifies its meaning from 'speech to individuals outside the home sphere' to 'speech to literate English-speakers in general'. Thus adapted, the belief has the disabling and prescriptive effects that arise from its embodying a half-truth and being therefore untrue. Public speech, and by extension the public speech of poetry, has potential for good as well as for harm. The poet who is aware of this – who knows that his poems may do harm or good to himself or others – can want and try to use his poetry, boldly and prudently, to do good to both. Consequently, he is able to use it for this purpose, able to speak boldly to clarify the world for his generation or to emulate the greatest poets and become one of them. He can comfort or encourage the oppressed or despairing, build a poetic bridge between opponents, satirise or castigate tyrants, ridicule cowards, lift the hearts of his people, admonish his friends for their good or warn their enemies, glorify God or praise virtue. Great poets have done these things before him. But the poet who sees public speech merely as having potential for harm cannot want or try to use it for doing good, and cannot therefore write those and other kinds of poetry, unless by accident or forgetfulness. Many categories of address and theme are excluded *a priori* from his repertoire. He must confine himself to using language, nervously and carefully, so as to avoid doing harm – keeping to safe themes and modes of address, and doing good only in this negative, protective manner.

Then again, when the maxim 'Whatever you say, say nothing' is applied to the poetry of a poet published in London and New York, 'say nothing' modifies its meaning. The 'saying nothing' of the poet, who is by profession a public speaker and addressing literate people in general, is different in kind from that of a County Derry farmer – a private person, for whom speaking to individuals outside his home sphere is merely an activity among others. Still, however, for the poet as for the farmer, the maxim provides a practical guide to the safe kind, and kinds, of public speech, which by avoiding doing harm to himself or others will benefit both. This can best be seen by observing how the maxim works, first in its native setting, then on poetry.

As a rule of everyday life, 'Whatever you say, say nothing' prescribes not literal silence but a kind of silence: effective silence. If need be, speech is permitted, but it must be an unnatural, uneasy, fearful manner of speaking, which is careful to negate the real function of speech by conveying, effectively, 'nothing'; that is, nothing of importance. The something (of importance) that is not to be communicated is home affairs: information about the life, thoughts or intentions of the speaker, his family or his community, as the case may be. Speaking so as to 'say nothing' about these matters means either keeping the talk to other, trivial matters, or, if an important matter is pressed on the speaker unavoidably, making no clear, quotable statement about it but dealing with it evasively, noncommittally, peripherally, and with the help of riddle devices – ambiguity, half-saying, inconsequential anecdote and so on. The putative receivers of this artful speech are strangers to the home sphere, however defined, including, therefore, on occasion, neighbours with whom a competitive relationship exists. Its purpose is at least to protect, at most to further, the interests of the speaker, or of his family or community.

Applied to poetry, the maxim produces formally the same speech pattern. The poet speaks as if speech were a minefield, and therefore unnaturally and uneasily, the language craft taking precedence over the contents. He 'says nothing' by avoiding saying anything about important matters. But important matters, in the speech of a public speaker, means matters of interest to his audience – which for a poet comprises literate people in general. Let us call such matters general matters. So the poet says nothing by avoiding clear, quotable statements (in plain or figurative language) about general matters: the human condition, current affairs, the state of his country or the world, men, women, history, the future, nature, beauty, fear, love, death, and such like. Instead he speaks about particular matters (himself, his feelings and memories, incidents from his domestic or family life), historical titbits or esoteric subjects (words, the poet's craft, abstruse conceits, etcetera); and if pressure from within or without forces him to deal with a general matter, then he evades the issue, and manages to be noncommittal, by keeping to peripheral aspects, converting these when possible into private matter, and employing riddling devices from quip, hint and irony to strained allegory. Applied in this manner to his poetic speech, the maxim achieves its purpose for him. By refraining from pronouncements on general matters, he avoids saying things that might encourage people to think or act wrongly, prevents the harm to his own creative activity that might come from getting involved in media controversy, and escapes the damage to his poetic career that would result from offending powerful or influential people. In short, by saying nothing he does no harm and – if he is a talented poet – some good to himself.

'An unnatural, uneasy, fearful manner of speaking.' As in everyday life, so in the poetry it is the manner of speaking, *as an overall performance,* that is (necessarily) fearful, unnatural and uneasy. Within this overall unease, the degree of actual unease varies.

Obviously, it is greatest when the poet has perforce to fence with a general matter; but when he is dealing with particular matters, as he usually is, his anxiety is not so pressing, and it is minimal when his subject is, actually or virtually, language for its own sake. Thus, for example, in his 1977 interview with Seamus Deane, Heaney said, with reference to his poems about County Derry placenames, 'I had a great sense of release as they were being written, a joy and devil-may-careness.' They were, so to speak, a holiday from care for him; and similarly, it is not surprising that he wrote his most delightful, icily scintillating verse when he was translating the anonymous *Buile Shuibhne* into *Sweeney Astray*.

> I would live happy
> in an ivy bush
> high in some twisted tree
> and never come out.
> The skylarks rising
> to their high space
> send me pitching and tripping
> over stumps on the moor
>
> and my hurry flushes
> the turtle-dove.

Because the avoidance of general matters tends to lead to the poet's speaking a great deal about himself, and about matters pertaining to himself, it involves the risk of his boring people and of appearing at least self-obsessed, at worst vain. It is a gamble that ends up either by losing him his audience or, if he is a good enough poet, is lucky and becomes famous, by providing them with a subject that really interests them. In the latter case, fame makes his self and its inner workings into a 'general matter': for his audience in the first instance, but also for people who never read his poetry. His poetic speech about himself becomes the only, if limited, exception to his rule.

A poetry that deliberately says nothing about the world is a poetry akin to silence. To be more explicit: because it says nothing about the world, it is silent in it – not heard by it, and not affecting it, because silent on its concerns. But because it is silent, not by accident, but by the poet's design – not because he could not say something about the world, but because he will not and artfully does not – it has an inner tension that fascinates its readers, a compressed intensity, a lucid-opaque quality, as of an exotic mask or icon.

I think I have outlined the most striking characteristics of Heaney's poetic speech, and shown how they fit together. When I say that he has avoided clear statements about general matters, I mean – lest I be misundersood – that none of his poems, nor a part of any of them, makes such a statement. It follows that his poetry conveys no structured worldview and is in this sense intellectually poor. Those readers of his poetry who believe it 'says something' about old-fashioned rural life, married life or the Northern Ireland conflict may be surprised at my implicit denial of this. Married life is, after all, a general theme, and so also, if in much more limited ways, are old-fashioned rural life and the Northern Ireland conflict. But a moment's reflection will confirm that neither 'old-fashioned rural life' nor 'married life' is the subject of any of Heaney's poems, and that none of them contains any statement, plain or figurative, about those or related matters. What many of the poems do is to present, with the poet's accompanying feelings, a remembered scene or incident from what readers, especially when they have read several poems with similar themes, might call 'old-fashioned rural life', 'married life' or 'a love relationship'. Much the same applies to his treatment of the Northern Ireland conflict. However, because this conflict has played such a large role in Heaney's reputation, and because there are confused ideas about it outside Ireland, a more extensive clarification seems called for.

Occasionally, commentators on the relevant poetry relate it

not to 'the Northern Ireland conflict', but to 'the Troubles' or 'the violence' in Northern Ireland or 'Ulster'. To get things in order, let us first set down what conflict has been going on in six counties of Ulster these past twenty-one years. A political, partly violent conflict has been going on, on Irish soil, between Irish nationalism and British nationalism, between people of the Irish Tricolour and people of the British Union Jack: on the one hand, about 600,000 ethnic Irish or 'Catholics' (Heaney's people) and, on the other hand, the British government and about 900,000 Ulster British, or 'Protestants', who take pride in their 400-year history as 'No Surrender' colonials. Broadly speaking, the members of the Irish community have been struggling to win recognition, in political terms, by Britain and the Ulster British, of their non-British, Irish identity – what Heaney was concerned about for himself personally when he wrote *An Open Letter* in 1983 objecting to being included in an anthology of British poets – and the British side have been resisting this demand, while making minor concessions. Important subthemes of this central drama are the general rise from subservience to self-confidence of the Six-County Irish during the past twenty years; the relative decline in self-confidence and power of the Ulster British; and the hunger strike of 1981, led by Bobby Sands, which for months, while ten men demanding better prison conditions slowly died, stirred the world. Neither the main drama nor these likewise dramatic subthemes have shown up in Heaney's poetry, except where, in one veiled passage in 'Station Island', the funeral of a hunger striker in the poet's home place figures.

What the poetry does copiously allude to is another subtheme, the armed conflict between a small section of the Irish community and British forces and their supporters which, because of its noisy drama and lethal character, has come to signify 'the Northern Ireland conflict' internationally. More fully described, it is an armed struggle, with many noncombatant casualties, between on the one hand the Irish Republican Army and some smaller republican groups and on the other the British army and police, and loyalist paramilitaries (whom the police also pursue). The declared aim of the IRA is to break Britain's will to hold Northern Ireland, thereby achieving a British withdrawal, while the declared aim of the British government, with the support of the Ulster British, has been to defeat the IRA and hold onto Northern Ireland while a majority of its citizens so desire. Tacitly, at the same time the IRA and the loyalist paramilitaries (Ulster Volunteer Force, Ulster Defence Association) are fighting for local mastery. That is the 'Northern Ireland violence', and those are the main issues – easily understandable and known to everyone in Northern Ireland – that are at stake in it. It will be ended, ultimately, as it could have been years ago, by decisive political measures giving due recognition to both communities.

When, in 1984, Seamus Heaney delivered the Pete Laver Memorial Lecture at Grasmere on 'Place and Displacement: Recent Poetry of Northern Ireland', he felt called on to defend the response to the violence by some Northern fellow poets, and implicitly by himself. He said:

> 'Pure' poetry is perfectly justifiable in earshot of the carbomb but it still implies a politics, depending on the nature of the poetry. *A poetry of hermetic wit, of riddles and slips and self-mocking ironies,* while it may appear culpably miniaturist or fastidious to the activist with his microphone at the street corner, may be exercising in its inaudible way a fierce disdain of the amplified message, or a distressed sympathy with it. [Italics mine.]

Heaney's own poems in response to the conflict have gone further than 'hermetic wit, riddles, slips and self-mocking ironies'. They have included, for example, accounts of being stopped at an army checkpoint, of seeing a column of motorised troops traversing his countryside and his feelings on the matter, and of killings of individuals known to him and his feelings about them. In no instance, however – not even in 'Ministry of Fear' which without the fudging, might have been a luminous statement about the Stormont police state – does he depart from his standard practice of avoiding clear, quotable statements about general matters. His poetry says nothing, plainly or figuratively, about the war, about any of the three main parties to it, or about the issues at stake. Nor, indeed – quite apart from saying – is anything *suggested* about the war except that it is sad, rooted in history, often ruthless, and connected with the oppression of the poet's people and sacrifice to a goddess. Of course, in the minds of readers, especially if they are at a distance from the scene, the poems about prehistoric bodies in a Jutland bog, and about particulars of the Northern Ireland war, may fuse together as 'poems about irrational violence'; and that is certainly their collective, tendentious suggestion. But Heaney says nothing about irrational violence, and all he suggests about it, generically, is that it is evil and sad: an insight that we hardly need to read poetry for.

In the characterisation of Heaney's poetry, its lack of statements about the Northern Ireland conflict is not very important; of much greater significance is its nothing-saying about matters of common human experience, whether perennial or contemporary, or about life in the Republic of Ireland where Heaney has been living these past nineteen years, most of that time in Dublin. Compared with the amount of world (all of it) that the poetry of great poets speaks about, very little world is spoken about in his poetry. But inasmuch as the Northern Ireland conflict was so to speak handed to him, and pointed its historic finger at him, his silence on it – imposed like all his silence by his belief in the harmful potential of public speech – has, as he knows and has said, been fateful for him as a poet. Truly, in refusing it as a theme, he 'missed/The once-in-a-lifetime portent' that of itself could have made him great and – what matters most to poets – remembered forever. His painful awareness of this, poignantly expressed, makes 'Exposure' one of his best poems.

I am neither internee nor informer;
An inner emigré, grown long-haired
And thoughtful; a wood-kerne

Escaped from the massacre,
Taking protective colouring
From bole and bark, feeling
Every wind that blows.

Who, blowing up these sparks
For their meagre heat, have missed
The once-in-a-lifetime portent,
The comet's pulsing rose.

Besides saying things about the world, poetry can represent or show it. Even if it is silent about it, and speaks only about particular and private matters, it can represent the world by making its representations of these matters representative, so that they stand for more than their particular content. Goethe said to Eckermann: 'The poet should seize the Particular, and he should, if there be anything sound in it, thus represent the Universal.' Poetry can do this with its feelings, as with its depicted scenes and incidents. It can still, by this means, be rich in meaning. Are the feelings and sentiments expressed in Heaney's poems part of common experience, so that they mean something personal for literate people generally? Do the scenes, incidents and situations that are depicted, straightforwardly or allegorically, convey a larger meaning than their particular content? These are the silent, 'nothing-saying' ways in which a great painting speaks about more than the subject it depicts. For example, a run-of-the-mill work of Dutch genre painting may depict much the same scene as a Vermeer, but it remains an image merely of that scene, while the Vermeer *means* both that scene and the human condition, or some aspect of it.

The *Phoenix,* Dublin's equivalent of London's *Private Eye,* regularly carries brief reviews of books, plays and films in a commonsense vein that takes no account of established reputations or critical conventions. Its review of Heaney's last book of poems, *The Haw Lantern,* was as follows:

> It's a fair bet that this is the only poetry collection most people will buy this year, such is the hype surrounding this pricey 50 pages of verse (Faber and Faber, £4.54). While the experts insist that Famous Seamus is one of the best English-language poets in the world, he certainly isn't the most accessible. Hands up, for instance, who knows what this means: 'I ordained opacities and they haruspicated.' Sometimes it seems that, like some 'Call My Bluff' enthusiast, Heaney reaches for the word that will obfuscate rather than elucidate. It requires much cleverness to do this properly, and Heaney's genius is that, though the words may baffle, they sound rather ... well, poetic!
>
> But while our revered bard's literary and intellectual gymnastics may impress, it is very difficult to respond on an emotional level to this collection. In most of the poems, it is a struggle to discern what he's on about, and there is very little here that encapsulates a common, day-to-day feeling or sentiment that might be shared by his less gifted audience.

This review is interesting, incidentally, because it conveys how the fame of 'Famous Seamus' is commonly seen in the city where he lives: with satisfaction that this (by now) local poet, and Irishman, has made it to the top, and with a bemused sense of wonderment both at the degree of the fame and at the fact – Ireland was not consulted on the matter – that Heaney rather than one of several other Irish poets of the past or present has been selected for such exaltation. Both these sentiments are shared by the present writer, and indeed the second has given rise to this investigating essay. But what pertains directly to the question I am discussing is that *cri de coeur* in the last few lines of the review, as of people who went to their poet looking for bread and got stones.

In Heaney's collections up to *Field Work,* there were many poems in which the feelings and sentiments meant something, emotionally, to ordinary people. The subjects and diction were straightforward, and the accompanying feelings of tenderness, wonderment, disgust, sorrow, guilt, anger, and so on, intelligibly grounded. But as Heaney's reputation has grown, and as he has directed his poetry more to the academic audience gathering around him, especially in the USA, and to poets (in the latest collections, quite a number of the poems are either dedicated to another poet or writer, or deal with a dead one), the number of extremely esoteric poems has been growing also. By 'esoteric' I mean accessible in practice only to a small number of people with special knowledge, or not even to those. Apart from much of *The Haw Lantern,* the Sweeney poems in *Station Island* are a case in point: in most of these, even the professional interpreters can only surmise what the poet is on about, let alone feeling. Some of them read like clues to a sophisticated crossword puzzle, and the suspicion arises that Heaney, seeing how well Joyce did out of it, has likewise decided to keep the professors busy. What, for example, was this 'hermit' up to?

> As he prowled the rim of his clearing
> where the blade of choice had not spared
> one stump of affection
>
> he was like a ploughshare
> interred to sustain the whole field
> of force, from the bitted
>
> and high-drawn sideways curve
> of the horse's neck to the aim
> held fast in the wrists and elbows –
> (from 'The Hermit')

Scattered throughout the work, after the first two volumes, are moderately esoteric poems, dealing with placenames, words, the poet's craft, Greek mythological themes or obscure historical incidents. Educated literary people who are interested in language for its own sake can find pleasure in many of these; but the pleasure is largely confined to this elite. One way or another, there is an excess of poems that do not stand on their own feet – do not yield their meaning, or their full meaning – without some introduction, background knowledge or elucidating commentary such as the commentarists supply, or Heaney himself supplies in his prose works or at a poetry reading. To cite an example chosen at random, 'The Stone Verdict' begins as follows and, after an abstruse 'stone verdict', ends without identifying the subject.

> When he stands in the judgement place
> With his stick in his hand and the broad hat
> Still on his head, maimed by self-doubt
> And an old disdain of sweet talk and excuses,
> It will be no justice if the sentence is blabbed out.
> He will expect more than words in the ultimate court
> He relied on through a lifetime's speechlessness.

It is almost unfair to inspect for universal meaning the many fine Heaney poems that depict a person or persons in a setting. The infusion of such meaning into a particular reality requires the poet to be concerned primarily with his subject, and with the soul or inner life of a person depicted, and generally speaking Heaney has different concerns. The busy language in the foreground makes the subject it is depicting into a fragmented background, and the persons figure as workers, as opaque physical presences, or for their character traits. Where, very occasionally, the language quietens and makes way, the universal appears.

> Walking with you and another lady
> In wooded parkland, the whispering grass
> Ran its fingers through our guessing silence
> And the trees opened into a shady
> Unexpected clearing where we sat down.

I think the candour of the light dismayed us.
We talked about desire and being jealous,
Our conversation a loose single gown
Or a white picnic tablecloth spread out
Like a book of manners in the wilderness.

(from 'A Dream of Jealousy')

When all the others were away at Mass
I was all hers as we peeled potatoes,
They broke the silence, let fall one by one
Like solder weeping off the soldering iron:
Cold comforts set between us, things to share
Gleaming in a bucket of clean water.

(from 'Clearances' 3)

When several readings of 'Sunlight' (see p. 133) have rendered the language lucid, it comes close to being that image of a Martha-like loving woman that the poet perhaps wanted it to be. Usually, however, the subject is pinned so decisively to its particularity and physicality that I am reminded of those programmatic poem titles of Wallace Stevens's – 'The Plain Sense of Things', 'Not Ideas about the Thing but the Thing Itself', 'Of Mere Being', 'The Course of a Particular' – and of these lines from that last poem:

The leaves cry. It is not a cry of divine attention,
Nor the smoke-drift of puffed-out heroes, nor human cry.
It is the cry of leaves that do not transcend themselves . . .

Heaney's scenes and incidents from the Northern Ireland violence do not transcend themselves. People familiar with the scenario recognise the depictions as representative of it, but their meaning for them ends there: the poems offer them less insight than they already possess.

Good poetry, like good painting, can be poor in world and meaning. A painting of a vase of flowers, of a toad on a computer disc, or of a domestic scene that does not transcend itself, can be good art. But like good poetry that 'says nothing', and does not mean much, it is minor art.

Of course, Heaney's reputation, like that of any well-known poet, is based not only on what his poetry says or expressly represents, but on what it suggests, intentionally or otherwise, about the world and himself. Whatever its deficiency in world, it conveys willy-nilly a world image. Readers note absences, presences and emphases: impressions are transmitted, values and valuations intimidated. Similarly, a self or persona appears or is enacted through the work, all the more so because it is so self-absorbed.

The most striking features of the world image that Heaney's poetry suggests are materiality and non-transcendence; a world that is mainly rural and silent, without peopled landscapes; the goodness of the material earth, of primeval slime and the rustic past, of work, marriage, friendship and rootedness in family; the sadness and evil of violent death; the compulsive pull of an individual's cultural roots and tribal attachment; the doubtful value of commitment outside the domestic sphere; and the very suspect pull of communal or patriotic loyalty. The only major public matter that figures, the Northern Ireland conflict, is conveyed impressionistically as a sad, atavistic, tribal feud, in which, as in a bog, the soldiers, police and prisons of the rational state flounder. The self enacted in the poems is a painfully introspective, well-read countryman, in wellingtons, squelching mud. He delights in words, wordlore, wordcraft and earthy things; practises private and familial tenderness; feels concern and occasionally anger about public matters, but holds back guiltily from action or commitment; supports Amnesty International; heeds his roots and tradition; relates to others singly (one would not know that his rural home contained eight brothers and sisters); and holds back, humbly and cannily, from pronouncements on human life and the matters that concern people.

Overall, then, Heaney's poetry has many elements that seem likely to appeal to contemporary academics, and none likely to repel them. Most Eng. Lit. and Am. Lit. academics are liberals (more precisely, left-liberals), and as such they would find the suggested world image according pretty closely with their own, and the performed persona close to their preferred self-image. For the great majority of them, living in England and the USA, the simple rural settings and bogs confirm their idea of Ireland, provide comfort in a brittle world, and are relatable to well-known recent poetry in their own literatures. The Northern Ireland matter conveys to them, agreeably, the *frisson* of a sensitive soul impinged upon by civil violence, along with good reasons for not caring about the issues at stake. The poems with difficult words and Irish allusions, and those with esoteric themes and rarefied feelings, challenge them engagingly as literary interpreters – justifying them by giving them work to do. The lack of singing melody, the ripple and thud of chill concordances appeal to their mandarin purity of taste, assuring them that there is nothing spurious, nothing merely emotional or sensual, in their appreciation. The poet's humble silence on the general matters of mankind pleases them because it accords with their scepticism about 'human nature', and because it is fitting for a provincial not to pronounce above his station. Doubtless all these satisfactions for his academic audience have helped Heaney, decisively, to his high standing. In the introduction to Carcanet's *British Poetry since 1970,* the publishers, Peter Jones and Michael Schmidt, write:

> The academy – schools and universities alike – has modern poetry by the throat. The market for books of poems is now preeminently academic. No new poet is safely established until he is on a syllabus.

There is much less in Heaney's poetry for the non-academic reader of contemporary poetry, who still exists in Britain and, disproportionately, in Ireland. Consequently, his popular following needs explaining. Like his critical reputation, it was founded on the combination of exciting verbal craft with rustic themes. The rustic themes were attractive for their own sake. In England the taste for them was maintained by Wordsworth's poetry, and renewed in this century by the Georgians. A television soap about a country vet doing his rounds among old-world Yorkshire farmsteads is a long-time popular favourite, for its milieu as much as for its animals. In Ireland, Patrick Kavanagh ploughed the rustic furrow with popular success, and opened the eyes of country boy Heaney to its poetic potential. In 1989, *To School through the Fields,* a collection of prose scenes from remembered farm life by a housewife, Alice Taylor, was the biggest Irish bestseller of all time; at last hearing, 170,000 copies had been sold,

When word went out that *North* dealt extensively with the Northern Ireland conflict, Heaney's popular appeal spread wider. As the English critic Blake Morrison testified in *British Poetry since 1970,* it caused great excitement in London. 'It met with the kind of acclaim which, in Britain at least, we had ceased to believe poetry could achieve.' Over 6,000 copies were sold in the first month, 'a figure which outdoes even Larkin's *The Whitsun Wedding* and Hughes's *Crow*'. In Ireland those who hoped for Yeatsian statements were disappointed. But many, particularly in the Republic, whose own attitudes to the war were ambiguous and cautious derived wry pleasure from Heaney's acting out, vicariously, their state of mind and their personal policy of 'Mind you, I've said nothing' – another Irish saying about nothing-saying. There was wry admiration for him as a 'cute hoor': cleverer than his Dublin fellow poet Tom Kinsella who, it was said, plummeted in Anglosaxondom after the blunder of *Butcher's Dozen,* which bitterly rebuked the paratroopers who shot the thirteen in Derry; or the Northern poet Padraic Fiacc, whose raw war poetry, often imbued with polemical sentiment, gets left out of the London anthologies.

In the eighties, as Heaney became more vatic, and a decreasing number of his poems offered pleasure to the ordinary reader, it is likely that sales were maintained both by his books being prescribed for courses and, as the *Phoenix* review suggests, by the reputation itself and the media hype attending each new book. It is probably true, in Ireland, that Heaney is the only poet whom many people buy or give as a present – meaning that they buy him not so much for his poetry as because he is the most celebrated poet or the book of the month. Similarly, people who normally ignore rock or pop music will, when U2, Enya or Sinéad O'Connor make a noise in the media, purchase a record out of curiosity or to be with the crowd. The plain fact is that Heaney's poetry, apart from the earlier poems on rustic themes and some of the poems about family members, is not the sort that appeals to most people who find sustenance and delight in poetry. They like rhythmic, melodic language, comprehension on at most two readings, and the memorability that arises from this. The poetry that they treasure most – literally by carrying it in their minds – is poetry that combines those qualities with common kinds of feeling, and with clear statements, plain or figurative, about things they have experienced, thought about or dreamt of: things that interest them, in short. No one today needs to write like Shakespeare, but that poet, though four centuries old, still fills the bill.

However, granted that Heaney's poetry has many qualities likely to please the academics, it is not yet clear why, from London to California, they have elevated him above all Irish poets since Yeats, and above all his British and American contemporaries. In view of the known range and possibilities of poetry, and the kinds of poetry from the past that we now judge great, there is still a question as to why an uneven body of lyrics, many of them well-made and beautiful but lacking a structured worldview, saying nothing about general matters, covering a repetitively narrow range of themes, and growing obscurer as they increase in number, should be regarded so widely, not as good minor poetry, but as the nearest contemporary approximation, in English, to what poetry should be, and the equivalent of great poetry. The question is sharpened by the knowledge that the great majority of literate English-speakers have stopped reading poetry – in the USA, almost everyone, outside the academy – that much of Heaney's work, especially in the later books, is not the kind of poetry that has a wide appeal, and that his miniaturism offers people much less than poetry can offer them. So it is a matter of understanding not just the reasons for a literary judgement, but also the decision implicit in it that the separation of poetry from life, and therefore from people, will continue and grow greater.

II

> The reasons for this change from a vernacular to an academic mode of composition may also be the reasons why, after Plautus and Terence . . . vernacular comedy received little new blood; drama became a literary art, and popular entertainment was provided by spectacles and physical contests.
>
> E.F. Watling in *Plautus: The Rope and Other Plays,* 1964

I mentioned at the outset that Eng. Lit. academics are a category almost identical with poetry critics. Certainly at the top that is the case, and there is a further professional overlap. Increasingly, over the past forty years, poets have themselves doubled as academics, most notably in the USA, but also in Britain and Ireland. Heaney, holding two professorial chairs, is himself an outstanding example. In Helen Vendler's *Faber Book of Contemporary American Poetry* the biographies of 25 out of the 34 poets include academic employment, and of the 23 living poets, 11 are professors of English, 5 are academics in some other capacity, and one was for a time. Consequently, what we are in fact investigating is the literary judgement of what might be called, on the analogy of the military-industrial, the academic-poetic complex. It is this complex, with its representatives, regular or occasional, in the general media – and its judgements broadcast by those media – that has made Heaney in effect its transatlantic poet laureate.

In order to get to the top today in poetry, transatlantically, there are three prerequisites which a poet must fulfil, and Heaney has fulfilled all of them. The first is to write only or mainly lyrics, and preferably fairly short ones. The idea has been put around that the lyric is what poetry essentially is, and that narrative, satirical, philosophical or dramatic poetry, and long poetic works generally, while they may continue to exist and sometimes to merit praise, are not necessary for the health of poetry. Poetry is now generally written about as if it were synonymous with lyrics, and the two words are often used interchangeably. Lyrics, moreover, are the kind of poetry suitable for printing in newspapers and magazines, and for reading on television. When people go to a poetry reading, it is lyrics they expect to hear.

Second, the poet must actively manage his career, with particular attention to the fact that we live, as we are so often told, in an age of public relations and mass communications, and in a free market economy. Heaney has done this well. Unlike many poets he has regarded poetry as a career to be taken as seriously as any other, and he has used his intelligence and personal charm accordingly. He has noted and responded to the signals of his socially changing and geographically shifting audience. Though living in Dublin, he has been careful to maintain his Northern Ireland persona. Accused by some of condoning Irish republican violence, he 'balanced' with a poem to mark the assassination of the British Ambassador to Ireland. In choosing the poems for selected editions, he has been guided by political as well as aesthetic considerations. Above all, he has been an assiduous communicator about his work, thereby ensuring that critical writing about it is interspersed with explanations and critical comments of his own.

The third prerequisite is hinted at by the poet and critic Marvin Bell, writing in the *American Poetry Review* (May–June 1990): 'Much of our [American] official criticism grows on the East Coast, and looks to the Old World, perhaps unconsciously, for cultural signals.' He adds: 'Puritanism may apply: it seems to be

flourishing . . .', but of that more anon. To get to the top, transatlantically, in poetry, you must reach the top first in London.
Heaney accomplished this.

To begin with, along with Mahon, Paulin and others, he was
one of the 'Northern Ireland poets' who, from the late 1960s
onwards, were being hailed in London as the rising hope of British
poetry. They were hailed as that because Northern Ireland is
British and they were publishing in London; their matter was
new to many there; and their vigour and quality stood out in
the tired British poetry scene, where the muted postwar epoch
was fizzling to a close. Heaney, who won prizes in London with
his first book, *Death of a Naturalist*, emerged as their leader. In
Faber, he had, to quote a London poet acquaintance, 'the only
poetry publisher who has got his act together'. From 1969
onwards, when the violence put Northern Ireland daily in the
news, it came to seem the most exciting, because embattled, place
for a poet to be. In 1972 Heaney moved south to near Dublin.
His reputation had not been enhanced by his second book, and
he had begun to be typed, even caricatured, as a rustic bard of
farmyards and country lanes. But his stock rose again in 1972 with
Wintering Out, which offered fresh, vibrant language and a couple
of hints of Northern violence. Then, with *North* in 1975, he
delivered the 'war book' that London was waiting for, and that
made him top poet in Britain. Blake Morrison, in the essay I
referred to, 'Speech and Reticence: Seamus Heaney's *North*' writes:

> The book had barely come back from the printers before various
> funding bodies were rushing to cast their cheques at Heaney's
> feet. *North* was made the Poetry Book Society choice; it won
> the Duff Cooper Memorial Prize and the £1,500 W.H. Smith
> Memorial Prize; it was gushed over on television and radio. . . .
> A sceptical observer might have suspected that there was rather
> more to the acclaim for *North* than appreciation of the book's
> literary merits. . . . For some years, in a new version of the old
> cry 'Where are the war poets?', critics had been calling for a poetry

that would 'deal with' the Northern Ireland 'problem', and in the reviews of *North* there is an almost audible sigh of relief that at last a poetry of stature had emerged from the 'troubles'.

'A poetry of stature' not least because two of its most striking characteristics, its nothing-saying and its poverty of meaning, were prized poetic qualities in London critical circles. Morrison continues:

> At the same time it was noticeable that . . . hardly anyone seemed interested in what it was that Heaney had to 'say' about Northern Ireland. Indeed the suggestion seemed to be that while it was good to have a poet like Heaney 'involve himself in' the Ulster troubles, his poetry was valuable insofar as it could not be seen to be making statements: poetry, after all, should not mean but be.

Perhaps Morrison's citation of Archibald MacLeish's dictum is not without irony – he himself is critical of this view of *North* – but what matters for our purpose is his account of the prevailing view. Somewhat further on, in a sentence that sums up neatly the two main currents that had joined to make Heaney's poetic, he explicitly integrates Heaney into the postwar English mainstream of poetic reticence.

> Having grown up in a community, the Catholic minority in Ulster, where to speak openly is a dangerous activity ('whatever you say, say nothing' as one of his poems has it), and belonging as he does to a modern poetic tradition which distrusts poetry that too explicitly 'states', Heaney is loth to wear the mantle of the political poet . . .

Morrison is inexact when he suggests that the English reticent tradition shrank from 'too explicitly stating': it shrank, generally, from explicit statements about large or general things, not about the self and small, particular things. But the point of what he says is that in Heaney the poetically adapted speech behaviour of County Derry Catholics fused, happily, with the similarly adapted speech culture of the English military-administrative caste. Thomas

Foster, in his book, remarks on the 'terseness' of an early Heaney poem, and says that 'it recalls a characteristic tone in contemporary British and Irish verse: defensive, tight-lipped, understated'. From 'characteristic' subtract 'Irish'; the operative word is 'British', and more precisely, English. Foster continues:

> One thinks of a similar hard edge in Jon Silkin's 'Death of a Son' or any number of poems by Philip Larkin, Charles Tomlinson, Geoffrey Hill, Roy Fuller, Kavanagh, and Hughes. While the British may have learned that pose and attitude from Thomas Hardy, Edward Thomas and the Georgian poets, as well as, according to Larkin, the privations of World War II, Heaney and the . . . Ulster Irish have learned to hold their tongues from extra-literary affairs.

Actually, the special virtue of Heaney that was sensed, rather than identified in London, was that he went one further than reticence by practising nothing-saying, or effective silence. Larkin, for all his reticence, had occasionally allowed himself clear statements about the human condition. In that respect Heaney trumped him, just as in his poems reflecting the Northern Ireland conflict he trumped the other English top player, Hughes, who had strongly influenced his early poetry. Where Hughes, deviating from the genteel English mainstream, had offered sinister violence, imaginatively, in his animal poems, Heaney provided it not in animal but in human form, and not imagined but actual – as actual as the television news. To crown it all, and to speed the transatlantic crossing, Robert Lowell, then the reigning poet of the American academy but living for some time in England, described Heaney in the *Observer* as 'the best Irish poet since W.B. Yeats'.

The upshot was that *North* was rocketed to New York with the labels 'the best that Britain can offer' and 'according to Lowell, the best since Yeats'. Heaney had a certain reputation in the USA based on his early bucolic poems and their Frostian echoes. 'Digging', with its present-participle title recalling Frost's 'Mowing', 'Mending Wall' and so on, became and has remained his best-known poem there. People were grateful to him for 'bringing the theme back into poetry', something that had never been noticed in Ireland or Britain where the 'theme' had never disappeared. Already, before *North*, his reputation in London had helped; now that book's triumph there ensured that it was received enthusiastically in most of the US journals, mainly academic publications, that review poetry. Henceforth Heaney was up front in the East Coast poetry stakes. But *North* did not bring him to the top there, let alone in the USA generally – that would not happen until the eighties. He rose to that eminence partly because of his continuing British reputation, his teaching in Harvard, and the gratuitous advantage of being a foreign poet. 'You know the four great poets in this country in recent years?' an American poet said to me ironically. 'Heaney, Brodsky, Milosz, Walcott.' More decisive, however, was the fact that Heaney's work was congenial to the United States poetry establishment – particularly to its queen, Helen Vendler – and that he worked, successfully, to make it more so.

Given that poetic modernism in English was pioneered by Americans, it is not surprising that, by comparison with Britain where there is little, and Ireland where there is none, poetic theory plays a big role there. In this respect, and with various groups of poets practising different isms, the American poetry scene is more like central Europe than the British Isles. To a degree that must have surprised Heaney, this world of theory, especially on the East Coast, accommodated his kind of poetry. If it wanted puritanism, the cool chastity, emotional restraint and guilty introspection of his work supplied it. MacLeish's 'A poem should not mean/But be', which had eased the way for him in London, had even more force in MacLeish's home country. Since the fifties the most celebrated American poets had been writing a downbeat, cerebral, hermetic (though often loquacious) poetry that literally meant little or nothing to the great majority of literate Americans, so that meaning little or nothing had become, effectively, a defining attribute of contemporary poetry, and the doctrine that this was how poetry should be, a justification of the reality. As for silence, in that same 'Ars Poetica' MacLeish said:

A poem should be palpable and mute
As a globed fruit

Dumb
As old medallions to the thumb,

Silent as the sleeve-worn stone
Of casement ledges where the moss has grown –

Pulsing through the American academic-poetic world, since Pound and Williams, Ransom and Jarrell, had successively asserted and developed it, was a poetic theory that made particulars, for their own sake, the core of poetic creation: poetry was about 'concrete particulars', the purpose of literature was 'the knowledge of particulars'. The composer John Cage had got himself into the dictionaries of quotations, under the heading 'Poetry', by writing, in a book called *Silence*: 'I have nothing to say and I'm saying it and that is poetry.' More to the point: 'Vendler doesn't like poems that *say* something', wrote Bruce Bawer in 1989, in a long critique of *The Music of What Happens* in the *Hudson Review*. Even if he then added '– or, more accurately, she's very strict about the ways in which she thinks it is proper for a poem to say something', he had conveyed, with the first statement, the impression she gives.

Field Work, Heaney's next collection after *North*, was recognised by the critics as 'Heaney Lowellising', and it contained an elegy to Robert Lowell. In the year it appeared, 1979, Heaney taught for a term in Harvard, and the following year his selected poems and selected prose were published. In 1981 Helen Vendler came out strongly for both in the *New Yorker*, one of the few general magazines in the USA that reviews poetry. Plath, Berryman and Lowell had created a vogue for painful, personal 'confession' in verse, and Heaney's keenly felt soul-searching had fitted well with this. Now, in 1985, in *Station Island* he supplied a full, penitential session of it, perhaps not so keenly felt. Again in the *New Yorker* Vendler approved. Then, after *The Haw Lantern*, she presented her ultimate accolade by using a Heaney phrase as the title of her new book (her previous book title was from Wallace Stevens).

Bruce Bawer calls Vendler 'the colossus of contemporary American poetry criticism ... [she] looms hugely over the ever-shrinking landscape'. But the full significance of her wholehearted acclaim for Heaney is not apparent from her *New Yorker* articles. Probably because these were for the general public, they confine themselves to explaining background, summarising, commenting lightly and praising highly, without discoursing on poetry as such or her own ideas about it. There are a few significant indications in some expectable phrases: 'evil, violence and our individual helplessness in history'; 'a barer, "adult" aesthetic: "things founded clean on their own shapes"'; 'ritual sacrifices, of which the Ulster murders on both sides are simply recurrences, are tribal customs defeating all individual reason or endeavor'; 'free from a superficial piety'; 'another source of fracture and culpability'; 'thorns of conscience and apprehension and moral revulsion'; 'to devote himself rather to the ardors than the pleasures of verse'; 'extraordinary descriptive powers – dangerous ones'; 'Heaney's lines [are] not corrupted by pure linguistic revel'. There are hints there, but we are not given a rounded picture of the kind of poetry Vendler likes, the kind she values most highly and why, and therefore the kind of contemporary poetic elite she was receiving Heaney into. Only when we know that, as she reveals it in her fully professional writing, can we understand what being a top poet in the USA means, and how well Heaney, especially in his later books, qualifies as one. But Vendler's poetic has an additional interest. During the eighties, as poet, professor and critic Heaney adopted Vendler's view of poetry and developed

it, and this has been influencing both his poetry and his apologia
for it.

In *The Music of What Happens* Vendler writes about John Ashbery.
Because he is her favourite living American poet, her opening
description of his work is interesting.

> It seems time to write about John Ashbery's subject matter. It
> is Ashbery's style that has obsessed reviewers, as they alternately
> wrestle with its elusive impermeability and praise its power of
> linguistic synthesis. There have been able descriptions of its fluid
> syntax, its insinuating momentum, its generality of reference, its
> incorporation of vocabulary from all the arts and all the sciences.
> But it is popularly believed, *with some reason,* that the style itself
> is impenetrable, that it is impossible to say what an Ashbery poem
> is 'about'. An alternative view says that every Ashbery poem is
> about poetry – literally self-reflective, like his 'Self-portrait in a
> Convex Mirror'. *Though this may in part be true,* it sounds thin
> in the telling, and it is of some help to remember that in the code
> language of criticism when a poem is said to be about poetry the
> word 'poetry' is often used to mean many things: how people
> construct an intelligibility out of the randomness they experience;
> how people choose what they love; how people integrate loss
> and gain. [Italics mine.]

Poetry that has doubtfully a subject is like abstract painting: words
added to it tend to thrash about and flounder. Here, and in the
following seventeen pages of Vendler on Ashbery, I am back in
the sixties, reading one of those French art critics who could
surround the work of a voguish abstract painter with a volume
of very similar prose.

However, if that passage merely suggests Vendler's idea of good
poetry, another essay in the same book deals directly with the
matter. She is discussing the views of three American writers
who want poetry to have 'a strongly mimetic and a strongly
communicative value'. In addition one of them, Robert von

Hallberg, wants 'a directly civic value', while the others want 'an ethical value'. 'But I myself', she writes, 'think aesthetic value, properly understood, quite enough to claim for a poem.' (Clearly, here and in what follows she is equating poetry and 'a poem' – from Homer, Lucretius and Juvenal to Dante, Shakespeare, Goethe, Dryden and Yeats – with lyric poetry.) She writes:

> What [a poem] represents, ultimately, is its author's sensibility and temperament rather than the 'outside world' – but of course that sensibility and temperament have been shaped by the historical possibilities of the author's era. Thus, in representing a sensibility, the poem does represent a particular historical moment. The poem ingests, it is true, the outside world (which it uses for its images, its symbols, and its language), but it does so, as Marvell said, in order to color everything with the mind's color, reducing to zero ('annihilating' said Marvell) the entire creation into its own mentality.
>
> > The mind, that ocean where each kind
> > Doth straight its own resemblance find;
> > Yet it creates, transcending these,
> > Far other worlds and other seas,
> > Annihilating all that's made
> > To a green thought in a green shade.

As is evident from the text, Marvell did not say that a poem does that, but that the mind does it; in a garden, to be precise. It is noteworthy that Vendler here equates 'a poem' with a mind. She goes on to explain that, of course, 'all kinds of ethical and civic topics turn up in poetry, as do trees and flowers and ladies' eyes; but they are all material for the transformation into green'. Granted that what she means to say is that a poem is similar to, and represents, a mind at work on its environment, this might seem to imply that a poem is like any thoughtful discourse. But elsewhere she makes clear that she does not favour a poetry of ideas – that would mean 'saying something' – and Bawer writes of her: 'Time and again in Vendler's essays, language-as-action wins the day.' In sum, her ideal poem might be described as 'conclusionless thinking in active language', or a vigorously verbal musing. As for communicative value:

> Because language is the medium of poetry, and language cannot, when used according to any of the possible rules of its coding, not communicate, there is, it seems to me, no need to worry about poetry's 'communicating' itself. All poems grow easier with time, even *The Waste Land*. And there is no need to worry about 'universality' or speaking for everyone.

In her previous book *Part of Nature, Part of Us,* published in 1980 – the year before her first article about Heaney – Vendler tells us more about the notion of poetry that is adumbrated in the above. In an essay on Robert Lowell, she describes what poetry is when it is 'grown-up' and therefore, presumably, most truly poetry. Lowell, she writes, began with the youthful belief that poetry needs religious vision, the poet as questing pilgrim, resonant Hebraic denunciations and the well-made poem. But in his late poetry, which is 'seemingly mused rather than written, ruminating not spontaneous', he came to a better understanding and practice. Vendler lists the characteristics of this 'musing' poetry, beginning with 'profoundly irreligious' and ending with 'exempt from the tyranny of the well-made poem'. Around the middle are these two: 'addressed not homiletically to an audience, but painfully to the self' and 'private rather than public'. She concludes: 'It is in this sense Chekhovian. In fact, reading the complete Lowell is rather like seeing Dostoevsky grow up to be Chekhov.'

A private musing addressed, painfully, to the self, and expressed in active language: that seems to be the core notion of really good poetry that runs through Vendler's discourse. And it seems to me that we have here another instance of justification after the event. Certain persons by getting their verses published rank as poets; and some of these, judged very good or the best by the academic-poetic complex, are producing quantities of verse that mean little or nothing to ordinary literate people: they are obviously not speaking to them, nor trying to. *Ergo,* poetry at its best is not public speech, but private musing addressed to the self. As a delivered product, it is *published* private musing. Since the verse in question was, presumably, written for publication, this is a fiction; but it is a useful fiction because it explains everything. No one expects somebody's musing to himself to mean much to others; it has its private syntax, its own unique and personal way of connecting meanings and words. Logically, moreover, if a number of poets are at it, it needs Vendlers, hundreds of them, to interpret it and 'teach' it. In short, the poet *par excellence* becomes a sort of ruminating, groaning shaman, delivering oracles that his academic acolytes interpret to the students within the temple and the heedless multitude beyond the gates.

Heaney qualified in Vendler's terms, and he worked to qualify better. Obviously he had the 'active language' and the 'pain'. For the rest, it was a matter of how you conceptualised and described poetry which, though published to wide audiences, said nothing about general matters, and therefore cancelled itself as genuine public speech. For Vendler it was musing directed to the self and, as such, poetry at its best. Quite early in his career, Heaney had hinted in his poem 'Thatcher' that poetry was a work of rumination and measuring. Neil Corcoran, in his book *Seamus Heaney,* finds in some poems in *Wintering Out* and *North* that 'the poet's "I" is detached from ordinary social circumstance, withdrawn to solipsistic meditation, ruminatively entranced . . .' The fact is that much of Heaney's poetry in the seventies could be regarded as private musing or meditation – with any intrusive general views censored out – rather than as public speech that, in the County Derry manner, 'said nothing'. But Heaney, with long Irish and English traditions of poetry as public speech behind him, had hesitated to commit himself to the 'private meditation' concept.

Now, in response to Vendler's high valuation of such poetry, he did so, and the result can be noticed in the increased self-absorption and indifference to readers in *Station Island* and *The Haw Lantern*. Significantly, the first blurb of a Heaney collection to describe his work as 'meditative' is that of *Station Island*. Since then he has been consciously not speaking to us, even to 'say nothing'.

In Britain and the USA, the poetry that prepared the way for Seamus Heaney was the mainstream poetry of consumer capitalism. It is as a practitioner of this forty-year-old tradition that he is judged pre-eminent transatlantically. Before that, between the world wars, modernism had been predominant. Yeats, Eliot, Pound, Auden, MacNeice and others were making clear statements in poetry both about particulars and about the human condition, the state of the world, and other matters of general interest. Other poets, such as Marianne Moore and Padraic Colum, confined themselves to particular subjects. In these respects, poetry was in a normal condition. What the leading poets said, explicitly or in eloquent images, about the world and man under liberal democracy and capitalism was by and large negative, and tending to discourage attachment to the ideological, political and economic status quo. Then the Second World War and the poetically confused forties came and went. When poetry regrouped in the fifties, under the aegis of consumer capitalism, its mainstream no longer reached outwards towards the world and common human experience but dealt predominantly with the fractured and put-upon self, particulars in the self's environment, and poetry. Tight-lipped, suffering poets remembered childhood tenderly, and watched wives moving in rooms and performing household tasks. Philip Larkin lacked even those consolations.

The consumerist form of liberal capitalism, which emerged in the fifties and reached maturity in the sixties, was marked by an extension of the public power over the lives of people. The Power, as Tom Wolfe calls it in *Bonfire of the Vanities,* was now increasingly a corporate power, comprising all the major institutions of society. Its extension of control was aided by the new technology of computers, television, and faster communications generally, and by larger and better-equipped police forces. The state bureaucracies grew in size and regulated more. 'The media' became a phrase in the language. Led by television, and feeding off each other, the media were a sort of bureaucracy of public information and entertainment, pervading all of life, reconstructing it into an image world, and promoting uniformity of thought, speech, dress and behaviour generally. The private patrons who had funded modernist poetry, and provided it with its magazines, were now replaced – for all but the exceptional poet who had private means – by foundations, universities, radio and television.

Within this context of corporate power, on both sides of the Atlantic the academic-poetic complex took shape, and in taking shape selected and defined two broadly similar poetic mainstreams. In their diction, the length and nature of their poems, their allusions and so on, the selected poets responded, as poets do, to the needs of their patrons, now principally the academy and the media (with the former predominant in the USA). True, when the poets looked at the new mass affluence and its trappings, they took a sour view of it and reflected this occasionally in their verse. But they did not thunder, and their grumblings registered decorously as poetic disdain for philistine values. Occasionally in the USA, when some powerful faction sanctioned it, a poem would reflect, in the meditative manner, contemporary events or concerns touched by the poet's feelings. But clear light thrown on the human condition, or a voice raised memorably to exhort, decry, console or celebrate in the general interest, was a rare event in poetry. In short, just as mainstream philosophy in English had withdrawn from illuminating the human condition, so now virtually did mainstream poetry. Maverick philosophers and poets apart – and these were effectively marginalised – illumination was left to the journalists and their experts, the politicians and pop psychologists, and the priests whom dwindling congregations heard. Had Plato believed that the poets of his republic could be persuaded to such reticence, he would have recommended, not that they be banished, but kept – and paraded on state occasions as ornaments of the regime.

Just as the kind of poetry that Heaney practises is a product of the consumerist era and must be seen in its context, so too must be seen the critical theory that supports this poetry and judges Heaney's work the best contemporary example. As consumerism extended and corporatised the public power, it carried out a massive assault on Victorian ethics. Victorian poetry may have ended in the early years of the century, but the puritanical morality, legitimised by religion, that we call Victorian had endured for several decades longer. Now this morality was driven, by propaganda, the devaluation of savings, and legal enactments facilitating libertinism, from its bastions in personal money management, drinking habits and dress, and from its chief stronghold in the family and sexual relations. And because it had used religion as its justification, and made purity of the soul and eternal salvation its overriding purposes, now religion too – for the first time in English-speaking countries – was declared an illegitimate intruder in the public domain, and human reality was redefined as effectively physical and non-transcendent.

The upshot was that puritan morality, which had shaped American culture from the start and British middle-class culture for a century, became a homeless outlaw, searching with its religious zeal intact for new purposes and habitations. As the sixties passed into the seventies and eighties, it found its most popular new purpose in the pure, disease-free body, and its most popular habitations in the movements for healthy food, real ale, organic farming, unchlorinated water, clean air, smokeless lungs and slim figures – with slimming, jogging, aerobics, squash and marathons supplying the requisite pain. Its antipathy to sex found ideological lodgements in radical feminism and homosexuality. PC, Political Correctness, guaranteed purity of mind and language to intellectuals. Inevitably, in view of this drift of things, a fellowship of literary critics and related poets – principally in the USA, but with notable adherents in the British Isles – gave the displaced puritan morality a literary cause in the cult and pursuit of the puritan poem.

More precisely, what this influential clerisy hankered after was the puritan poem, new style. The puritan poem of earlier times was distinguished by pure and lofty sentiments, and by aspirations beyond this corrupt world to God or some spiritual reality. New style, it aspires to no transcendence, and its language is conceived of and treated as materially as language allows. As Gerald Dawe, poet and critic and a Belfast Protestant, put it to me some years ago, 'Poetry is now about words and how they look and how they sound.' In addition, the current critical ideal of the puritan poem is fed by two goals carried over from modernism: the 'autonomous, self-referential poem', and 'pure poetry' in the sense of Mallarmé and George Moore: poetry untainted by human intellect and the concerns of man. The ideal might be represented by two overlapping images. On the one hand, it is a poem that stands there like a Puritan – correct, self-contained, unsensual, pained by the world and himself, and disdainful of charm and communication because to be right is enough. But it is also a poem like Wallace Stevens's bird in his 'Of Mere Being', if we read his 'human' correctly as 'shared by mankind':

> A gold-feathered bird
> Sings in the palm, without human meaning,
> Without human feeling, a foreign song.

In sum, the good poem, aesthetically and morally speaking, embodies in shifting proportions the socially indifferent moral rightness of the puritan character and a crystalline, effectively silent beauty. In practice, either with a touch of the other will do.

After two decades of consumerist poetry, as the waters were thinning, Seamus Heaney appeared from a new, untapped place of puritan culture, where bombs were exploding. Garbed in Victorian poet's dress, and with peasant vigour and instinct, he made poems that were remarkable from the start – and grew more so as he learned from New England – for their embodiments of those two prized elements. Even 'foreign', as of the Stevens bird song, applied literally to his principal themes, to much of his diction, and to the communal life his poetry reflected, as these were perceived and read in London and the US universities. It is not, of course, that Heaney has achieved the ideal – no human poet could – but he has approached it near enough to thrill those who seek it – as an embodiment, outside this corrupt world, of a goodness not available within it.

When the goodness of poetry, conceived in these ideal terms, has become a quasi-religious value for the dominant academic-poetic sect, no other 'good' of poetry can matter to them, let alone take precedence. If the pursuit of poetic goodness, as they conceive it, and the exalting of it when it appears in Heaney or another encourage poetry to move even further away from life and people – extending the parched American landscape to Britain and Ireland – then they may regret this, but they will do nothing to prevent it, and they would consider any attempt to prevent it philistine. The welfare of poetry, in the terms defined, must remain the sole concern of those who have charge of poetry.

This, naturally, raises questions that will not go away. What good to people is this goodness of poetry? Has poetry, has the puritan lyric, any intelligible social function, and if so what? How can poets who 'say nothing', and leave the world in darkness, do good socially? In a civilisation that prides itself on its social concern and its democratic culture, these are pointed questions. They preoccupy Seamus Heaney, not least because he would like to believe that his work does good to people, and in particular to those Six-County Irish whom he keeps looking back at over his shoulder and feeling guilty about. He said to Thomas Foster:

> If you come from a situation where truth and justice are not
> generally at work, and you are a product of that contorted place . . .
> you have some imperative that comes with your vocation to deal
> with that. That's a fundamental demand that writers from the
> North of Ireland face, it's a demand from within themselves, to
> discover a path into proper thinking, action, and composure.

'Action' is the painful word there.

Heaney knows that his belief that public speech is dangerous
and potentially harmful has prevented him from doing good to
his people, or to people generally, in the ways that such good
can be done by publicly-speaking poetry. He knows that by keeping to safe themes and by 'saying nothing' he has in the world's
terms done good, positively, only to himself. He suffered, as every
Northern Ireland Catholic did, during the long agony of the Long
Kesh hunger strike – and suffered doubly because he wrote no
poem about it. Two of the dead hunger strikers, Francis Hughes
and Tom McElwee, and the priest Oliver Crilly, who did most
to try to get a settlement for the prisoners, came as it happened
from his home place, Bellaghy. Like any Six-County Catholic,
he has among his friends, acquaintances or relatives men and
women who are in the IRA, others who have spent years in jail
as political prisoners, or suffered otherwise in the struggles of the
past twenty years. He is as conscious as anyone of how the war
in Northern Ireland projected him to an attention and fame that
no equally good poet from Galway, Yorkshire or Tennessee could
possibly have enjoyed; that there is a war because there is an IRA;
and that what Bernadette McAliskey said years ago of John Hume
and his moderate nationalist party, the SDLP – that they had 'rid-
den to power on the backs of the IRA' – might with much truth
be said of himself. Aware of all this, and that he cannot, because
he will not, depart from his chosen path of poetry, Heaney asked
himself during the eighties: Is there not, nevertheless, some way

in which poetry that says nothing and seems socially indifferent can do social good?

He has worked on finding an answer to this, and come up with a mystical one which is not easy to pin down. At its core is the Vendler idea of the poet as ruminating, world-reflecting shaman, but developed and given a socially beneficial dimension. There is some hint of it in the passage I quoted on page 143 from Heaney's Pete Laver Memorial Lecture of 1984, in which he says that 'a poetry of hermetic wit, of riddles and slips and self-mocking ironies . . . may be exercising in its inaudible way a fierce disdain of the amplified message, or a distressed sympathy with it'. This seems to mean that a poetry that says nothing about contemporary social events may be doing something relevant to them silently, that is, imperceptibly. Five years later, in his inaugural lecture as Professor of Poetry at Oxford University, Heaney dealt more fully with the matter. The lecture is entitled 'The Redress of Poetry', and much of it discusses how poetry does social good by redressing ('setting right, making up for') what is wrong in the world. Heaney does not here answer the question about poetry's social usefulness comprehensively. Because he is thinking about poetry, such as his own, that avoids speaking about the world, he does not touch on what many would regard as poetry's principal social service, namely, the illumination of life so that people may see it better; its struggle, in the common interest, against darkness and confusion of perception. He deals exclusively with, and argues for, the usefulness of poetry in what might be called the mechanical sense, as a force in the world of active politics.

A few preliminaries set the tone. Plato's 'world of ideal forms provides a court of appeal in which the poetic imagination can seek redress against the affronts of the prevailing conditions'. Sir Philip Sidney argues that 'if nature's world is brazen, then poetry's world is golden in despite of it'. We get closer to the point when Heaney, having discussed Wallace Stevens's views, concludes that Stevens purveys the 'received wisdom' that poetry, while 'not intervening in the actual', constitutes a 'benevolent symbolic event, for poet and audience alike'. That, says Heaney, is true in an artistic sense, but 'not politically speaking, within the shiftings of the world of power'. He continues:

> Politically speaking, the redress of poetry does not reside in its placing of a symbolic truth in the balance against a historical situation. That is all very well as an aesthetic project, but it will not satisfy either party in the actual vehemence of a conflict. For them the redress of poetry would consist rather in poetry's renunciation of complexity and self-division and its embrace of one or other side of the question, without ambivalence. Its redress would be in the simple act of adding leverage to one or other arm of the scale.

Here the question about poetry's usefulness to people narrows to one about the redress it can offer in a political conflict; and it must be said that Heaney's description of the kind of 'redress' that 'either side' would expect from poetry is somewhat simplified and caricatured. Citing some concrete examples, he instances that 'if you are an Irish poet in the wake of the 1916 executions, the pressure will be to revile the tyranny of the executing power'. In such cases, he suggests, the poet should disappoint the expectations of his own side: Yeats, for example, was right 'to see the English government as a body who might keep faith'. (Oddly for the reader, Heaney does not mention the celebration of the Rising and its leaders in the poem he is citing here, 'Easter 1916' and in other Yeats poems.)

He continues: 'Although such actions frustrate the common expectation of solidarity, they do have political force, all the more so because they are directed against the grain of the usual. Their exacerbation is the very guarantee of their effectiveness.' The argument here is difficult. Their 'effectiveness' as what? As redress? Is 'going against the grain of the usual', that is, disappointing one's own people, how poetry effects redress? The question is pertinent, because Heaney goes on to say that such actions are 'particular instances of a general law' enunciated by Simone Weil in her book *Gravity and Grace*; and this law, which he quotes, speaks of a rather different kind of redress. Simone Weil writes:

> If we know in what way society is unbalanced, we must *do what we can to add weight to the lighter scale*. Although that weight may consist of evil, in handling it with this intention, perhaps we do not become defiled. We must have formed a conception of equilibrium and be ever ready to change sides like justice, 'that fugitive from the camp of conquerors'. [Italics mine.]

Heaney, remarking that this is obviously inspired by 'Christ's paradoxical identification with the plight of the wretched', quotes Weil again and comments that 'her whole book is dominated by the idea of counterweighting, of balancing out the forces, of redress – tilting the scales of reality towards some transcendent equilibrium'. He continues:

> And in the activity of poetry a similar impulse persists, to place a counter-reality in the scales, a reality which is only imagined but which nevertheless has weight because it is imagined within the gravitational pull of the actual. This redress of poetry comes from its being a revelation of potential that is denied or constantly threatened by circumstances.

Compared with the clarity of Weil, this is murky. 'Weight to the lighter scale' has disappeared. Heaney seems, while formally assenting to Weil, to be veering back towards Stevens's view – previously rejected as insufficient – that poetry's social service lies in its being a non-intervening but socially benevolent symbolic event. This impression is strengthened by another passage somewhat further on:

> In the fully realised poet, what Simone Weil perceived as the necessary principle of counter-weighting or redress will be inscribed in the poet's imaginative signature. To put it another way, the best poetry will not only register the assault of the

actual and the brunt of necessity; it will also embody the spririt's protest against all that.

In both the passages just quoted, there is an echo of what Helen Vendler said above about a poem reflecting events in the historical world as they register in the poet's mind. But whereas she said that this *can* happen, Heaney says it should or must. He repeats this in the last passage of the Oxford lecture, which relates directly to poetry's 'redress'.

> [Poetry] has to withstand as well as to envisage, and in order to do so it must contain within itself the coordinates of the reality which surrounds it and out of which it is engendered. When it does contain these coordinates, it becomes a power to which we can have redress: it functions as the rim of the silence out of which consciousness arrives and into which it must descend. For a moment, we can remember ourselves as fully empowered beings.

Simone Weil was a mystic whose mysticism was intellectually disciplined by Christian doctrine. In the passages that Heaney quotes she clearly recommends, as a rule of social virtue, that we should resist the weight of worldly power pressing on us to conform to it, and instead throw our weight, in a literary sense or otherwise, onto the weaker side of the scales of power, even if this means involving ourselves in evil. Heaney in his Oxford lecture speaks as a freelance mystic, outside the framework of an ordered doctrine of reality, and one has to guess at the meaning of what he is saying. While he signals assent to Weil, his ensuing exposition of the redress effected by poetry does not paraphrase her injunction, but veers back towards the non-interventionist and symbolic social relationship that has always been at the core of his own poetic. (This would not have surprised T.S. Eliot who said that the poet, as critic, always tries 'to defend the kind of poetry he is writing'.)

Heaney seems to me to envisage the poet's beneficent social

action on the analogy of the monk in an enclosed religious order, who, Catholics believe, helps to atone for the world's evil – to assist Christ in the world's redemption – by his detachment from the world, his chastity, and above all his life of meditation and prayer. Heaney's repeated injunction that the poet must reflect the affairs of the contemporary world in his poetry – but in his own way and without intervening – corresponds to the monk's promise, much prized by the faithful when they receive it, that he will 'remember' or 'include' their worldly concerns and 'intentions' in his prayer.

Given belief in God, in the efficacy of prayer, and in the sincerity of the monk's dedication, it is easy and indeed logical to believe that through the processes of the spiritual economy the monk's prayer effects good in the world, atones for evil, stays the punishing hand of God. It is not so easy to believe that, with no part in the transaction for God or a spiritual economy managed by Him, a man of no proven virtue, perhaps even a bad man, effects social redress – corrects the world's imbalances – by meditating and delivering verses that 'contain the coordinates of the surrounding reality'. But within the community of professor-poet-critics who have fashioned a cult of veneration and exegesis around the puritan poem, and around the poet who generates and delivers it, such belief is probably possible; and it is to these, who share that fellowship with him, that Heaney was speaking in Oxford. By supplying them with what looked like an exposition of how poems that 'say nothing', and are poor in world and meaning, nevertheless do good in the world, he reassured them about what some of them must realise is a serious public relations flaw, even rational deficiency, in their poetic enterprise. For that, doubtless he earned their gratitude, and a renewal of their conviction, on both sides of the Atlantic, that he is the best poet laureate they could have.

Having now pondered my way through the phenomenon of

Seamus Heaney's fame and status, I am left admiring the skill and grace with which he has pursued his chosen profession, and used his luck, in a time and under conditions which he did not choose. Starting out, he did not know that the poetry business at the top in consumer capitalism is a verbal, emotional and intellectual circus; but having found out, he signed on and mastered all the acts – poetic, critical, professorial, oracular and mystical.

POSTSCRIPT

For a time after I had finished this essay I was worried by Catullus. I had argued that poetry, to be great, must include treatment of general matters either by direct or figurative statement or by the use of particulars to represent universals. Yet Catullus's reputation rests on poems that deal with particulars that remain particulars, and I consider him a great poet. The problem was resolved for me when I realised that poetry about ungeneralised particulars can, if it is well crafted, be made great by *passion:* that passion is the other ingredient of great poetry. That Heaney's poetry lacks passion goes without saying, though it has frequently been remarked on. Not unrelated to this is something else I missed and that was subsequently pointed out to me. Heaney is not, as I suggest at the beginning of section II, a 'poet doubling as an academic' – as are so many contemporary poets, especially in America – but a professional academic who is also a poet. Teaching literature in a university was his first occupation, and, in college or university, with a short intermission, he has continued in it all his life. Finally, with regard to what I say about his poetry being silent, readers may be interested in Susan Sontag's 'The Aesthetics of Silence' in *A Susan Sontag Reader* (Penguin, 1983), where she discusses silence as an aim and feature of much modern art.

9
LEFT,
RIGHT IN THE
NEW EUROPE

I N IRELAND PERIODICALLY, people call for a realignment of Irish politics 'on a left/right basis'. It would make things so much clearer, they say. I very much doubt it.

Already before the collapse of the Marxist-Leninist regimes in Europe, some confusion and nonsense existed in the political terminology that we inherited from the nineteenth century: not only left/right/centre, but also liberal, conservative, socialist, etcetera. Now the collapse of those regimes has brought these words and their meanings into utter chaos, so that anyone writing about contemporary politics must henceforth make a choice. He can ignore the chaos and muddle on, guided in his use of political labels by cliché and emotion, without regard for commonsense or coherent meaning; or he can try to restore sense and consistency to the language he uses. What follows is a descent into the chaos and an attempt to find a way out.

Muddle existed already prior to and apart from the East European events. It was and is widely assumed that a party called Conservative must be conservative in mind and practice. This is assumed, regardless of the evidence. That is why many have screwed their minds into believing that Mrs Thatcher's whirlwind, destructive assault on the postwar British consensus is

From the *Irish Review* (Winter 1990)

somehow 'conservative' in nature – an expression of 'conservative' political philosophy. Or take the term 'left'.

On 17 July 1990, the *Irish Times* published a debate on the future of socialism between Eoghan Harris and Justin Keating, under the heading 'Where Should the Left Turn Now?'. 'The left' there meant socialists and people of the socialist tradition. But an article in the current issue of *Krino,* the Galway literary magazine, quotes the American feminist Andrea Dworkin as saying, 'Pornography is the graveyard where the left has gone to die.' Here 'the left' means not socialists at all, but left liberals – usually called 'liberals' in the USA. They are being criticised for failing to take a stand against pornography.

In Western Europe in the decades following the Second World War, 'the left' included parties that called themselves socialist or social democratic and upheld the heritage of liberal freedoms, as well as the communist parties and regimes of Eastern Europe which trampled on these. The Swedish Socialists, who managed liberal capitalist Sweden for decades (and were really left liberals), belonged to 'the left'. So did the Soviet Communist regime which confiscated all property, ran a one-party state and a command economy, sent millions to concentration camps and killed millions of its citizens, employed a pervasive thought police, created a new privileged class, persecuted Christians and Jews, and continued the Russian domination of many subject peoples. Consequently, 'the left', as a collective term, had no positive political meaning. In effect, it meant merely parties and regimes opposed to the right or using socialist or left-liberal language. The latter was all they had to do – speak a dialect of 'left language' – to show they were the former: anti-right, and thus left. By doing that, regardless of what else they did they were of 'the left'. So the political left was not what you might imagine, but simply people using anti-right forms of language.

Last March, when I was in East Germany during the election campaign, I was confronted with some of the newer confusion.

The Christian Democrats were being described in the media, East and West, as 'conservatives'. In fact they were campaigning to change the state and its institutions from top to bottom, and ultimately to abolish it. Promising 'freedom and prosperity', they wanted East Germany to adopt the West German way of life, complete with rampant consumerism, social market economy, and a high degree of public sexual licence. The communists, on the other hand, renamed the Party of Democratic Socialism (PDS), were characterised by patriotism towards the German Democratic Republic (GDR), and a protective intent towards the existing institutions, poorer people, and sexual morality. (The GDR maintained public decency in sexual matters: no sex shops, pornography, striptease or general flaunting of sex, such as exist in West Germany.) In short, the PDS based its campaign appeal on GDR patriotism, on protective and puritanical ideals, and fear of change. It was obvious to me that it was the conservative party, and that the Christian Democrats were liberals. If we take account of the Social Democrats (SPD) who tried to their cost to occupy both positions simultaneously, then the SPD was liberal–conservative; or left-liberal in relation to the centre-liberal CDU. (The Liberal Party was right-liberal.)

In the Soviet Union now, 'leftists' are communists, or others, who strongly favour private property and the free market economy. Those who want to uphold the Marxist-Leninist institutions are 'the right', or 'conservatives'. For people who think 'conservatism' is an ideology in contemporary politics, and that Thatcherism adheres to it, this would seem to put these Marxist-Leninists in the same camp as Thatcherites and Christian Democrats. But to complicate matters further, in an article in the *Irish Times* on 23 July 1990, Conor O'Clery referred to the extreme wing of Pamyat, the Russian nationalist organisation, as 'far-right fanatics'. On the face of that, Pamyat extremists would be in the same part of the political spectrum as the Marxist-Leninists, Thatcherites and Christian Democrats only more so – 'further right'. Which is truly a muddle.

Let us try to clear the ground.

Liberal capitalism, to give it its full title, is the politico-economic system which exists in the Western world, and which has triumphed successively over conservatism, fascism and socialism/ communism. When it is called 'capitalism' for short, the adjectives 'liberal, individualistic, pluralist, consumerist' are tacitly understood. Strong bureaucratic centralism (with or without a federal structure), a degree of state enterprise, and liberal democracy are generally connoted. Also understood, in the Western world, is a system that pays workers decent wages and, to a greater or lesser degree, subsidises the poor; in other words, welfare capitalism, to some degree.

Liberals have always been, and are, persons who support liberal capitalism, but with a variety of nuances and roles. Like any other developed ideological position, liberalism has a right, centre and left, though this fact is often obscured, in English, by the use of the term 'liberals' to designate left liberals only. Roughly, right liberals, such as US Republicans, British Conservatives or Continental Liberal parties, support capitalist economics whole-heartedly and want the minimum feasible of social welfare expenditure. Left liberals, such as Labour and Social Democratic parties, and successful Socialist parties in capitalist countries, are critically supportive of capitalist economics and stress maximal social welfare. Left liberals also regard thorough secularisation – the complete removal of religious values from law and politics – as a good thing, whereas right and centre liberals have reservations on this. (On the Continent, right liberals, in economic matters, are at one with left liberals on this point.) Again, right liberals are less inhibited than left or centre liberals about the resolute use of state power to put down subversion or to promote the state's interests internationally. Left liberals often criticise this. Finally, while right liberals may condone authoritarian or military regimes, left liberals oppose these unless they use Marxist rhetoric.

The open conflict between right and left liberals buttresses the capitalist system by seeming to display in action its much-trumpeted virtue of freedom of expression, or tolerance of dissent. Particularly useful in this respect is the fact that left liberals predominate in the capitalist media, and carry on a continuous carping criticism there. The resulting din of 'critical opinion' serves to hide the fact that liberals are intolerant of illiberal views and criticism.

Conservative, as a political term, originally described people who stood for the landed interest, traditional rural life, clerical, military and aristocratic values; had a worldview to support this stance; and resisted the changes sponsored by liberals ('modernisation', the Industrial Revolution). The word has continued to be applied senselessly to people who lack those characteristics, practise liberal politics and are not resisters of change (often the reverse). Usually this is because there is a convention of applying the term, regardless of the facts, to those who oppose Labour parties, socialists or left liberals, or who are inspired by a religious philosophy. But all established political groups are conservative in some respects, and any of them can, in certain circumstances, be generally conservative for a long period. Sense and clarity require that, party names apart, 'conservative' be used only in its literal meaning of 'wishing to conserve the existing order substantially, and resisting proposed or occurring radical change'.

Socialism, whether in the tradition running through Thompson, Owen and Proudhon to Connolly and Russell, or in its Marx–Engels formulation, has always meant a political and economic system different from liberal capitalism however modified, and based on control by workers of their labour and of the added value arising from it. It has also meant, in both versions, the attainment, after a brief period of radical reorganisation, of a condition of greater personal freedom for everyone than that afforded by liberal capitalism. *Socialists* means people who have this (anti-liberal) aim and programme.

The Right/Left Myth. In the wake of the Enlightenment and the French Revolution, the French liberal bourgeoisie created this myth, which was adopted throughout the Continent. The anti-liberal conservatives accepted it, but with reversed values. It was a Manichean view of the world that saw it divided between a principle of Good and Light, and a principle of Evil and Darkness, which were at war. Viewed from the Left perspective the Right, the enemy of man, was everything old, religious, dark, backward, tyrannous, and the Left, the good of man, everything new, non-religious, enlightened, progressive and free. The Right was originally embodied by the Catholic Church (in Eastern Europe also the Orthodox Church), absolute monarchy, aristocracy and the military castes attached to these. The Left, from the start and subsequently, was incarnate in all reasonable, progressive, agnostic and atheistic people. The Right was *noir, schwarz,* black; the Left *rouge, rot,* red. Opposition to the Right and victory over it were the meaning and purpose of history. This myth was firmly established long before socialism became a significant political force.

The defeat of socialism. As time passed, absolute monarchy and aristocracy exited from the scene; liberalism absorbed conservatism and divided into right and left wings; socialism challenged capitalism; the left liberals continued to articulate the Left idea, but now with a sprinkling of socialist language; and the Right they opposed was embodied by the Catholic Church and right liberals, who included nationalist imperialists.

Capitalism weakened socialism by making pre-emptive adjustments in its own practice. It destroyed it by persuading the majority of West European socialists that Left loyalty in the cosmic struggle of the Left against the Right must be their primary value, that the issue of socialism versus capitalism was, accordingly, of secondary importance, and that speaking Left language (left-liberal-social-democratic or plain socialist) was the overriding indicator of Left adherence. The agents of capitalism in this persuasive process were the semi–socialist–talking left liberals.[1] Their success, as recruiters for the solidarity of the Left, led to the destruction of socialism in two stages.

First, the great majority of West European socialists became emotionally committed to the Left struggle primarily, and lost awareness of what they were really about. Without fully realising it, and believing they were still 'true to the faith' – they were, to the Left faith, and still hated black and wore red – they became 'left-wing' adherents and managers of capitalism, and gave up the struggle to replace it. Second, when a Muscovite tyranny speaking extreme socialist language established itself in the USSR, and similar tyrannies later appeared in east-central Europe as far as Berlin, the great vocal bulk of the West European Left (left liberals and nominal socialists) spoke of these regimes, and treated them, at least with critical respect, at most with admiring enthusiasm. Left loyalty demanded that those in the West who spoke for the Left and socialism should at least recognise these Left-speaking tyrannies as 'really existing socialism', as 'socialist countries', and not reject them as fascistic, oligarchic despotisms that mocked socialism's historic aim and promise. If they had done that, the good name of socialism would have been saved; but it would have meant agreeing with what the Right was saying, if not precisely in the same terms; so it was impossible for Left loyalists. And then, in 1989, the people came out on the streets and shouted that 'really existing socialism' was everything the Right had been saying and worse. And the Marxist-Leninist regimes fell in ignominy.

The net result? On top of the already accomplished dis-appearance of socialism from West European politics, there was

1. An interesting, latterday example of the left-liberal line in action occurs in the title given by the *Irish Times* to the debate on socialism mentioned above. Although in the wake of the events of 1989, the debate between a man who had previously called himself a socialist and another man who still did was really about the future of socialists and socialism, the title chosen, 'Where Should the Left Turn Now?', made the future of 'the left' the issue.

a worldwide smearing of the concept 'socialism', disgrace for those who gave critical respect or more to 'really existing socialism', and the general collapse, barring waffle, of the 200-year-old socialist project.

Remaining uses of 'left' and 'right'. If for no other reason than the fact that in the USSR the orthodoxy that was once indubitably 'left' is now 'the right', there is no future in a pan-European context for a usage of 'left' and 'right' based on the Right/Left myth. In this respect too, the modern age has ended. For all we know, a few years from now Orthodox Christianity will have become again the bonding ideology of the Russian state, and atheism will be branded there as 'backward'.

It seems to me, however, speaking tentatively, that 'right' might still be usefully employed to mean 'fully endorsing an ideological or political position'; and 'left' 'endorsing it with some dissent'. That seems to work, not only with 'right liberal', 'left liberal' – with respect to liberal capitalism – but also with 'right conservative', 'left conservative', and 'right communist', 'left communist'. That last pair do express the existing division of opinion in, say, the Soviet Communist Party, with 'left' indicating, as it actually does now in Moscow, a critical deviation from orthodoxy towards the free market, private property, etcetera.

10
GETTING TO KNOW
DUBLIN 4

D UBLINERS REGARD THEIR CITY as being divided principally
into a northside and a southside, with the river Liffey as
the rough dividing line. The southside, particularly when taken
to include the borough of Dún Laoghaire which extends from
it southwards, is on the whole much more affluent than the northside. Moreover, it contains many important institutions: the Dáil
and Senate, government buildings, the Republic's two biggest
universities, the national television and radio service (RTE), most
of the newspapers and big hotels, and the headquarters of many
important companies and banks. The southside jokes about the
northside: 'Why did the southside woman marry the northside
man? To get her handbag back.' 'What is a northsider in a suit?
A bus conductor.'

Since the early to mid-eighties, the name of a postal district
in the heart of the southside, Dublin 4, has come to signify a
powerful force in Irish politics. This symbolic usage was invented
by the Mayo journalist John Healy, in his column in the *Irish
Times* during the FitzGerald government of 1982–87. The literal
Dublin 4 is characterised by old, leafy suburban roads and contains,
besides a number of embassies, the Royal Dublin Society

Paper read at the Fourteenth Lipman Seminar on Ireland, Ruskin College, Oxford,
April 1992

showgrounds, RTE, University College Dublin, some research
institutes and the Chester Beatty Library. But Dublin 4, in the
political sense, is understood to include a much wider area of
southside life. It is perceived as a powerful social group with a
characteristic mentality and agenda, which is located in South
Dublin, exists largely outside parliament and the government of
the day, but includes varying proportions of both.

So far, Dublin 4 has escaped analysis by political scientists and
has been described only in impressionistic terms. Healy, writing
from a West of Ireland perspective, depicted the FitzGerald-led
Dublin 4 of the mid-eighties as a smug and inward-looking coterie,
unsympathetic and inimical to the values and welfare of the rural
West, and of rural and small-town Ireland generally. Healy died
in January 1991. Towards the end of that year *Jiving at the
Crossroads*, a best-selling book by a young Roscommon journalist,
John Waters, treated Dublin 4 at some length. Once again, the
basic perspective is Western. The author, who grew up in the
small town of Castlerea, County Roscommon, first encounterd
what he was later to recognise as 'Dublin 4' in the guise of RTE
radio voices.

> At some point in the late seventies or early eighties, when we
> in the West of Ireland became conscious for the first time that
> the voices on the radio and the television were not our voices,
> we automatically began to think of them as Dublin
> voices . . . What we really felt was that they were not saying things
> with which we could sympathise, and they certainly did not seem
> to sympathise with us. They lambasted us for our conservatism,
> for our backward notions of politics, for our profligacy with public
> money.

Later, in the mid-eighties, when Waters came to Dublin to work
for a rock magazine, he realised that there were two Dublins:
the 'real' Dublin, on the northside, which was a visual and human
wasteland, and 'official Dublin', on the southside, known by the
name of 'Dublin 4'. It was in the latter, he discovered, that most

of the people he had heard on the radio belonged. On the last page of his book, Waters describes the RTE television election studio as situated 'in the geographical as well as the spiritual heart of Dublin 4'. But before that he has had a stab at giving body to 'this something real but nebulous in the language of modern Irish politics'. Writing of his first encounters with it, he says:

There were as many definitions of 'Dublin 4' as there were perceptions of it. Its most general usage, however, was as a pejorative term to describe what was effectively a new class of people, whose principal characteristic was perceived as a stridently professed aversion to unreconstructed forms of Catholicism and nationalism, but in particular to Fianna Fáil, and most especially to Charles J. Haughey.

By 'nationalism' there, Waters means Irish nationalism. At the time, he and his family were Fine Gael supporters, but they would later switch to Fianna Fáil – by far the largest of the political parties, with support from all social classes but especially the less well-off.

Dublin 4, writes Waters, could also be seen as synonymous with the people who frequented certain pubs and restaurants between the Shelbourne Hotel and Jury's Hotel, 'the equivalent of what in London were known as "the chattering classes": people who, through their jobs in the media, the civil service and the professions, were in a position to influence the direction of society in an intravenous manner . . .' Dublin 4 had 'many of the qualities of a country village' but without the disadvantage of a village hierarchy to put you in your place. As such it was initially attractive to this young man from a small town. He continues:

There were those who held that the term defined a class of people who regarded themselves as the social and intellectual élite of modern Ireland, but who ideally would have liked to have been born somewhere else. Others saw 'Dublin 4' as a new bourgeoisie, a class of people who had transcended their own class and background, who were out to culturally colonise the country . . .

On the one hand, it was 'an attitude of mind'; on the other, 'a generation that had been reared to the promise of an Ireland free from the grip of history and religion', and for whom 'rural Ireland' was 'a darkness on the edge of town'. To an extent the Ireland that Dublin 4 wanted 'had already been brought about in its imagination. All that was required was for the rest of the population to agree to lie down and die.'

While angrily rejecting Dublin 4's view of the Republic outside Dublin as a dark, priest-ridden place peopled by stunted halfwits, Waters concludes his main treatment of the subject on a mellow note:

> But ultimately, if we were honest, 'Dublin 4' was a part of all of us: the part of our brains that wanted Ireland to be different, better. . . . We all needed some escape from reality, but in the creation of a whole section of society that had allowed this tendency to dominate its thinking, there was scope for seriously deluding ourselves.

As a Dubliner who grew up on the northside, lives on the southside, and does not belong to Dublin 4 but knows it well, I recognise Waters's images of it. But its precise nature, in social, political and ideological terms, remains to be defined. I became interested in the matter while working on two articles about Ireland and the Maastricht Treaty and at the same time reading Waters's book. In my analysis of European Community politics in Ireland, I came to the conclusion that there was a class of people in Dublin, but predominantly on the southside, whose present and future interests were bound up with Ireland's being and remaining a member of the European Community, or Union as it was now to become. Using a term that I had come across in the analysis of black African states, I called this class the 'state class'. Moreover, I argued, in view of the Republic's bad experience in the EC hitherto, and our worse prospects in the Union, there was a divorce between the interests of this state

class and those of Ireland generally. During our membership of
the EC, since 1972, our general economic condition had
deteriorated: 40,000 fewer people were employed; we had
acquired a crippling public debt; economic emigration was heavy
during the 1980s until recession abroad stopped it; and by early
1992 our unemployment rate had reached 20 per cent of the
workforce and was still rising. Maastricht, I believed, on top of
this, would be disastrous for us as a society.

While writing these articles, I concluded with some surprise
that the 'state class' I had identified was identical with 'Dublin
4'. The articles were published in the *Irish Times* on 4–5 February
1992, with that identification of Dublin 4 figuring as a passing
remark. As it happened, three other small items relevant to the
Dublin 4 question appeared in the same newspaper in those days
– between 31 January and 11 February. It seems to me that the
four items together, all of them stemming from Dubliners, offer
a basis for clarifying the nature of Dublin 4.

The main political event around this period was the final
resignation, after many battles for survival, of Charles Haughey
as leader of Fianna Fáil and Taoiseach. On 8 February Paul
Gillespie, the *Irish Times* foreign editor, enumerated the features
that had made Fianna Fáil something of a 'populist' party:

> It may be seen in the attempt by Fianna Fáil to combine tradition
> with modernisation; in the belief that it is possible for the periphery
> to control the modernisation process; in its anti-intellectualism
> (an attitude apparent more with the media than with the artistic
> and literary intelligentsia during the Haughey years); in its appeal
> to 'the people' against the establishment – Dublin 4 – which was
> certainly reciprocated so far as Mr Haughey was concerned.

Here we find Dublin 4 equated with 'the establishment'. This
is unsatisfactory on two counts. The word 'establishment', which
is little used in contemporary Ireland, denoted in its original,
English usage a powerful group of people who, among other

things, epitomised Englishness or Britishness; and the same is suggested, *mutatis mutandis*, when the term is applied in say a French context. But Dublin 4, far from epitomising Irishness, is in conflict with this concept and even with the word. (To cite a simple verbal example: in the language of Dublin 4, 'an Irish solution to an Irish problem' is a cant phrase meaning 'a remedy that is intrinsically undesirable and reprehensible and which should not be attempted'.) Furthermore, whilst Dublin 4 does include much or most of what might, in more normal circumstances, be called the Irish establishment, a fair number of people who belong in that category are not part of Dublin 4.

Nuala O'Faolain, writing a week before Gillespie, depicted the anti-Haughey element in Dublin in more explicit terms. A north-sider who moved to the southside, she is generally a staunch exponent of the Dublin 4 line, but departs from orthodoxy in having a soft spot for Haughey personally as distinct from politi-cally. In this special article she was recalling the reactions she had got from certain people when, a couple of years previously, in her account of an interview with Mr Haughey, she had described his cultural interests:

What kind of a fool was I, to be taken in by his fine talk? What kind of a journalist, to let him off the hook? And above all, how could I give any credence to his pathetic cultural pretensions? The implication was that I'm as much a vulgarian as he is. 'But then, you're both from the Northside . . .', one man said to me.

   This was from the kind of people who live in biggish houses and who've had sons and daughters in the professions as long as there's been a Catholic middle class. Themselves, they wouldn't [as does Mr Haughey] live in Georgian mansions or buy whole islands or plant rare trees or try to reintroduce eagles. They live cautiously, only breaking out the sherry when the son-in-law is appointed consultant. Their snobbery about Mr Haughey comes disguised as moral indignation. An indignation that extends to most of their compatriots. After all, *they* should be running the country. It is not just painful to them, but baffling, that Mr Haughey has been running it instead. The only explanation they can offer is that the majority of the Irish electorate is mad.

There is no explicit mention here of Dublin 4, but some features of the description are certainly characteristic of it: the (implicit) southsideness, the middle-classness, the hatred of Haughey and the snobbery dressed up as moral indignation – indignation that not only Haughey but people, specifically most Irish people, can be so uncouth, primitive, wrong-headed, etcetera. I hear echoes of the ironic title I gave a book about Ireland in the mid-eighties, *Nice People and Rednecks*, the 'nice people' being what I then called the 'Dublin liberal bourgeoisie', and 'rednecks' most of the remaining Irish. However, whilst the people O'Faolain is describing could belong, at least in part, to Dublin 4, they are not socially or occupationally typical of it. Dublin 4 is middle-class, but not typically of the upper sort; nor is it confined to people of Catholic background. South Dublin, as it happens, contains the largest concentration of Protestants in the Republic. Moreover, its occupational spectrum embraces much more than the classical professions.

Appearing between O'Faolain and Gillespie, my articles on Maastricht suggested that Dublin 4 could be seen as the 'state class', which I described as follows:

It is a class in the sense that it comprises people who feel they share – and actually do share – values, and a common interest, that distinguishes them from the nation generally. It includes a growing majority of the political class – higher civil servants, government advisers, MEPs, Brussels lobbyists, top party officials, and the majority of Oireachtas members in all parties except Fianna Fáil; also people who derive substantial income or status from the institutional appurtenances of a typical modern state, whether in the 'national' television and radio stations, the 'national' airline, press, university system or art gallery, the 'national' banking and courts systems, or in the provision of 'essential national services' such as electricity, telephones and road-building.

I went on to remark that the state class, or Dublin 4, 'functions, politically, as a party, both inside and outside the Oireachtas, and has the national media as its "party press"'. During the past twenty years or so, the Dublin media have shed the political and ideological pluralism that once characterised them, and have developed a single Dublin media line on all major issues, domestic and foreign. Their priority issues, their advocacy and deprecation, derive from what is called the 'liberal agenda'. It is therefore plausible to see these media, with minor exceptions (the *Sunday Business Post* occasionally, the fortnightly *Phoenix* regularly), as the voice and propaganda of a single group or class.

A state class is different from a national establishment in two ways. It consists only of people who service or are nurtured by the state, and it is not organically connected with the nation or society it commands but floats above it, exists apart from it. On reflection, I think it possible that the Irish state class, as I have defined it, may not be exactly identical with Dublin 4, may still include some people who do not belong to Dublin 4. But it is a matter of 'still', for Dublin 4 is an upwardly mobile and growing group. Moreover, there can be no doubt that it relates to the state rather than to the nation.

'The state', conceived of as an intrinsically secular, non-religious and therefore benign being, has always been a god-term in Dublin 4 diction. Dublin 4 people speak as if the state belongs to them as of right, shares their nature mentally and morally, and is illegitimately possessed by Fianna Fáil – or at least Fianna Fáil as it has been hitherto. They urge it to be influenced in its laws and actions by themselves, by their 'liberal opinion', and by all who abroad and in Northern Ireland think like them, rather than by the Catholic Church, or rich Irish businessmen, or what some call the nation. In particular they warn it against the Catholic Church, which embraces the great majority of the nation.

Assiduous in discovering and playing up 'Church–state conflicts', they always cheer on the state to win. Their extreme elements want our pluralist education system (Catholic, Protestant, Jewish and interdenominational, under the Department of Education) to be replaced by a single-ethos, secular state system. And until recent events in Eastern Europe, and even more recent scandals in the state-connected business sector, Dublin 4 exhibited a vaguely leftish tendency in favour of state-sponsored commercial enterprise (of which RTE is one instance).

A week after my *Irish Times* articles, on 11 February, the newspaper published a somewhat jokey letter from a reader in the depths of South Dublin. Not disputing the identification of state class and Dublin 4, the reader, Mr Tom Doorley, said:

> It is quite clear that the State Class or Dublin 4 Class comprises all those who are not the Plain People of Ireland . . . So, quite clearly, the State Class comprises a tiny group. Mr Fennell is a little coy about spelling out the State Class's identifying characteristics – or perhaps he regards these as being too obvious to mention.

I had in fact been explicit about its occupational characteristics. What Mr Doorley meant is its ideological identikit, which he went on to supply, obliquely, by sketching the 'Plain People of Ireland':

> The PPI are noted for their firm stand against foreign games such as soccer, their aversions to foreign filth (much of James Joyce's canon was written on the Continent) and foreign soap operas. They are, for the most part, daily communicants and attend confession weekly. They are happy to agree that sex is for procreation and certainly not for enjoyment (even simultaneously and at the same time). They have a tendency to dance at the crossroads and have a wonderful facility with the Irish language.
>
> Not so the State Class . . . I'm worried, though, by Mr Fennell's

strong implication that this State Class may be infiltrating the more progressive elements in Fianna Fáil.

If I had not directly made that last point, I certainly insinuated it: the state class, alias Dublin 4, has been making progress in detaching, or winning over, leading members of Fianna Fáil. Moreover, Mr Haughey himself was paralysed by his attempt to embody the 'plain people' *and* to placate Dublin 4. But the main interest of that letter is that, in its jokey way, it describes the two groups into which Dublin 4 sees the Republic divided. On the one hand there is the great, ordinary mass: fans of the Gaelic Athletic Association or GAA (the largest sports organisation by far), xenophobic, painfully religious, Victorian in matters sexual, rurally traditional, and enthusiasts of the Irish language. On the other hand there are themselves, Dublin 4 people, who are proud to be none of those things. The unspoken subtext of this reactive and negative self-definition is that they, Dublin 4 people, are like normal, modern, consumerist people in London and the Western world generally.

What is reflected there, by means of a grotesque caricature of most people in Ireland today, is the mental set of those middle-class Dubliners who since the sixties have defined themselves as liberals, and who in the early seventies became known as 'Dublin liberals'. The word had not been a term in Irish politics since the British Liberal Party ceased to function in the country. For the great majority of Irish people for 150 years, the democratic Catholic liberalism of mainstream nationalism, of the new state and the Irish Constitution, had been as natural as the air they breathed and consequently not remarked on. In the Free State and then in the Republic the ideological differences had occurred almost entirely within this liberal consensus, and had expressed various degrees of commitment to the nationalist and socially redistributive objectives of the Revolution. This new, unqualified 'liberalism' of the sixties was a confluence of two currents: on the one hand, the new sixties brand of left liberalism in the Western world generally – secularist, social democratic, consumerist, extending the 'rights of the individual' to the removal of all restrictions on consensual sexual behaviour; on the other hand, and partly arising from the economic failure of the fifties, scepticism towards the political and cultural heritage of the Revolution, and consequently towards Irish nationalism.

The neo-liberals redefined ideological division in the Republic in terms of the Gilbert and Sullivan song: whoever was not a liberal had to be a conservative. But the difference from nineteenth-century English usage and similar usage elsewhere was that the people described as 'conservative' – they included all upholders of the previous liberal consensus, of the Revolution and of the Constitution – had not chosen the description, either as a party name or ideologically. The neo-liberals simply imposed it on them, fleshed it out with 'traditionalist' and 'reactionary', and through their growing ascendancy in the national media made it an exclusively pejorative label in the public discourse. 'Irish society', thus tagged, became 'a bad thing'. The few in the Republic who insisted they were socialists were reckoned by the liberals to be 'liberals' at heart, and generally were. Indeed, the small Marxist-Leninist Workers' Party, known colloquially as 'Stickies', made it their business to infiltrate the media, and were popularly regarded as providing the well-drilled core of 'liberal' hardliners in RTE and the *Irish Times*.

By the eighties, when Dublin liberalism had become the Dublin 4 syndrome, it was pursuing a well-advertised programme called the 'liberal agenda'. Under the influence of the right-liberal economic policies of British Prime Minister Margaret Thatcher and US President Reagan, it acquired, in economic matters, a right wing which, in 1985, produced a party, the Progressive Democrats, formed by dissidents from Fianna Fáil.

The 'liberal agenda' is a proposition as well as an agenda. It is the proposition that progress for the Republic of Ireland means removing every taint of Catholicism and of Irish nationalism from its public life and institutions and accommodating itself to Britain, the Northern unionists and EC Europe, while retaining a state apparatus in Dublin. In a shorthand that anyone in the Republic in recent years would understand, this boiled down to divorce, more condoms, easy on abortion; support the EC, unionist demands, British policy in the North and revisionist history-writing; bash Charles Haughey, Fianna Fáil, the Catholic Church, the Constitution, the IRA, Sinn Féin, the GAA, Irish Americans, and all those ignorant, deluded people in northside Dublin and 'rural Ireland' (the rest of the Republic) who support that sinister man or one of those benighted organisations. It was the agenda, to requote John Waters, of 'a class of people . . . who ideally would have liked to be born somewhere else'. Of late, there has also been a tendency to bash corrupt big businessmen, with particular attention to rich businessmen connected with Fianna Fáil. Haughey's conspicuous wealth and the suggestion that it was the result of shady dealings have formed part of the motivation for the Dublin 4 vendetta against him.

I think that Dublin 4 is now in focus. From the start, Dublin liberalism has had adherents, including some prominent politicians, throughout the city and the Republic. But by far the largest and for obvious reasons the most powerful concentration of them is in South Dublin. Moreover, it is from there and by them, via the national media, that the 'party line' is set and promulgated. 'Dublin 4' denotes this socio-ideological group. At its simplest and least tendentious or controversial, it is the South Dublin liberal middle class. More precisely, it is the large and powerful segment of the middle and upper-middle class in South Dublin that is committed to the liberal agenda, and which acts as mobiliser, mouthpiece and platform for all who share this commitment.

Despite its pretensions, the neo-liberal agenda is anything but progressive. It opposes the 150-year-old endeavour to achieve and maintain the intellectual, cultural and political autonomy of the Irish nation in all of Ireland. In place of the self-definition of independent Ireland which it rejects, it proposes no new independent identity, but rather a renewed general merging with British wishes and cultural norms, and blind obedience to what they term 'Europe'. Thus it reneges on the Revolution and regresses to provincialism. Notably, it acquiesces in the material status quo, give or take a few rich entrepreneurs. In particular, it fails to address positively Ireland's two crippling disorders: the chronic insufficiency of the economy – rooted in the still-imperialist structures and still-dependent mentality of the postcolonial state – and the long war caused by the persistent British refusal to recognise adequately the Irish nation in the North. To the 3 million Irish people marginalised by forced emigration or unemployment at home, it offers contraception, divorce, abortion. To the long war it contributes yelps of outrage and torrents of sympathy when Protestant or English civilians are killed, indifference or 'serves them right' when Catholic Irish are killed, and practical mindlessness – 'can't bear to think of it'.

None of this would matter much if the liberal agenda were merely competing in the Oireachtas and the media against ruling progressive policies and against other minority agendas of various ilk, or, to put it differently, if the neo-liberals were concentrated in the Midlands or Kerry. What makes their agenda matter, disproportionately, is that they are concentrated in the few square miles on the east coast where the power of the state and the mass media are concentrated; that their reactionary, complacent and thematically peripheral programme is the *only* coherent national agenda being actively pursued; and that it is pressed daily on citizens and government by the national media and much of the political class. The massed pressure encounters a mass of recalcitrant voters; an irresolute government wavers between. The result is a political paralysis that prevents a progressive agenda gathering force, let alone winning power.

A progressive agenda would give priority to the two crippling disorders – the economy and the war – and redefine Ireland in refurbished terms as a distinct, self-governing nation. Depending on electoral circumstances and real demand, it might or might not include such matters as divorce, contraception and the abortion question. But if it did, they would rank in their proper place, not centrally, and the approach to them would be pragmatic and in the context of the common good, free of the secularist, anti-Catholic and anti-national animus that inspires the liberal agenda. As they are now presented, enveloped in that animus, by advocates indifferent to the Irish common good, they have, and are felt to have, threatening implications for a nation so denuded of the distinguishing and bonding features that a nation needs that its Catholic morality and practice are its only substantial ethnic definers. And this felt threat, in the absence of a vigorous, state-led nationalism, injects a more than moral motivation – a zeal bordering on the desperate – into the militant Catholic organisations that oppose 'divorce, more condoms, easy on abortion'. In short, in the absence of a progressive agenda of government, zealotry meets zealotry head on.

For the generation now in their twenties, Dublin 4 represents the sixties generation: those who made good in Dublin in that decade, created a distinct ethos to go with their new-found affluence, and held on through the straitened decades that followed. Allowing for the accretions to their ranks that have occurred since the sixties, that is an accurate picture. The sixties boom, which extended until the oil crisis in the early seventies, was produced by the last positive and successful agenda of government, that of Lemass, that the Republic has known. For the first time a large number of Irish Catholics, especially in Dublin, were able to do very well in their own country. The boom lifted to affluence a new middle class that reached eagerly towards the liberations then being trumpeted by swinging London. The *Irish Times*, which had been failing, seized the opportunity. Switching to the new consumerist liberalism and adapting it to local circumstances, it took the lead in providing the new, uplifted Irish with an ideological buttress. RTE television, which started in 1962, followed that lead. Its personnel, who were themselves mainly and increasingly middle-class South Dubliners of the new wave, took their cue daily from the newspaper that catered for them. The old Radio Éireann had been broadly nationalist but otherwise neutral. Now its successor RTE radio became a junior partner to the television station and gradually, through personnel replacements, adopted its ideological line. In the seventies, as independent periodicals such as the *Leader* and *Hibernia* disappeared, the *Gleichschaltung* of the media was completed. The *Press* and *Independent* newspapers, and new weeklies and monthlies that appeared during the seventies, followed the *Irish Times*/RTE lead.

It must be said that what happened with this new Dublin middle class – the course it took, the attitudes it struck as it embraced its new faith and created Dublin 4 – points to a failure of the founding fathers of independent Ireland. The failure derived from a deficiency in patriotic worldly wisdom; more precisely, worldly foresight. The revolutionaries might have foreseen that sooner or later, if their project for Ireland were to be successful, a new, thoroughly native class of educated, well-to-do people would surely emerge, particularly in the capital. Like their counterparts in other nations, even the smallest, they would want to see themselves as different from, and superior to, the general throng. They would need the airs, manners and coherence of an elite, they would need a snobbery, however civilised. Given Ireland's modern history, which had lacked, especially in Dublin, a native, nationally educated and nationally minded social elite – a normal European bourgeoisie-cum-smart-set – the failure of the founding fathers was their failure to provide from the start the nucleus of such an elite so that later, as a socially climbing class emerged, it would have a contemporary, native model to imitate and could affirm its distinction and practise its snobbery within the nation's social framework. To put it differently, the young Irish state needed Pádraig Pearse as its first Minister of Education; two or three well-endowed schools in the style of St Enda's, including one for girls; a *grande école* of the French sort drawing on the best teaching talent from the Continent; and a privileged lifestyle for its graduates, guaranteed by the state. Pearse was intelligent enough, cold-blooded enough and English enough to plan this; he was also stubborn enough to have overcome the resistance of his utopianly egalitarian colleagues. Because no such measures were taken, the educated Catholic middle class that came to affluence in Dublin in the sixties had no option but to become old-fashioned people with old-fashioned, pre-revolutionary attitudes, rendered in sixties swingers' guise. They had little recourse but to express their sense of difference and their snobbery in terms that were largely a throwback to Protestant-colonial and English precedents, and consequently antagonistic to the existing Irish nation. It was no accident that the newspaper that first gave them ideological affirmation, and that rose to life again through them, was Dublin's only surviving 'Protestant' newspaper, which still to this day, out of piety to its past, prints the 'Church Notes' of the Protestant churches weekly.

Three political events in the early seventies favoured the Dublin liberals' rise to power. The first was the deletion by referendum from the Constitution of the clause recognising the various Churches by name and the 'special position' of the Catholic Church as the Church of the great majority. This was done under pressure from the liberal media and to placate the Northern unionists; the alliance between the two groups was already forming. The net effect – for, of course, it did not placate the unionists – was to leave constitutionally vacant that 'special position' in the state to which the Dublin liberals aspired. The second event was the Republic's accession to full membership of the European Economic Community (EEC). The liberals were not alone in wanting this. The farmers wanted it for monetary gain, the political class because they could conceive of no alternative and wanted to join a privileged club. 'Since Britain is joining, we must join,' the Taoiseach, Jack Lynch, reiterated. The entire Dublin media supported membership. But for the Dublin liberals EEC membership had particular attractions. Alienated from what Ireland meant, they were situated at the centre of its highly centralised state and media, and already had strong footholds both in the media and in the political class. Full membership of the EEC would mean pressure on the Republic to shed its Irishness and to conform to the West European individualist norms to which the liberals aspired. It would also yield them material benefits and supportive connections that would make them less dependent on their fellow countrymen. In short, in Dublin, as in other capitals of the EEC, the seeds were sown of a state class that would be bound more to its counterparts than to its country.

The third event of the early seventies that helped the liberals on their way was the coming to power of Liam Cosgrave as Taoiseach. With the IRA waging war in the North, and support for it growing in the Republic, Cosgrave felt called on to emulate his father in the assertion of the state's law and order against militant republicanism. Consequently, under his Fine Gael–Labour coalition of 1973–77, liberal Dublin had a field day for its anti-republicanism (not yet for its anti-Catholicism). It applauded the government as with obsessive zeal it pursued republican organisations, their fellow travellers, real or imaginary, at home and abroad, and any utterance that might be construed as sympathetic to them. Conor Cruise O'Brien spancelled RTE and intimidated the press; Patrick Cooney did a Robespierre as Minister for Justice; and Garret FitzGerald, as Foreign Minister, struck hard on the Irish-American front. The government circulated a blacklist of people who, because of their known republican sympathies, were ineligible for employment in the public service. The Gardaí, long respected for their comparative gentleness and decency as a police force, were now told to get results at all costs. Part of the cost was the notorious Heavy Gang. In an increasingly routine way, prisoners were beaten up, even in non-political cases. It was current black humour that if your phone was not tapped, you must be a very uninteresting person. In short, the Republic came so close to being a police state that, on the election night in 1977 when O'Brien and Cooney fell and Jack Lynch won an overall majority for Fianna Fáil, citizens of all parties, everywhere, danced and sang.

A personal anecdote will illustrate the liberal climate of those years. In 1977, as a lecturer in Politics in University College Galway, I had been invited by the Irish American Cultural Institute to do a lecture tour in the USA. My lecture at all the venues was to be 'The Northern Conflict: Irish Proposals for a Solution'. Irish diplomats in the USA made two approaches to Eoin McKiernan, director of the institute, to inform him that the Irish government disapproved of the invited lecturer. After the second intervention, which was more forceful than the first, the institute felt obliged to cancel the tour. Subsequently I learned the reason for the ban from Garret FitzGerald himself, who had been a prefect in the Jesuit school I attended. A year previously, the Irish consul-general in Boston had visited a seminar on Northern Ireland at Amherst College, Massachusetts, in which I was a participant. In conversation with this lady, at a late-night drinking session with others present, I had used the words 'your tyrannous government' and the remark was filed.

For the South Dublin liberals, those years of the mid-1970s had been a taste of righteous power by proxy. In the 1980s, through a combination of circumstances, they became a righteous power in their own right and drew attention to themselves as such, as 'Dublin 4'. Their path to pre-eminence was smoothed by a succession of inert governments whose only notable net achievement, by the end of the decade, had been to alleviate the financial aspects of an economic crisis that recalled the grim fifties, before Lemass. First, tens of thousands emigrated annually; then

there were hundreds of thousands unemployed. Dublin 4 filled
a vacuum of ideology, political vision and political will. Another
reason for its conspicuousness was that for more than four years
in the mid-eighties, it had one of its own, Garret FitzGerald, as
Taoiseach, and most of his government, in addition to the media,
were committed to the full liberal agenda. With the state thus
effectively in its pocket, those years were an Eden of sorts for
Dublin 4. Apart from a couple of painful exceptions, to be mentioned presently, South Dublin liberals felt that things were going their way. Referring to 1985, John Waters writes, 'It was
around this time... that in faraway Roscommon I noticed the
radio becoming increasingly shrill.' In that same year, an Australian
poet, Vincent Buckley, who had visited Ireland several times,
wrote this in his book *Memory Ireland*:

> [Ireland] has been asked to lose its national memory by a kind
> of policy, in which politicians of almost all parties, ecclesiastics
> of all religions, media operators, and revisionist historians co-
> operate to create (and let us hope they do not need to enforce,
> for if they need to, they will) a new sense of corporate identity.
> This sense contradicts the immediately preceding one (the one
> based on the rising of Easter 1916 and its aftermath), which proved
> first so exhilarating then so wearying to its generations, some of
> whom had fought to realize it. Ireland is not a nation, once again
> or ever, so the new story runs, but two nations: maybe several;
> it does not have its characteristic religion – or, if it does, it ought
> not; it does not have its characteristic language, as anyone can
> see or hear; it has no particular race or ethnic integrity. Ireland
> is a nothing – a no-thing – an interesting nothing, to be sure,
> composed of colourful parts, a nothing-mosaic. It is advertising
> prose and Muzak.

It was an Eden of sorts for Dublin 4, but an Eden complete with
serpent, and the serpent had a poisonous sting. Twice, in two
constitutional referenda – about adding a 'pro-life' amendment
and removing the anti-divorce clause – the South Dublin liberals,

working with the government and the national media, took on the 'Plain People of Ireland' and, to the fury of the liberals, lost.

In sum, the eighties won them recognition as the main extra-constitutional power in the state, and hammered them in the heat of battle and the chagrin of defeat into an intensely self-conscious and embittered fighting force. Only in 1991, when one of their own, Mary Robinson, was elected President of Ireland, did Dublin 4 begin to feel slightly reconciled with Ireland and its democratic institutions. The *rapprochement* inched forward tentatively when in February 1992 the Supreme Court decided that the much-hated Eighth Amendment to the Constitution, which was intended to exclude abortion forever, actually permits abortion in certain circumstances.

The extreme and enduring bitterness of Dublin 4 people after their defeats marks them out from other Irish groups and parties who lose in the democratic process. But it is understandable in the light of their characteristic view of themselves and of those who disagree with them. Seeing themselves as 'enlightened' (their word) and therefore truly rational (really human) and morally good (sensitive, compassionate, requiring strict honesty from the power-ful, deeply appalled by evil actions), they regard people who disagree with them as mentally darkened and morally delinquent (irrational, ignorant, uneducated, blinkered, brainwashed, crooked, fanatical, bigoted, hating the light – all this with the suggestion of inhuman). Dublin 4 speech about, or to, those who think dif-ferently, regularly uses such terms with that overtone. It also employs the southern English locution, 'I (or one) just can't understand how ...' – intended not as an admission of mental incapacity, but as an assertion of intrinsic difference and superiority. It follows that disagreement with Dublin liberals is not, in their view, an occasion for liberal tolerance, a normal accident of human society for which democracy caters by pluralist media, a variety of parties, elections, referenda and majority decisions, but rather a sin against the light. And victory over the liberals by their opponents (the dark, inhuman forces) is a grievous moral disorder, a wrong of cosmic import, to which baffled bitterness is the due response.

The key to understanding their group psychology lies in the double effect of their liberal enlightenment: that it makes its recipients, they believe, both truly rational and highly sensitive – especially to unreason and evil. As a result, their reason is of the 'hot', not the 'cool' kind. This explains the recurrent mass hysteria that they manifest in hyperbolic language and, occasionally, panic action. February 1992 witnessed notable instances of both in the matter of the pregnant fourteen-year-old girl prevented by an injunction of the High Court from travelling to England for an abortion. For years before this incident, several thousand Irish women and girls annually had been going to England to have abortions, without any interference from the Irish legal authorities. The High Court injunction (later lifted by the Supreme Court in its momentous judgment) was made in the extraordinary circumstances of the case in question. But the *Irish Times* editorial of the following day compared the Republic to Ceausescu's Romania and the Iran of the ayatollahs. Reprinted in the English *Guardian* and taken up around Europe, it set the tone for ten days of Dublin media hysteria. Moreover, on the same day as it appeared, and perhaps spurred to action by it, a group of South Dublin women activists went to the airport and set up a 'pregnancy testing station' for females boarding aircraft. Quite simply, shocking unreason or evil makes Dublin 4ers gc haywire, so that the assertion of their counter-values, in the face of either, can and does take very emotional and even irrational forms.

Hardened by the combats of the eighties, and feeling beleaguered by a hostile hinterland, the South Dublin liberal middle class are not, as so often with liberals, ideologically lax. Membership is determined by strict adherence, give or take an item or two, to the liberal agenda for Ireland as the right way forward. That is the defining bond. Subscribe (as many Irish people do) to one or two, even three items but demur at the agenda as a whole, or at its general thrust, and you do not belong to Dublin 4 which, as John Waters recognised, is tight-knit, like a village community.

One could find other apt comparisons: a messianic political party, a fundamentalist religious sect. Most apt, perhaps, is a con-fraternity of well-catechised, 1950s-style Irish Catholics, com-plete with clergy and an obsession with sex. Granted that it is an analogy, not a definition, much about South Dublin liberalism can be better understood if it is viewed as a secular religion, com-peting with and trying to replace Ireland's two other main religions, Catholicism and nationalism. (Divorce, abortion, the public downplaying of 1916, the denationalising, successively, of the political parties and the Catholic bishops, are counters in this, the basic struggle.) While competing with its rivals, however, Dublin 4 is similar to them in many ways, and understandably so. Its airs and attitudes may be aped from Protestant-colonial antecedents, but the people doing the aping are of Catholic na-tionalist stock and culture. Consequently, their liberalism, like its historical rivals, has its dogmas, saints, martyrs, penal laws, freedom struggle, bishops (what the *Sunday Business Post* calls 'liberal ayatollahs'), preachers, and laity. The 'clergy', upper and lower, are supplied by journalists, broadcasters and media pets (ideologically sound politicians and spokespersons whom the media regularly present). Together, these form the actively committed and evangelising core. With the laity, as with many laities, it is more a case of passive affiliation. Most Dublin 4ers are not active ideologues but well-dressed, well-educated, middle-class people with an orthodox cast of mind, set of attitudes and simple faith, that are nourished daily by their 'clergy', and activated – into facial display or doctrinaire utterance – only when some alien attitude or utterance disturbs them.

The similarity to Catholicism is greater than to nationalism,

and what is evoked is often Catholicism in its medieval and early
modern forms. On 26 September 1981, the liberal leader, Garret
FitzGerald, in his first term as Taoiseach, declared a 'crusade' to
implement the liberal agenda. Next day, the *Irish Times* led the
choir of approval with an editorial containing three triple 'hurrahs'
and two single ones – a remarkable secular echo of liturgical
alleluias. The role of inquisitors is filled by RTE interviewers
when, in full view of the faithful *et pour encourager les autres*, they
arraign say, a Catholic bishop or a pro-life activist (republican
activists are banned), and call on them to account for their thought
crimes. Media witch-hunts are directed at offending individuals.
Occasionally, massed media campaigns, conducted night, noon
and morning for days on end, recall the old six-day parish retreats
with hellfire sermons. Like them, these spiritual offensives exhort
their target audience – the 'Plain People of Ireland' or one of
their organisations – to feel guilty, repent and confess. When a
campaign climaxes with an opinion poll showing that a majority
have declared themselves 'converted', it is like nothing so much
as the last night of the old retreats when the packed congrega-
tion held up lit candles and declared in fervent unison: 'We re-
nounce the devil and all his works and pomps.' Frustratingly,
however, for the new clergy as for the old, ordained sort, these
media conversions often turn out to be just as temporary as their
Catholic forerunners.

Seen in this light, Dublin 4 has its humorous side. But for the
majority of citizens of divers views who are subjected to the massed
harangue, it is of course terribly boring and, worse, intimidating.
So much is it the latter that if, for example, someone on a TV
panel mentions the harangue and says it is oppressive, a subversion of democracy, a travesty of pluralism, or suchlike, that person will be told afterwards, by letter, phone call and words on
the street, that he or she is 'courageous', and thanked for it –
though he or she has merely spoken their mind and said the
obvious in a liberal democracy.

But to return to definition: once we have established Dublin 4's identity, concretely and non-controversially, as the South Dublin liberal middle class, its identity in socio-political and historical terms, its role identity, remains to be determined. I have suggested 'state class', in the black African sense, perhaps in the emerging Euro sense, or at least such a class in the making. Historically, Dublin 4 recalls that earlier Irish state class, the eighteenth-century Protestant Ascendancy, which had a similar relationship to the mass of the people, a similar special position and outward dependency.

Alternatively, Dublin 4 may be seen as Ireland's latest modernising vanguard, and there is some truth in this, but with important qualifications. What is classed as modern has always been determined in, and promulgated from, the biggest capitalist power centres. Consequently, 'modernisation' means the reproduction of that elsewhere, to a greater or lesser degree, under nationalist or provincialist auspices. Measured in these terms, Dublin 4 is at most a superficially modernising movement, because of its concentration on ideological and symbolic values and its lack of interest in economic and scientific development. It must also be distinguished from a nationalist modernising vanguard, such as Fianna Fáil was in the 1930s and again in the 1960s, and ranked as a radically provincialist one: renewing after a nationalist interlude the overall thrust of modern Irish history.

Lastly, in postcolonial terms – which in the light of Ireland's recent history are perhaps the aptest – Dublin 4 is a powerful sector of the national bourgeoisie which, opting out of the nation but clinging to the hard-won state, has reverted to the role of colonial bourgeoisie. By the same token, it is an eloquent pointer to the state of the nation in the Republic of Ireland. Powerful neo-colonial bourgeoisies emerge only in postcolonial nations that have lost their sense of direction, their self-love and their will to be. In this perspective, Dublin 4 is the symptom not the disease, the bulbous growth on the paralysed body politic, the balloon filled with Ireland's collective emptiness.

One way or another, given their growing political predominance, their expanding hold on the state and their attitude to the rest of the nation, the South Dublin liberal middle class is ominous for the Irish people. John Waters has written of them, 'It was as though they had decided that the country outside Dublin was a millstone around the neck of the capital. If we did not have these mucksavages to contend with, maybe we could have a decent standard of living.' And reading their thoughts to their logical conclusion: 'All that was required was for the rest of the population to agree to lie down and die.' A hundred and fifty years ago the population nearly did that; now, with potato blight well under control, forced emigration is a more likely ethnic cleanser. This year, as we move towards the 'irreversible', periphery-draining European Union, the mechanism is being set in place.

But if the prospect for the nation is ominous, for Dublin 4's Little Irelanders it is bright. That same European Union that threatens the nation offers them an assured and indefinite upkeep. 'Ireland' is part of the deal, and they have hold of the nameplate. A vision beckons them forward, its name is Luxembourg, and its features rejoice their hearts. Population 350,000; full member of the EC; gets its slice of the cake and its share of the freebies; hosts the Presidency regularly; has a high standard of living and no unemployment; has divorce and abortion; no mucksavages to contend with.

POSTSCRIPT

Micromania. Strange, perhaps, that I should mention it as a postscript, when it has been a notable feature of Dublin 4 since the sect's earliest emergence. At the start of the 1960s, as for a hundred years before that, a Dubliner viewing the world from South Dublin still saw Ireland and Irishness as vast. 'Ireland's spiritual empire', as it was called in the public discourse, embraced the Irish communities in Scotland, Wales and England, the farflung Irish millions in the USA and Australia, the Irish in Argentina, the thousands on the mission frontiers in Africa and Asia. Within the span of this Irish world, where the sun never set, but it rose on churches called St Patrick's, even Dubliners, though they supplied fewer of the emigrants than other parts, felt a particularly vivid and grateful closeness to 'our Irish-American cousins'. And within the island thus conceived of as 'mother country' to many millions, Dubliners saw Irish everywhere from Antrim to Kerry, called the Northern nationalists 'our people in the North' and regarded the unionists as ours potentially – if they would come to their senses. The sect intensely disliked this spaciousness of Irish being – so unlike them, so threatening to their enterprise – and set about demolishing it. The first to fall was the great framework, the 'spiritual empire'. Mawkish talk, they said, and, inasmuch as it referred to exiles who were mainly Catholic, sectarian to boot. With our compliance they erased the phrase from public discourse, and we lost its consciousness. Then when the North boiled over and 'our people' were assaulted and we called them 'our people', the sect, grown more powerful, rapped us again. 'The unionists are "our people" too,' they said, 'they are all, all "our people".' So both they and we stopped calling any people in the North our own. Then it was our transatlantic cousins. Foolish, ignorant people, the sect pronounced, people with mad ideas about Ireland and, worse, supporters of the IRA and therefore enemies of Ireland. So in Dublin we stopped cherishing them, lost our sense of kinship with them, even learned to feel ashamed of them. The sect, who held the stage and microphone, could do these things. 'Rural Ireland,' they intoned liturgically – meaning the Republic outside Dublin – 'We can do without rural Ireland and everything it stands for. Rednecks! Ugh!' Articles Two and Three, they are now saying, 'must go because the unionists say so, and say so with good reason. It is provocative for Dublin to lay claim to Ireland beyond the border.'

Micromania: the pursuit of smallness as a psychic imperative. It comes from their so desperately wanting Ireland and the Irish to be like them – in everything, even size.[1]

1. For long after the February 1992 hysteria, abortion, and the legal and political tangle surrounding it, continued to figure prominently in the 'national' media. The divide between the priorities of Dublin 4 and those of the Republic generally, as well as the illusions of the former about the latter, are vividly illustrated by the opening sentences of a new weekly column on the provincial newspapers introduced by the *Irish Times* on 13 April. Like a traveller reporting home on a fabled foreign country, Kathryn Holmquist, an American resident in South Dublin, writes thus: 'The prevailing view that the moral outrage of the public stems from rural Ireland was revealed to be a myth on reading the latest issues of local newspapers. The bank strike and other job-related issues dominated the headlines in 11 cases. There was not one lead story on the abortion issue in the 16 local newspapers reviewed and only three news stories on the subject.'

11

INTELLECT
AND NATIONAL WELFARE

The achievement of political-constitutional
independence is the beginning and not the end
of the task of national liberation.

Gearóid Ó Tuathaigh

Ich vermochte nur wenig. Aber die Herrschenden
Sassen ohne mich sicherer, das hoffte ich.

Bertolt Brecht

IN HIS GREAT WORK *Ireland: 1912–85*, Professor Joe Lee devotes
most of his final chapter to an assessment of the Irish performance since partial independence. While he is primarily concerned
with economic performance, he takes in social and political
organisation – which he sees as intimately connected with the
former – and some aspects of the conduct of foreign affairs. It
is a comparative assessment in which the criteria are the perfor-
mances of other small north European nations, and the finding
that by this measure we performed poorly. In pursuit of an
explanation Lee devotes eighty pages to the intellectual factor.
Here his premise is that good national performance depends on
the nation's intellectuals' providing a rich supply of new social
thought, and on the effective use by the policy-makers of this
resource of knowledge and ideas. Social thought, in this context,
means thought dealing with Irish society in its various aspects;

it embraces sociology, social psychology, economics, political science, linguistics, and the interpretation of history as a guide for the present and future. But also, and primarily, it means synthetic social thought, 'the most demanding specialisation of all', which brings the various strands coherently to bear on the state of Ireland. Joe Lee is not, it should be noted, examining whether the Irish in this period were interested in general ideas, produced them or used them. He is concerned only with the specific matter mentioned: the supply of knowledge and ideas about Irish society – by native intellectuals, or in their default by foreigners – and the use of these social ideas by Irish policy-makers.

He finds that the supply of social thought by Irish intellectuals was comparatively very poor; that disproportionate contributions were made by foreigners who visited Ireland or settled here; and that the mainly nationalist policy-makers of the new state showed little interest in such thought about Ireland as was produced, and were slow to demand or organise the production of it. In this last respect they improved somewhat, for a brief period, when they were reacting to the economic crisis of the fifties and launching the First Programme of Economic Expansion. But their normal practice, not only in policy-making but also in legislation, has been to follow English doctrines and examples uncritically – while British national performance was falling behind the rest of northern Europe.

Even if the picture Lee presents is, as he says, that of a bleak intellectual landscape, it is valuable and empowering because it fills out a neglected aspect of our national self-knowledge and reveals a radical defect in our collective functioning which, once revealed, we can consider how to repair. While we are addressing that, I want to point out a gap in the picture, and then partly fill it with some detail that will make the picture more complete and the landscape even bleaker, but still reclaimable. My additions are drawn from fairly continuous work, experience and observation on the supply side, at the coalface, since the

mid-sixties. Having made them, I will set the picture in a broader
historical context by relating the notion of 'social thought' to
nationalist thought and the Irish intellectual tradition.

Between the production of social thought and the effective
use of it by policy-makers, there exists, in the normal order of
things, a mediating factor which Lee touches on only tangen-
tially, and without stating its vital, dual role. I refer to the processing of the thought from its raw *produced* state into intellectual
currency. This is done by the functioning intellectual community,
the informal parliament of thought and judgement, which discusses
the new thinking as it emerges and decides how much of it, in
what shape, will enter the nation's intellectual currency: either
as ideas generally shared, or as ideas adopted for use and development by a recognised sector or party.

Like most parliaments this informal one is organised, as it were,
in two houses, one small, the other large; but unlike most
parliaments, membership of the houses overlaps. In the smaller,
academic house, comprising the community of thinking resear-
chers – not all of whom work in institutions of teaching or research
– the new ideas are critically discussed by means of specialist journals and books, and at professional get-togethers. At the same
time or slightly later, in the larger, public chamber they are
discussed in public by the nation's entire intellectual community,
which includes, together with professional thinkers, all who are
interested in ideas. This discussion, being public, takes place in
the mass media of communication; specifically, in those sections
and organs of the mass media, including books, that are directed
to thoughtful audiences. (An example of the sort of book I mean
is W.J. McCormack's *The Battle of the Books,* which discusses
literary-political ideas of the seventies and eighties.) It occurs also
at informal intellectual events such as public workshops or
seminars, and summer schools which have broad agendas. Being
a critical discussion, a discussion that is also an assessment, it
includes responses, agreements, debates, amendments and informal

ballots, all of them both written and oral. (Obviously it involves much more than book-reviewing, which, though it can serve to get things going, can also be a decorous burial ritual for good new thought.) Normally, that is, when the intellectual community is functioning fully and freely, it is this broad, public discussion that produces the nation's partly stable, partly changing intellectual currency.

To clarify what I am talking about, let us look at three scenarios in which Irish thinker X publishes important new social thought and processing does not occur. X publishes his thought as a long article, based on a lecture he has given somewhere. Being an article, it is not reviewed, but during the subsequent year three scholars in their own publications refer readers to it without comment, and a journalist, in the course of a newspaper article, attacks it briefly. Subsequently, writing and thinking go on as if X's thought had never appeared. Again, X publishes his thought as a book which is widely reviewed, more than half the reviews being favourable, some mixed, one hostile; X is interviewed about his book on radio. But apart from footnotes or remarks in lectures that refer audiences to the book's existence, subsequent writing and lecturing draw on the same stock of ideas as before. Finally, X publishes his thought as a book that is widely and favourably reviewed in all the media. The author is interviewed in a newspaper and on radio, and, in a television programme for thoughtful viewers, four intellectuals discuss his ideas for half an hour, with a great deal of head-nodding and only one strong dissenter. X's book wins a valuable prize. Papers read at two conferences during the following year discuss X's book from several angles, and are followed in each case by a response from X himself and a lively debate among those attending. But since X is a native son, and the members of the intellectual community believe that native thought, however brilliant, cannot be a real way of seeing things, least of all their own lives, and cannot therefore point the way for public policy, they do not adopt X's thought into their currency of ideas. They continue thinking about their nation and the world by means of good old reliable imported thought, freshening it occasionally as the foreign fashion changes, and adopting X's way of seeing things only ten years later when a book by an Austrian, translated from the German, becomes the rage in London and is hailed by a British cabinet minister as 'setting the pace for all future development'.

Because Lee – who could not do everything – does not deal explicitly with the processing factor in the intellectual economy, he does not assess to what degree such scenarios have been enacted in Ireland since the 1920s. The question would be: to what degree did the intellectual community discuss, academically and publicly, such new social thought as was supplied, and by a process of agreement, modification and rejection introduce a portion of it into the national intellectual currency? Lee's narrative contains some of the basic data for such an assessment. He deals with the formative role of the journal *Irish Historical Studies* in academic history-writing, and mentions the *Irish Statesman*, the *Bell*, and the *Leader* (edited by Desmond Williams) as important disseminators of ideas to general readerships. For several decades after 1922 – in contrast, for example, to Swedish practice – major Irish scholars did not contribute routinely to newspapers. Irish newspapers up to the sixties had meagre intellectual content. Radio Éireann and the academy kept their distance from each other until the start of the Thomas Davis lectures in 1953. Academics appear frequently on television, but usually in debate about some controversial topic of the moment, where profundity of thought is neither called for nor appreciated. All this and more is in Lee – tantalisingly skirting the question posed above, and its subquestions. Book reviews apart, were the social ideas launched by one intellectual discussed critically by others, in academic forums and in such mass media as were available? Did the broad intellectual community, including academics, freelance thinkers and intellectuals working in the mass media, function as an informal public institution – as an intelligentsia – debating new social thought, organising discussions of it, and adopting it, selectively, into the intellectual currency? Did the intellectual community, in other words, do its job? If so, to what extent, in different periods? And finally, in so far as there has in fact been since the 1920s a changing currency of ideas in Ireland, to what degree was this change due to Irish critical sifting of new thought, native or foreign, rather than to the uncritical adoption of new, imported ideas?

As I have suggested above, the processing of new social ideas has two important functions. In the first place, as anyone who thinks of ancient Athens, postmodern Paris or Dublin at the beginning of the century will readily understand, it provides the nation with an intellectual life. Few would dispute that having or not having an intellectual life is one yardstick of national performance. Having it, moreover, is a value quite regardless of whether the ideas under discussion and judgement are used by the national policy-makers. The collective, disputatious pursuit of a true view of the polis is its own value and justification; all the more so if it is done with a view to the polis's welfare. But the public noise and stir of this intellectual pursuit, and its evident passion, give it additionally an educative role and value: making it, without leave of the official policy-makers, an educator of the nation.

Second, the processing of ideas ensures that good new social thought is persuasively presented to the policy-makers and, if adopted by them, implemented or (in the case of external policy) actively pursued. The processing does this by making the new social thought current, which means, in a democracy, both politically usable – even advantageously so – and politically pressing. Because it means the latter, it is unlikely that the new thinking, once adopted formally as policy, will remain mere fig leaf or intention – will not be executed. The pressure that the ideas exert, as part of the regular political discourse, works against that. This link between the processing of ideas into currency and their implementation as policy is shown by default when policy-makers make a policy, nominally, out of ideas that have been ignored by the intellectual community. They do this, exceptionally, when an unwelcome political necessity compels them, and the need is simply to 'have a policy' rather than be without one. Then, because the ideas adopted lack the force of currency, the policy is stillborn, effecting little – dead words on paper. It follows that any judgement of Irish policy-makers as consumers and appliers of new Irish social thought would in fairness need to investigate not only whether, and in what quantity and quality, such thought was produced, but also whether the intellectual community did its processing job.

Lee's inattention to the processing factor in the intellectual economy is the likely reason for a large omission in the more recent period of his eighty-page intellectual history. Earlier he has considered, and rejected with arguments, the suggestion made by some that, in the decades from independence to the sixties, the Catholic Church had a seriously inhibiting influence on the production of social thought. But in his account of more recent times, he fails to give due attention to the emergence in the sixties of a quasi-church, the Dublin neo-liberals, whose occupation of the national media has been preventing the processing of benevolent new thought about Irish society – and therefore of most new social thought that has been offered, or is likely to be offered, by Irish thinkers to Irish policy-makers. The consequences for the national welfare can be imagined and are, indeed, recorded in the title Lee gives to the final chapter of his historical narrative, covering the period up to 1985: 'Drift: 1969–?' Drift, in humans beings, is literally mindlessness.

Because for nearly twenty years the main communications media have been occupied by the neo-liberal sect, we have only gradually perceived the sect's real nature, what it is driving at and with what effects. By now its more obvious features are widely recognised, and Lee catches several of them when he refers (p. 655) to 'the shallowness of much liberal thought, fashionable in the media, and reeking with condescension towards the "peasantry", defined to include virtually everyone who dared query their assumptions'. That catches the (land)lordly airs, the echoes of Ascendancy, the media connection, and the intolerant, big-city antagonism towards 'rural Ireland' (meaning the Republic outside South Dublin). The liberals give out about 'Irish society' because they see it as a burden and a threat. Opposed to its inherited Catholicism and nationalism, they have written off the Irish nation, but value the state called Ireland because its power – like the national media and themselves – is highly concentrated in Dublin, and its nameplate gives them seats at international conferences. They value it particularly because, under their influence and at their urging, it is embarked on a course of provincial bending to London, the unionists and the EC that is cleansing it of Irishness, making it theirs, and rendering it docile to their agenda. Their disproportionate power and success is due largely to the fact that since the end of the Lemass era they have been the only major group in the Republic pursuing a clear agenda resolutely; in this sense, the liberals have been the Republic's counterpart to the IRA in the North. Their agenda is driven by a rootless, absolutist individualism which claims for them, individually and collectively, a greater sovereignty – not 'under God' – than that which democracy and the Constitution ascribe to the nation. To hammer home their slogans and promote their aims, they use the united Dublin media. All this is more or less recognised. What I am adding is a hard-won insight into the crippling effect those same media have had, and are having, on our intellectual life, on our national policy-makers, and consequently on all aspects of our national performance.

In matters intellectual the principal agents of neo-liberal policy in the media are the intellectuals who work there, most of them as editors or producers, some as columnists, presenters or interviewers. They are assisted by others of their choosing, intellectuals or not. There are the media pets, the ideologically reliable politicians and others who are regularly brought to utterance because their utterances advance the cause. For example, a woman I met in Dublin a few months ago, who had had an unfortunate marriage and wanted a divorce, told me how she was used under five different names and with various home locations 'from Howth to Greystones', when RTE radio was pushing divorce. There are also the broadcasters and journalists who are simply streetwise about fashions in ideas, who know what is 'in' and what is 'out' and speak or write accordingly. But directly or vicariously, it is the intellectuals with full-time jobs who determine the media's policy with regard to ideas, and who have therefore been the effective executors of neo-liberal thought politics.

A process of selection and replacement that began in the sixties and by the eighties was virtually complete gave most of the relevant jobs in front line or back room to men and women with the appropriate convictions and priorities. That they promoted the neo-liberal topics and ideas went without saying, and was publicly obvious and generally noted. Less obviously, but with equal effectiveness, these media intellectuals have been doing what they could to prevent benevolent new thought about 'the nation' or 'Irish society' being publicly discussed.

This was partly because, being the people they were, they were simply not interested in ideas of that kind; they found them distasteful and boring. But accompanying this lack of interest was fear: fear that if such ideas gained currency they would nourish and strengthen the nation, influence policy-makers, and lead to a pro-national agenda which would replace the liberal one. So it was a matter of defending the neo-liberal ascendancy and interests. They have taken particularly stringent measures when the social thought was of the 'synthetic' sort, coherently embracing all the main aspects of the nation's life, for they rightly sensed that this was the most dangerous kind. John Hume, speaking at the MacGill Summer School in Glenties in 1991, testified to their success when he said that summer schools 'fill a gap which has emerged as the media have virtually annihilated serious debate'. Although he exaggerated the role of summer schools, he was right about the 'annihilation', particularly with regard to the serious debate of social thought.

All this I have observed closely and learned, while witnessing the treatment accorded to my own thought and that of Tom Barrington, Ray Crotty and others. By a route leading from naiveté to dismay, and through misunderstanding to insight, I have learned not only that the media intellectuals have been imposing this veto, but also how they do it. I can think of no better way to convey my findings, graphically, than to tell the story of the learning process I have gone through while living the life of a free-thinking intellectual in late-twentieth-century Ireland. However, because my story has much in common with that of other citizens of the Republic who were similarly occupied during the same period, it will do more than convey my findings. It will serve as a paradigm, recognisable to many, of the disorder that some of us particularly, and most of us to some degree, have experienced in these mindless years.

In half a lifetime of thinking and writing about Irish public affairs, my central value, shared with Irish patriots of the past and present, has been the welfare of Ireland. I started, and continued for a time, with certain normative assumptions which I believe I was justified in making, and which anyone engaged in similar work has a right to make.

Thinking and writing, creatively, about the welfare of one's nation means – once the thinking is done – submitting new, relevant discourse for discussion by the nation's thinking and writing members. The discourse, with its burden of new ideas, is about values and applications of values that the thinker believes are relevant to the national welfare. Submitted to his fellows, it is two things simultaneously. Personally and informally, it is a request for discussion, because discussing ideas is the bread of his mental life and he needs to have his ideas discussed in order to check their validity and come nearer the truth. Socially and formally, it is a portfolio of new designs for the nation's intellectual currency, which is in constant need of renewal and re-minting lest it grow thin, worn-out, hackneyed and incapable of inspiring or sustaining a successful national life. The thinker hopes his ideas will enter the currency through a critical public discussion of them in which he participates. His ultimate hope is that, this having happened, his ideas, or most of them, in their original or modified forms, will pass from being current to being realised, culturally and politically, in the nation's life.

Knowing the chances of the game (several of his design ideas may be inept, he will have opponents who are intelligent or powerful or both), he accepts that some of his sketches may be rejected in debate. And again, knowing the chances of the game and what is legitimate and illegitimate in it, he accepts even, in the back of his mind, that all his ideas may fail to make it into the currency – even as the coin of a recognised school or party. Only one thing he does not accept, because he knows it is against the unspoken rules of communal membership and particularly against the norms of the thinking and writing fraternity, and that is that his ideas will not be subjected, with attribution, to public discussion and debate. Or rather, he accepts that rebuff and deprivation only in one specific circumstance, namely, that the values to which his ideas relate, the 'reference values' which show through in them, are not current in his society or in the wider culture to which it belongs: not current values, in short, but obsolete, esoteric or alien ones, and therefore – whatever their intrinsic worth or his bright ideas about them – non-values for his people now.

At the start, too, and for some years, I worked with optimistic assumptions about the specific roles that academics and the mass media would play in the public discussion and sifting of my ideas.

To an extent these assumptions derived from my actual experience, both previous to the mid-sixties and as the sixties finished and the seventies began. I remembered, for example, that, when I was a history student at University College Dublin and had outlined a radically new view of the Irish people in a student magazine, Professor Dudley Edwards, to my astonishment, publicly advised the class to read and discuss it. In 1969, when I had written some newspaper articles and delivered a publicised lecture which together offered new views of the Gaeltacht, of Connacht, and of how to save them, Mícheál Mac Craith, then a lecturer in University College Galway, edited and published this material, on his own initiative, as the pamphlet *Iarchonnacht Began*. Those writings, together with the activism and ideas of groups in Iarchonnacht and Dublin, led first to a debate in the media and in many public oral sessions, with intellectuals from the media, the academy and the nation generally taking part, then to a growing consensus for the new ideas, and finally to actions by public authorities and the language movement to implement most of them (though not the most important one). Almost, in its outcome, a Joe Lee dream scenario! In the sixties the national media were still pluralist, in the sense that, within a general Irish consensus, the newspapers and periodicals differed ideologically and RTE was ideologically a house of many mansions. Consequently, I assumed that in the matter of media intellectuals' promoting discussion of my ideas, or themselves actually discussing them, bias against my thinking in some quarters – resulting in inaction, hostile argument or misrepresentation – would be balanced by favourable bias in other quarters, with active and supportive consequences. I expected, in other words, that the intellectuals in the national media would function, with regard to my new thought, as a representative and facilitating part of a functioning Irish intellectual community.

Those were my assumptions at the start of a period in which I would write five books and eight pamphlets on Irish social matters, two Irish travel books in which some of my general thinking probably showed, and many relevant articles in newspapers and periodicals. My basic position from the start and throughout has been that, in the matter of Ireland, the proper task of Irish intellectuals and policy-makers is to think about the country, and transform it, in the spirit of the Irish Revolution. Consequently, most of the values I have written about or drawn on are to be found in the Revolution and its aim.

With regard to one area, my new thinking on the North, my assumptions about the media intellectuals were disappointed as early as 1971-72, when I was developing in my *Sunday Press* column a new analysis of the Northern problem, a new general formula for solving it, and an application of that: condominium or joint sovereignty. The media intellectuals ignored these ideas. As was to be the case throughout the succeeding years, their eyes were fixed on London, awaiting the 'next British initiative'; and when it came they discussed, and promoted discussion of, the British ideas endlessly. Indeed their irritation and scepticism were palpable when, in 1972, in a jurisdiction where they were not the media masters, the SDLP, after consulting with me, used my analysis and particular proposal in a policy document. But that experience merely dented my assumptions. It was not until the mid-seventies and subsequently, as the national media were ideologically homogenised and the 'intellectual' stratum filled with neo-liberal hacks, that my assumptions, first about the role of the media, then about the intellectual community generally, disintegrated. But it took time for me to register the new state of affairs, to realise that I had bumped against the Counter-Revolution, and to understand procedures and purposes very alien to liberal democracy and liberal pluralism.

When an ideological sect has a monopoly of the national media, it tends inevitably, without need of conscious decision, to prevent or minimise public discussion of those ideas it does not want discussed. Moreover, it can achieve this without preventing – as in the East European media when they were under Communist control – the occasional publication and airing of the unwanted ideas. In Dublin over the past twenty years, the neo-liberals combined the simulation of free public discussion with measures designed to smother unwanted thought. The appearance of free public discussion was created by means of chat shows, vocal studio audiences, phone-ins, letters-to-the-editor pages, panel discussions and similar forums. In each instance access was controlled and apportioned, and the agenda determined and weighted, by backroom *apparatchiks*; the chair (literally or figuratively) was occupied by a person, or persons, who could be relied on to keep discussion ideologically more or less on track, to have the last word, and to rebuke dangerous deviance. At the same time, and fully obvious only to those who were directly affected, measures were taken to prevent the public discussion of unwanted ideas. The measures fell into three categories representing increasing degrees of repression, and could therefore be applied selectively according to the requirements of each case. The first and second degrees were: *silence*, simple or manu-factured – little or no response was made to the new ideas, or little or no action taken to promote discussion of them; and *dismissal* – the ideas were curtly represented as impractical or irrelevant. Both these techniques, which in pluralist circumstances are employed against different sets of ideas from varying stand-points, were now employed by the entire collective of media intellectuals, with their chosen media pets and fronters, against a single target: ideas that neo-liberals were not interested in or feared. Finally, for very threatening ideas whose author pushed them insistently, there was the last resort: *excommunication* – the new ideas were represented as heretical and their author portrayed as a heretic.

Increasingly during the eighties I found this last method being applied to my ideas and to myself. From 1980 to 1984 I was again writing a column in the *Sunday Press*, and from 1983 onwards publishing books that summed up my conclusions since the sixties, my view of present developments, and my proposals for progressive alternatives. At the same time, due to the referendum battles of the eighties and the growing cocksureness of the liberal, revisionist, anti-nationalist band, the system of thought control was tightening. My ideas were being ranked as heretical and I was being classed personally as a heretic, with something like the mental, moral and social connotations that have attached to that concept in medieval Christendom, or to its equivalent, 'dissident', in modern totalitarian regimes. I felt the effect particularly after 1984, when I ceased writing my weekly column, and was therefore without any regular opportunity for clarifying my standpoint or defending myself.

Because of liberalism's traditional support for freedom of ideas, the media intellectuals could not operate openly in terms of 'orthodoxy' and 'heresy'. They achieved the same effect by tacitly substituting the notion of 'current values' (meaning neò-liberal values) for the former, and 'non-current anti-values' for the latter. Because their own values and their applications of them were, they insistently suggested, current among 'all right-thinking people', meaning people mentally and morally like themselves, those were the current (normative) values and as such worth discussing and hammering home at every possible opportunity. But values that did not thus qualify as 'current' were by definition not values at all, but mental aberrations or alien, evil principles. Within this framework, powerfully established by daily media propaganda, I was dealt with by public signals to the effect that my ideas related to values of the latter kind – non-current anti-values; that I was therefore myself an anti-value, and was consequently, as in the Church's rite of solemn words and extinguished candle, ex-communicated – not to be communicated with or commented on publicly, whether by argued reply, respectful discussion or debate. Of course, as with any heretic arraigned by the orthodox, smearing misrepresentation[1] and personal abuse were appropriate, and indeed called for, as displays of virtue and true faith. Needless to say, I am talking about the public sphere. Dublin being Dublin, and the Irish being Irish, personal relations, even with ideologically ruthless opponents, usually remained civilised and were sometimes grimly jocose. But I did occasionally feel my courtesy strained, and I recognised wryly my counterparts, and those of my opponents, in Vaclav Havel's plays about Stalinist Prague.

The excommunicating signals were delivered to the public generally, but took effect primarily among the chief concentration of the faithful, the media-ridden liberal middle class of South Dublin who had developed a symbiotic relationship with the excommunicators, and were often, indeed, their relatives, friends or neighbours. In this tight-knit mass the excommunicating signals from the hacks served both as pastoral guidance and as word to pass on.

The signals were of two distinct kinds, demonstrative and verbal. It was demonstrative, for example, when I was asked to take part in a so-called discussion programme so arranged that the chairperson and the other participants were of one (orthodox) mind on the main issue, and I alone had a different view, so that my odd-man-out position was 'demonstrated' and 'everybody' was heard rejecting both it and me as wrong. This device has become such a cliché of Dublin broadcasting that I mention it merely for the record. It has also ceased to affect me. Twenty years ago RTE used to invite me fairly frequently onto 'discussion programmes' (unlike print journalism, you cannot invite yourself; they do it). During the early eighties it was three or

1. A fairly recent one springs to mind because its hilarious blatancy made me memorise it and quote it frequently for laughs. It came from the RTE broadcaster Andy O'Mahony, chairing a radio discussion, at which I was not present, about my Seamus Heaney monograph which caused such a furore among the right-thinking. Referring to my ideas about what constitutes 'great' poetry, O'Mahony told the nation, 'He wants Paisley or Paisley-like statements.'

four times a year; more recently, once or twice, and I have finally stopped accepting. Why talk to people who are not interested in your ideas but merely in using or demolishing you? I get more interest from the BBC. Another demonstrative device was that a newspaper, say the *Irish Times,* when it had carried an article by me would publish either a shoal of letters attacking me and very few agreeing or reasonably arguing, or else no letters at all. True, in particular instances, that may actually have reflected the post received or not received, but I include it among the media's excommunicating signals on two grounds. First, the published letters often did not reflect the post received: in the past five years I have been sent about a dozen copies of unpublished letters of the supportive kind, or had telephone calls telling me about them, and only once heard of a hostile letter that the paper had not published. Second, the years of liberal occupation of the media had made many people slow to write a letter expressing public support for a dissident thinker; partly for prudential reasons, partly because they believed their letter would not be published. (Instead – often to my chagrin – they wrote to the heretic privately!) One way or the other, or rather, by both means combined, the effect was achieved: the letters page transmitted an appropriate demonstrative signal.

The verbal signals were of two overlapping kinds: negative diagnoses of my mental-moral condition and ideological tags with a negative mental and moral import. It was put around that I was a 'controversial' writer, a term innocuous enough in a pluralist setting, but which means in Dublin in recent years 'not right-thinking'. So widely did words to that effect become current among the right-thinking that, for example, at the last Irish Management Conference in distant Killarney, where I was one of a panel of speakers on 'Ireland, My Ireland', the chairman, an RTE broadcaster, could say in his gracious introduction that my ideas were 'considered by many to be idiosyncratic' but that I always accepted criticism courteously. (In plain terms: my discourse to the audience would be piquantly entertaining, and in the ensuing 'discussion period' their predictable demolition job – anything else or less being highly unlikely – would be accepted graciously by the speaker!) A Dublin friend told me recently, with concern, that her Dublin 4 circle regarded me (and Raymond Crotty, as it happens) as 'eccentric', which, of course, means 'not to be listened to', let alone argued with. Now clearly, to be controversial, idiosyncratic and eccentric in the eyes of the *bien-pensants* has – its entertainment value apart – more than mental implications: there is a hint of the disreputable. But the moral dubiousness lightly suggested by such signals was rendered more explicit by the recurrent epithet 'provocative', with its connotations of 'frivolous': DF 'always has something provocative to say' or, more crudely even if jocosely, 'does it to draw attention to himself'. And the opprobrium was rendered explicit and, indeed, solemn as with snuffed-out candle, by describing me in the national media over the years as a 'Provo', 'conservative' or 'reactionary' – terms that in the liberals' Manichean worldview denote all who, by disagreeing with them, are mentally and morally unspeakable (*to* or *about*; I never cease to wonder at the rich, subliminal expressiveness of colloquial English).

Finally, there has been a negative component in the excommunicatory process which fits into neither of the categories I have mentioned. Though often prominent in public attention in the past twenty-five years, I have never been interviewed, as a person, in any mass audience medium: in any of those series or slots where an interviewer tries to reveal to the public the person behind a public name. (I was the subject of such an interview only once, in the popular music magazine *Hot Press*.) The necessity of this 'negative exposure' for the excommunicatory process is obvious. Revelation of the many-faceted person, of the actual, dangerously persuasive man, would overthrow the arduous work of caricaturing him so as to prevent his ideas being discussed. I blush at the implied compliment: one not paid, during my lifetime, to even the most demonised politician!

I take 'demonised' from colloquial Dublin speech about what the media - the respectable media, not the gutter press of which we have little or too much - do to Irish politicians, and some others, whom they want to annihilate. 'Media witch-hunts' is another vernacular term. In an attempt, by similar analogy, to portray the reality we have been experiencing, I have referred to the neo-liberals as a 'quasi-church' or sect, and to their sharpest method of preventing discussion as creating heretics against a background of simulated orthodoxy. And behold, the vernacular is catching up on me: I have just been invited, from distant Sligo, to take part in a special event at the 1993 Yeats Summer School: a three-man panel entitled 'Heretics'. After years when the word seemed lost for good to history books or mere analogy, it has been whipped back to life by our secularist liberals and names a category of living Irishmen.

But my own case apart for a moment, it is interesting to pause and duly note the technique of this liberal interdict on free discussion that has figured so largely in the life of the Republic in recent years. The reasonable, even if not rational, criterion for 'ideas not suitable for general discussion' - namely, that their reference values are not current in the given society or in the larger culture it forms part of - has been hijacked and applied by a powerful sect which substitutes itself for Irish society, and its thought police for the free critical interchange of thinking and writing people. The decision as to which ideas refer to non-current values is taken by factional decree, not by democratic judgement. Note, too, how, in extreme cases such as my own, the clamping down on discussion of the unwanted ideas falls of necessity into disvaluing the person who is offering them, by calling him disqualifying names. The person in question is controversial, eccentric, provocative, conservative, reactionary, republican, fundamentalist, etcetera, and therefore (it is implied) his or her discourse, whatever it may say, and even if it concerns widely current values such as democracy, national independence, self-respect or media pluralism, is not discussible 'by right-thinking people', that is, not discussible at all.

Of course, in the ranks of the Dublin media during these mindless years, humanity, mental or moral, did not entirely die. As in Havel's Prague and other similar places in our time, there survived, despite the weedings-out and replacements, some men and rarer women who recognised the intellectual philistinism surrounding them and suffered it tight-lipped for the daily crust. Journalists who still believed in the principles their seniors had once taught them, intellectuals who remained aware of the media intellectual's proper role, they could not get discussed what the system did not want discussed, but they told me plainly or reticently of their unhappiness and, when they could, did little services, such as advising me how to go about getting a letter or article published, or seeing to its publication themselves.

But to return to the point. In my case as in others the name-calling took effect, and not only among the media-ridden. On persons less believing but streetwise, it had an effect akin to that of intimidatory police harassment. Just as newspaper readers who might have written supportively learned to think twice about it, so too people who might otherwise have publicly discussed my ideas felt 'warned off' doing so, lest a similar fate, a similar outcasting from the ranks of the right-thinking, befall them. For logically, whoever publicly discusses (that is, takes seriously, is courteous towards) odd, eccentric, reactionary, nationalist persons or their ideas must himself be a sneaking eccentric, *provocateur*, oddball, reactionary, Provo, fundamentalist, or at least arouse suspicion that he is. In short, for one reason or another, some brave souls excepted, the name-calling technique succeeded widely.

It succeeded even where it should least have succeeded, among the academics of the human sciences. Ensconced in their citadels of academic freedom, where it is their professional duty to sift through, discuss and assess the values and ideas thrown up by the society that pays them, they succumbed, with rare and brave exceptions.[2] Thus, for example, to cite only three fairly recent examples which I made it my business to notice and write to the respective authors about, you had Hilary Tovey and Damian Hannan discussing the current problem of Irish identity in *Why Irish?* (1989), Brendan Bradshaw writing his important critique of historical revisionism in *Irish Historical Studies* (Winter 1989), and Roy Foster, in his well-publicised lecture to the Cultural Traditions Group in Coleraine, in 1990, calling for a 'new' Irish nationalism as distinct from the traditional kind, all without any discussion of what I had published on those subjects in the seventies and eighties. Given, moreover, that I had pioneered the three themes, and that the colleaguely obligation in question applies particularly when one is writing in the wake of the pioneer, these failures to discuss my contributions were all the more conspicuous. But I mention them only as examples, and by no means suggest that they are more noteworthy than other, similar instances that preceded or followed them and which I shrugged off. Moreover, in fairness to Brendan Bradshaw, he did notice one of my two relevant essays in a footnote, and he did explain to me subsequently that he wanted to direct his argument, in professional historians' terms, at professional colleagues. To have invoked my support, he wrote, 'would have run the risk of *argumenta ad hominem*' being used against him. Precisely, my very point; quite regardless of the substance and merit of what I had written, and, for what it matters, as a Modern History MA to boot! Moreover, since 'support' has been mentioned, let me make clear that my primary expectation, as with any serious thinker, has never been to have my 'support invoked' – though anyone is welcome to do that – but to have my tentative effort at truth processed through critical discussion to argued acceptance or rejection as coin

2. Lest I overlook anyone, I hesitate to mention names, but the late John Whyte, Declan Kiberd, Joe Lee, Gearóid Ó Tuathaigh, Terence Brown and William J. Smyth must be mentioned.

of the intellectual currency.

One result of the effective action by the thought police, working through the national media, has been that my actual values, views and proposals, during nearly thirty years of writing, have been unknown, or very hazily known, in large sections of the intellectual community and to many journalists. And this, in turn, has had two consequences. Right-thinking or at least untainted persons, who were aware or unaware that I had argued something fifteen or twenty years ago – for example, that the communal division in the North is ethnic, or that the conflict there is not *sui generis* but has parallels throughout the world – could come out with it, all those years later, as their own clean discovery, without anyone mentioning, in print at least, its tainted origins. This sort of thing has on the whole given me pleasure, though of the wry sort. What has not pleased me is when, in such instances, some book reviewer or commentator welcomes this 'advance towards a truer view of things', quite unaware that it was available two decades previously. Then I feel that I laboured and wrote in vain, and I grieve at being thrust by fate into such a malfunctioning, discouraging and sluggish intellectual environment.

To be precise, I grieve at that, but in the specific matter of my new thinking on the North, I don't feel that I laboured and wrote entirely in vain. Unpredictable as a bolt from the blue, the great Long Kesh hunger strike dented the rule of mindlessness. By increasing the support for Sinn Féin, it created an 'unwelcome political necessity', namely, to stop Sinn Féin by producing a revamped Northern policy. The politicians hastened to organise the New Ireland Forum, the only major arena for the discussion of new ideas that the Republic has seen since the early seventies; and through the Forum and its report, my new thinking on the North shaped what has been since then – however lazily and surreptitiously pursued – the policy of the Irish government on a Northern settlement. What I had in mind when I said 'in vain' was the routine public discourse in the Republic, both on the North and on some other matters: it lumbers on as if these issues had not been radically rethought fifteen or twenty years ago.

I have traced the working out of my excommunication process up to the present so that its paradigm might be complete and this fact evident: that declaring a thinker a heretic not only prevents public discussion of his particular ideas but thereby, if his thought is of some substance, damages the entire intellectual economy. The reader can imagine what results when such instances are multiplied, as they have been in the mindless years.

Naturally, it was painful for me that my ideas were not being sifted, thrashed out and returned to me for argued rejoinder. But more painful still, and a much greater cause of spiritual malnutrition and loneliness, was the absence in my environment of *any* sustained discussion of any substantial new idea – discussion such as I might have got my teeth into. I felt this all the more keenly after my return to Dublin from the West in 1982. South Conamara and Galway city were not rich in publications or media that dealt in ideas, because they were not rich in publishers or media. But in speculative conversation – the 'foreign language' of the Conamara Gaeltacht helped in this – they were a free zone, a Wild West, where inheritors of two thousand years of untamed thinking, fugitives from Dublin's Ireland and rebels against its dogmatism, commingled gleefully. Back in Dublin again, I missed that, and from the great array of media and publishers got nothing that adequately compensated for it, let alone surpassed it. As the eighties advanced I grew accustomed to telling visitors from Continental Europe, 'This is a great city for theatre and music. There are lots of exhibition openings, book launches, the women dress well and are beautiful, and there's intense political talk. But it has no intellectual life, so don't expect any.' In journals such as the *Crane Bag* and *Studies* some small new ideas occasionally surfaced, but the journals did not promote discussion of them and no one else did. Hand-me-down and imported notions about man, the world, psychology, the consumer society, feminism, socialism and so on passed through the media, but apart from some debate about the nature of feminism these large themes evinced no disputation. The only aspect of human life that was publicly discussed with some interesting insights was its beginnings in the womb! Apart from the topics – contraception, divorce, abortion, Charlie Haughey – the ideas most talked about in the media were old ethnic and religious ideas that had been knocked about in Ireland for centuries with a respite of about fifty years in the present century. There was the cluster *Irishness: awfulness of (in life); excellence of, with reservations (in art); right and wrong kinds of; what is?* dating, respectively, from Giraldus Cambrensis, the Statute of Kilkenny and Shakespeare's *Henry V. Awfulness of (in life)* was thrashed out in all the media in many contexts: Irish mothers, Irish men, Irish lovers, Irish sex, Irish society, Irish nationalism, Irish politicians, Irish Constitution, Irish religion, Irish clergy. The last two overlapped with another cluster dating from the Reformation: *Roman Catholicism: harm it does; wrongness of.* And this, in turn, figured in various contexts: Catholic morality, authoritarianism and bishops, Catholic guilt, intolerance, marriage and so on. Probably the liveliest intellectual discussion, in which Dublin participated with Derry, Belfast and London, was that about writers, texts and critics of English Irish literature and the intersections of all these with politics and ideology – the kind of thing that W.J. McCormack wrote the book about. But it was a discussion that fed off itself endlessly, never broaching big questions or producing an idea that threatened your worldview or pointing towards action of any consequence. For that you had to rely on chance encounters with adherents of New Age or Alternative thinking, who constituted an intellectual underworld remote from the media and the academy.

When I realised, about eight years ago, that the thought police were managing to put my ideas in quarantine, I began to fight back, both for my ideas' sake and because I was aware that many people valued them. Their letters and phone calls told me so. In pubs and in hotel lounges, sometimes in supermarkets, they sidled up to me, shyly, to engage in conversation. I suppose the most satisfying thing to be told as a writer is that you have written something that for long lay unsaid in an unknown person's thoughts because he or she was unable to put words on it. And I doubt there is anything more shockingly beautiful and burdening, for man or woman, than to be thanked by an unknown letter-writer, or voice on the telephone, for existing. I have frequently experienced the former, and, on a few occasions, the latter. I was made aware that a sort of samizdat was operating: people were photocopying some of my articles and distributing them widely to friends and strangers. Because I was fed with all this, fed with the passion of many Irish men and women – passion of thanks for a spokesman or articulator, passion of frustration and anger at their values being ridiculed – I understand the passion and zealotry of my neo-liberal opponents. I understand why friends who consort with the sect ask me, 'Why do so many people hate you?' This has been, and is, a civil war for the mind, soul and body of Ireland. But my point is that the very humbling flow of appreciation which came my way made me feel responsible for more than my own ideas, and made me try all the harder to break through the barriers raised against them.

Since it had become clear to me, as to everyone, that the neo-liberals were anti-nationalists, revisionists, provincialists, I concluded that the main reason for their opposition to my thinking was that it smacked of nationalism. More to the point, I believed that their growing success in preventing discussion of my ideas was due to their effective smearing of them and me as 'nationalist', in one way or another. The media intellectuals and their assorted helpers had many ways available to them. Not only had they made 'nationalist' itself a pejorative term, but they had lumbered Irish nationalism with a series of interlocking pejorative associations, particularly 'traditional' – a favourite boo word – but also

'outdated', 'diehard', 'Catholic Gaelic', 'sectarian', 'Provo', 'anti-
English', 'anti-Protestant', 'Brits Out', 'violence' and 'mindlessness'. By these means they categorised Irish nationalism clearly
as a 'non-current anti-value', the dead opposite of liberal right-
thinking. Consequently, my fighting back consisted of trying to
convey to the thinking public, in spite of them, that my thought
was *not* Irish nationalism as represented by the propaganda; was,
broadly speaking, in the Irish nationalist tradition, but was not
'traditional nationalism'; dealt with values and ideas that decent,
sensible people throughout Europe, or in other postcolonial
countries, were concerned with; was not malign, but beneficent,
not old hat but fresh, new and very relevant.

With this in mind, in 1985 I published a book whose title,
Beyond Nationalism, was meant to speak for itself. Its contents made
clear that I considered European nationalism a failure; saw its
ideology as belonging to a modern, liberal capitalist worldview
that was a misguiding illusion; and for my own part had been
trying, since the early sixties, to achieve in place of this illusion
a realistic image of human life now. In 1986, in the Introduction
to *Nice People and Rednecks*, I described my more immediate purpose since the sixties as to replace existing Irish orthodoxies with
new, realistic thought, and I defined our primary need as bringing about 'in as many people as possible . . . an eruption of new
thought and speech about the situations and problems which con-
front them now, and of action in the light of that'. I found this
explaining and reiteration of what I had been about, and was
about, embarrassing and distasteful, but judged that the circumstances made it simply necessary. In that same year, 1986,
three young men, Dónal de Búitléir, Dónal Ó Brolcháin and John
Roden, had published an article advocating important changes
in our political institutions. After some months of the usual silence
had ensued, I wrote to them, and to five others who over the
years had produced new thought on the government of Ireland,
and proposed that we set up a club, the Constitution Club, for

monthly, public discussion of 'new thinking on Irish government'. The five others were Tom Barrington and Ray Crotty (both of whom had made prolific contributions), John Robb, Roy Johnston and Mícheál Ó Flanagáin. Of John Robb, Northern Protestant, I had written in the *Irish Times* in 1972, when his pamphlet *New Ireland: Sell-Out or Opportunity?* appeared, 'There is no other man whose stance in Irish affairs so closely resembles my own.' In my letter to them all, I wrote:

> We all believe that the question of how the Irish state is constituted is a matter of the first importance, particularly now. But we have found it very hard to arouse public interest or discussion on the matter – to initiate the movement from ideas to action. Some of us are tempted, perhaps, to give up the effort.

They agreed to my proposal and, in a joint letter to the newspapers, we announced the club and our intention to provide 'a centre and a forum for new thinking on government'. In November 1986 the Constitution Club began its monthly public meetings in Buswell's Hotel, Dublin. They continued, with a membership of about sixty and an average attendance of around thirty, for two years.

But in all of this and in similar fighting-back tactics, I was under a misapprehension. I had not grasped the real reason why my thinking and writing seemed so threatening to the thought police that they were determined to divert attention from it and exclude it from discussion.

When I reflect on the principal values that have motivated me in my writing on Irish affairs, the first that springs to mind is *true representation in language*. In other words, when the mind is using language rather than some other symbolic system, good intellectual work. This involves investigation of realities; reflection on them so as to perceive them clearly and without prejudice; respect for the meaning of words; and the careful matching of those meanings with reality as perceived, so as to present clear ideas and images.

Closely related to this is *true representation of communal realities*, that is to say, of communities. I value communities as the form which man, the social animal, takes naturally and for his health, when living in groups. These groups, each of them sharing a common life, are conscious of themselves and of neighbouring groups. When unhindered by external force or psychic damage, they are self-governing and self-maintaining. Their self-government is not only political but also intellectual and cultural: they shape their worldview, language and life autonomously. They are also, in so far as they know of each other and act justly, mutually recognising – this recognition being their mutual 'permission' to each other to get on with being and ruling themselves.

Nations are communities of a special kind and status inasmuch as they are both conscious of themselves and recognised more or less by others, as primary social units of mankind, representative embodiments of man. They are what has been called, since history began, 'the peoples of the world' – constituting the human world directly, without mediation.

The true representation of communal realities is effected by a combination of language – for example, naming the communities by their chosen names – with other symbolic systems or institutions: political, ideological, constitutional, monetary, etcetera. The net effect is to represent the world's communities to the world and to each other as communities in being, that is, with the communal attributes of recognition, self-government and so on. This is the good way for man to be, his way of being – provided that the persons who make up the communities are also recognising each other (through religions, constitutions, laws and customs) as the self-governing beings they are, under God and their communal authority. What exists then is a *world community of communities and persons*, the ultimate value I have consciously worked for.

Clearly, then, *humanity,* collective and personal, is a value for me. Human being, as distinct from half-being or vicarious existence; *human being celebrating itself* – singing, as single being, its particular song and, as multiple being, its chorus. All the opposites of provinciality – which is the predominant condition of modern man, and of Irish man to an extreme degree.

My deep affinity with the Irish Revolution must be obvious. The Revolution was powered by and inseparably connected with the greatest intellectual movement of modern Irish history, and it was conscious of that. Douglas Hyde, in his evidence to the Royal Commission on University Education in 1902, described the Gaelic League as 'the intellectual movement'. When Ireland lost her language, she 'lost her intellectuality'; restoring the language meant restoring Ireland's mind. The league's aim was 'to make Ireland intellectually interesting for the Irish', to turn their minds from looking elsewhere to thinking about Ireland. The league was in fact the core 'intellectual movement' around which a much wider movement of intellect, art and politics developed. For Pearse, in 1913, the league was 'the beginning of the Irish Revolution'; he and his comrades 'went to school' to it. MacDonagh, speaking to his courtmartial judges about the Easter Proclamation, said: 'From minds alive with Ireland's vivid intellect it sprang...' That Irish intellect, accumulated over thirty years and more, gave independent Ireland the programme that established it among the nations into the 1940s. The Dublin in which Hyde, Griffith and Yeats, Connolly and Pearse, AE, MacDonagh, MacNeill and others thought and wrote; where article answered article, journal, journal, and thinkers met regularly in houses to discuss; where the thinking was sifted, honed and developed by this interaction, and its subject was all human and superhuman reality – that Dublin remains forever to inspire, challenge, or shame us.

It inspired and challenged me. So did the aim of the Revolution: to win, by way of recognition by the British, 'permission'

to bring about a self-governing, self-shaping, self-maintaining
Ireland. Born into a state and society that were committed to
the fuller achievement of that aim, I was glad of that commitment because I found the aim worth working for. It was a matter of ending the abnormality, the ill-being, of a national
community (my own) existing as a province, and restoring it to
its natural, well state. And I was at one with Daniel Corkery who,
in 1931, in *Synge and Anglo-Irish Literature*, had reaffirmed the proven strategy of the Gaelic League by putting a normalised national mind at the basis of the enterprise:

> It was ... Lessing who did a man's part in giving the German
> nation confidence in itself and in its star ... Ireland's present con-
> dition is incomparably worse than Germany's ever was; and not
> one but a whole battalion of Lessings would be needed to establish
> a normal state of mind among us. One can but predicate not one
> Lessing nor a succession of them, but rather a succession of na-
> tionalistic movements, rising and falling, each dissolving into a
> period of reaction, of provincialism, yet each for all that leaving
> the nation a little more sturdy, a little more normal, a little less
> provincial than before.

Consequently, *Irish nationalism* has been a value for me.
Nationalism, as a modern phenomenon, has meant and can mean
various things; but Irish nationalism in the twentieth century has
meant essentially, and meant for me, making the Irish nation intellectually and culturally self-shaping, democratically self-governing,
and economically self-maintaining; that is to say, a nation doing
its normal business of being, well. More specifically, after 1922,
it has meant working on that project in four fifths of Ireland and
winning British recognition of the nation in the other fifth also,
so that the entire nation could be included in the normalising
process.

Obviously, a project conceived in such general terms at a particular point in history can subsequently be interpreted in various
ways without affecting its essence, only its accidents. In the light

of new experience and insights, terms such as 'nation', 'democracy', 'self-government' can be given more precise or fuller meanings; 'intellectually and culturally self-shaping' can be refined and expanded. Tacit elements of nationalist practice, such as pluralism, can be named and made explicit values. According as this rethinking and deduction from principles proceeds, there will be consequences for the application of the project, for its practicalities, its method. The net result, if the intellectual work is well done, will be to facilitate the success of the enterprise by making its application fit the facts.

With that worldview, those underlying values, and the mental attitude just described, I addressed my mind instinctively to the well-being of the Irish nation. So it seems true to say that the central values directly underlying my writing on Irish affairs have been *intellect, humanity,* and the *Irish nation,* and that the other values which came into play were derivatives of these.

Not surprisingly, then, I took the meaning of 'the Irish nation' seriously. Being a nation, it is a community, and a community is self-conscious. So I was led to define it as those who count themselves members of the Irish nation – who say their nationality is Irish and nothing else – rather than as the inhabitants of Ireland, which was and is the 'traditional' nationalist view.[3] A corollary I welcomed was the need to recognise verbally the principal other community in Ireland, the *Ulster British*, which by its own clear testimony does not count itself part of the Irish nation. I was glad to do this because the recognition of our British

3. It has been the 'traditional' view only since the mid-nineteenth century. Wolfe Tone, for example, took that view not of the actual, only of the potential nation, and he believed that 'the Protestants' would not willingly form part of it. Two sentences after his famous words about 'uniting Catholic, Protestant and Dissenter', he adds: 'Of the Protestants I despaired from the outset, for obvious reasons. Already in possession, by an unjust monopoly, of the whole power and patronage of the country, it was not to be supposed they would ever concur in measures, the tendency of which must be to lessen their influence as a party, how much soever the nation might gain.' *Ergo,* they would be forced to join it.

fellow countrymen for what they are is a necessary part of coming to terms with them about the government of Ireland. Then again, since a nation, as we all know, contains other communities, I had to diverge from Irish nationalist discourse and the Irish Constitution in their view of the nation as a community of families and persons. It is a community of communities which contains families and persons – and therefore, of course, a community of all three.

In the light of this, and of a world in which nations are patently interdependent, the central theme of the nationalist project was clarified. 'Making the nation democratically self-governing' means, in its external aspect, controlling the nation's interdependent relationships through domestic strength and appropriate alliances. In its internal aspect it means making the community as a whole, and the communities it contains, democratically self-governing; ending not only London's empire over Dublin, but the empire of Tricoloured Dublin Castle over the communities of Dublin and the rest of Ireland; in other words, annulling the internal aspect of Irish provinciality (or non-communality), as the political break from London was intended to end its external aspect. This requires, along with central government, *regional, urban and district self-government* as, say, in Denmark or Austria, and *dispersal of the national mass media* as, for example, in Germany or Switzerland.

I value all this, and have advocated it, not only out of justice to the nation's communities, but as an imperative for releasing the latent creative energies that are needed if we are to end our recurrent crises of emigration or unemployment by producing a satisfactory economy. Our inherited, imperial system of government was for obvious reasons designed not to release enterprise but to discourage it, and to induce dependency. While we retain it – even worse, increase its sway, as we have done – its effects will remain the same. Moreover, multi-centred self-government, if it is accompanied as today it must be by dispersal of at least the national broadcasting media, enables and encourages the full, multiform expression of the nation's intellectual and cultural potential. *Intellectual and cultural diversity* is a pleasure and value in itself.

It follows that there is a contradiction between our inherited state, whether viewed as 'imperial British state', 'modern state' or 'nation-state', and the aim of Irish nationalism. Up to the Revolution and beyond, Irish nationalism conceived its project in uncritical imitation of standard European nationalism, which created the modern state simultaneously with the 'nation-state' and used the former, an imperial construct, to forge the latter fictional entity. Fictional, because a powerfully disseminated myth declared the nation-state – in effect, a metropolitan power centre ruling a malleable mass of 'individuals' wrenched from disembowelled communities – to be 'the nation', when it was in fact the nation's coffin or, in some cases, the mass grave of several annihilated nations. In short, to make our nation truly self-governing, as Irish nationalism intended, we need a state fitted to its shape and functioning as its servant, not its crucifier.

To say that is to say no more than many European regionalists, and critics of the modern state or nation-state, have been saying for years. But I confess that, in my own case, a more radical commitment lies behind it. In opposition to the modernity of modern states pretending to be nations, I have valued, as my ultimate Utopia, another modernity or, if need be, postmodernity. I mean the kind of society towards which the anti-state forms of socialism – whether communitarian or syndicalist – aspired from the beginning of the nineteenth century. They were anti-state in the sense of being opposed to the state as it was typically presented, the 'modern state' functioning as a ruling agency above and outside the society of mutually relating, producing and consuming people; they were not anti-state in the sense of excluding national or international political organisation. In Ireland this tradition was represented strongly by Thompson and Connolly, more moderately by AE, and definitively by the idea of a 'cooperative commonwealth' in which the thought of all three joined; on the Continent, principally by Proudhon and what flowed from him. In its end goal, though not in its method of reaching it, it was at one with Marx's vision of the world that would follow the withering away of (modern) states. But I have allowed this, my ultimate Utopia, to show little in my writing on the grounds that, in an environment hostile to communitarian thinking, movement in that direction might best be secured by reticence about where I hoped it might terminate. (Moreover, a Utopia, being a Nowhere, is explicitly a land reserved for hoping; its value is that of a receding beacon drawing travellers forward on a good road.)

After the state our largest social organisation is the Catholic Church. My adherence to the democratic principle, and to the right of communities to be communities rather than self-conscious, dependent masses, led me to campaign for the application of both principles, insofar as practicable, to the Church's parish, diocesan and national structure. That was in the wake of the Second Vatican Council, when there was much talk of the Church as 'the people of God' and of creating representative bodies of the laity. *Church assembly*, as I called it for short, would involve the redrawing of diocesan boundaries so that they would correspond to real, present-day communities; the election of parish councils, diocesan councils and a national church assembly from among the general body of the faithful; and the allocation to them of various administrative and consultative functions. This, in conjunction with the reassertion of independent Irish intellect and a multicommunal civil democracy, is my understanding of a people risen, speaking and acting, at last, after centuries of repression by outsiders and of themselves by themselves.

It is apposite here to speak of *pluralism*. The word has been brought into general currency by the Dublin media, beginning with the *Irish Times*, and has been given an odd, tendentious meaning. It is used to signify a condition of Irish public life and institutions that does not now exist, but which it is desirable to bring about; a condition in which the remaining imprints of religious values are removed and neo-liberal, secularist values shape the nation: in effect, therefore, a single-ethos civil society characterised by secularism and 'non-Catholicism'. The fact that this false and – given the word itself – absurd meaning has remained virtually unchallenged is an indication of the present dire state of Irish intellectual life. The same applies to the unchallenged acceptance of the notion that pluralism does not now exist in the Republic. Pluralism means, simply, the institutional recognition, within an agreed consensus or accepted norm, of cultural and ideological diversity. Consequently, it neither means nor presupposes secularism, and has no special connection with religious matters. From the Roman Empire to medieval France, the Ottoman Empire, and Europe in our own day, it has been implemented in varying degrees within a variety of ideological frameworks, including the democratic Catholic liberalism of the Irish Constitution. The word was borrowed from philosophy where its opposite is monism, from the Greek *monos*, single. Applied to the public sphere, its logical contrary, which is never articulated, might be called 'singularism'.

The Republic of Ireland is run on a mixture of singularist and pluralist principles. We have what is called throughout the world 'political pluralism', a number of recognised political parties rather than a single one. The Tricolour is symbolically pluralist with respect to the Irish and the Ulster British. The educational system inherited from the British was pluralist and we have made it more so by the addition of multidenominational schools. There is a weak administrative pluralism in the local government system and a degree of linguistic pluralism both in the special administrative arrangements for Gaelic-speaking areas and in the legal status and public use of Gaelic and English. Until the clause recognising the major religious groups by name was removed from the Constitution in 1971, we had fully explicit – now it is implicit – religious pluralism. Constitutionally, there is pluralism of thought and its expression, but in fact ideas that run counter to the neo-liberal/anti-nationalist dogmas are repressed or marginalised in the public domain. The national media, once pluralist, have been singularist for nearly twenty years. Unlike the UK, we have no pluralism in law or in policing.

Valuing, as I do, noneconomic social diversity and the recognition of communities, I naturally value pluralism highly. I have urged its implementation, with a levelled playing pitch, in the sphere of ideas; I have also urged great increases in its application to communities in the Republic and to the two ethnic communities in the Six Counties and, in the contentious matter of divorce, a year in which those who want divorce can apply for it, followed by the introduction of two kinds of marriage contract, dissoluble and indissoluble, to cater for the two opposed views of marriage.

Peace in Ireland, as well as between the Irish and British, has always been a logical corollary of the success of Irish nationalism, and therefore one of its implicit aims. The war in the North these past twenty-two years has damaged the quality of Irish life severely and cast a shadow over our personal lives and over Ireland. Peace, so that we can get on with our lives and political struggles free of that shadow, has long been a national priority that we have not treated as such. (Our failure to do so has made us maintainers of the 'violence' that we simultaneously 'condemn'.) Peace requires that Britain and the Ulster British recognise the Irish nation in the North as well as in the Republic, and that the Irish recognise the Ulster British.

The most just way of doing this would be a united, independent Ireland which would give effective political recognition to the Ulster British; that would be full justice both for the Irish nation and for the Ulster British as a community sharing part of Ireland with it. But the cessation of armed hostilities can be brought about by something less than the full recognition of Irish national rights, and peace is a more urgent need than full justice. Consequently, we should be working publicly, resolutely, and by every possible means to secure such recognition of the Six-County Irish as would suffice for peace. In particular we should be using for this purpose the right to make proposals for the better government of Northern Ireland and have them seriously considered by the British, that was given us by the Anglo-Irish Agreement – and which is the agreement's only useful content.

The Gaeltacht, in the strict sense of the communities which spoke Gaelic, was a pearl beyond price for the Irish people. It has been lost, virtually, through the failure of the Irish state to give it regional and district self-government. That would have created a Gaeltacht political class which, with its vested interest in maintaining Gaelic as the vernacular within the region, would have taken the necessary legal and other measures to do so. We would then have continued to have what we will soon not have: our ancient language spoken, and being developed, by a living and working part of Ireland, and available to us, in this condition, for whatever use we should decide to make of it.

Irish nationalism was profoundly right in maintaining that, to be a healthy, functioning nation we must have *a language of our own*. A community *is* a community fundamentally through the bonding agency of a discourse peculiar to itself that has been developed out of its experience and way of seeing the world, a discourse laden with coded references to both. A community, and all the more a national community, that speaks (and thinks) of its affairs and the world in terms borrowed from the experience and worldview of others and not reworked by itself, is a maimed community, with weak bonding and consequently with a weak collective dynamic and ability to perform. Moreover, as Irish history amply shows, a community in that condition cannot assimilate foreign communities that lodge within it, whereas a community with a language of its own can do that.

In order to have a language of its own, a nation depends on

the leadership and work of its intellectual class in kneading a worldview and discourse out of the distinct national experience and location in the world and history. Hence the inseparable connection between creative intellectual work and national well-being, and the rightness of Douglas Hyde in describing the Gaelic League as 'the intellectual movement'. He was also right in believing that it would be easier for us to have a language of our own if we spoke our own tongue.

Irish nationalism as we inherited it from the nineteenth century and the Revolution valued and respected *Irish Catholicism*; that was one of its ideological characteristics. More precisely, its attitude to Catholicism – James Connolly is a striking example – was one of critical respect for what was simultaneously the religion of most nationalists, a major and distinguishing element of Irish culture, and the greatest civilising force in the country. On those last two grounds, and as a Catholic myself, I have maintained over the years, despite some dismay at how the Church is being led, a critical respect for Irish Catholicism generally. (For that aspect of it that might be called 'popular religion', I feel affection and humble reverence.) I was much impressed by something Joe Lee wrote on the matter ten years ago when he was discussing the present condition of the Irish Church:

> The conclusion that 'what the Church is experiencing is less a crisis of faith than a crisis of culture' may be a shade optimistic in a society where faith and culture are so intimately intertwined. It is precisely this close connection that makes the civic culture so vulnerable to a sudden decline in the role of institutional religion. However confined the role religion may play in shaping standards of public morality, however long it may have been domesticated in Ireland as 'convention rather than conviction', the very shallowness of 'traditional' civic culture leaves religion as the main bulwark between reasonably civilised social control and the untrammelled predatory instincts of sectoral and individual selfishness. If religion no longer fulfils its historic civilising mission

as a substitute for internalised values of civic responsibility, the consequences for society no less than for the institutional church are potentially disruptive . . .

Living in Dublin during the years since that was written, I have had ample occasion to observe the truth of it. The value of Irish Catholicism becomes palpably evident as its influence on lives diminishes and nothing emerges to fill the vacuum but security personnel and paraphernalia, more police and vigilantes, more courts and prisons, state allowances for unmarried mothers and deserted spouses, rape crisis centres, campaigns promoting condoms, the great and increasing sums of money which pay for all this, and windy, impotent moralising.

Democracy, by which we mean liberal democracy, is a method of government that operates according to explicit rules and tacit understandings. The willing acceptance of those rules and understandings is *the democratic mentality*. Socrates gave an extreme example of it when, condemned to death in ancient Athens, he refused an opportunity to escape on the grounds that, by becoming a citizen, he had accepted the Athenian democracy (such as it was) and would do so to the end. Most Irish people, though not called on to display it in such an extreme manner, have a similar, sporting attitude to the Irish democratic process. Because I share this attitude and consider it a value, I have defended on occasion some of the tacit understandings of our democracy. For example, that if you are on the minority side on some issue, you accept with good grace that democracy operates by majority decisions. So you accept, whatever your reservations or disgruntlement, that a majority decision is a fair decision of your community, and that the way to victory for your own convictions is to persuade (not browbeat) a sufficient number of your opponents; which involves, for a start, respecting them, their different convictions, and their right to hold them. Furthermore, that when citizens are elected to the Dáil they are both entitled and expected

to bring their personal beliefs to bear on their legislative decisions, and that it is undemocratic to suggest they are not entitled
to do this; and worse to wage a privileged propaganda war against
their doing so, because they are Catholics and you have a long
alien tradition of anti-Catholic prejudice to draw on.

'Irish identity', by which is meant *Irish national identity*, has
become a fashionable theme of media chat and literary joustings.
This reflects the severe crisis of identity in which we find ourselves
since we abandoned the satisfactory national self-definition that
we lived and worked with during the first half of the century,
and put Muzak in its place. But reflecting the crisis does not solve
it. A satisfactory national identity is of a different order from
'national identity' as a speculative theme. It is a possession, an
experienced and lived-with reality, something created, taken for
granted and used. It is a reasonably clear, accurate and lovable
image of the nation, which its members or the great majority
of them carry with them, subconsciously, in their daily lives.
Created by the words and symbolic acts of thinkers, poets, politicians and journalists, interacting with the people in the pursuit
of national goals, it is the distinguishing, bonding principle that
enables the nation to be, to act cooperatively, and to achieve.
Clearly it requires a more substantial content than 'those who
count themselves members of the Irish nation and of none other'.
It must include some positive linguistic, religious, constitutional,
territorial or kinship characteristic, or rather, a combination of
such features that distinguishes 'this people' from its neighbours,
and bonds them, in a manner yielding self-esteem. Every successful nation has it. Without it, a nation is as the Irish are now:
unbonded and in bits, not pulling together, paralysed, unable to
solve problems – some doing well for themselves, many
marginalised, even ejected. Those who say, truthfully, that 'I and
my friends don't see any need for an agreed image of Irish identity, we get on very well without it' do not alter the objective
need, merely shrug at it.

Fundamentally it is a matter of our intellectual and political leadership saying yes, heartily, to what distinguishes us from our neighbours, historically and now (our freedom struggle and our Catholicism), or of their creating a new national distinctiveness to which we can say yes heartily, or of their combining both those actions. While they do none of these things we flounder – not all of us individually, but the nation collectively – and we lose that respect of the world which we enjoyed during the first half of this century and for decades before that.

While they do none of those things, we have no real presence in *Europe,* let alone a respected place there. Only when *we* have regained a satisfactory image of ourselves will we be visible again to most Europeans as a contemporary European nation, rather than as hands reaching out from behind England for Brussels doles, or as bombs exploding on television screens. We will become visible again not only by figuring to the mental eye in Munich, Rome, Zagreb and Amsterdam, but because we will have the self-confidence to associate politically, emotionally and intellec-tually with our likes in Europe, with the other small European nations, and to make common cause with them. We will encourage and support them when they strike out for freedom, or must defend their freedom, not stand by dumbly, denying our history, as we did when the Baltic nations were struggling free of Russia and when Croatia was attacked by Serbia. Then, in Berlin, Rome, Vienna and Budapest, an Irishman will find his punt listed with the Greek drachma and the Portuguese escudo in the *bureaux de change* – as he does not now, deservedly!

I think that is a pretty accurate summary of the values that have motivated me in my writing on Irish affairs, and of my ideas about those values. What have you there, taking it as a lump? A related assortment of values and ideas such as many thoughtful people in Ireland and, *mutatis mutandis,* in other liberal democratic or postcolonial nations, are, or might well be, concerned with. More specifically? Contemporary Irish nationalist thought. More explicitly? Intellect directed critically and creatively to the present condition and future welfare of the Irish nation. More concisely? Intellect directed benevolently, critically and correctively to the condition of the Irish nation. Or, to use Joe Lee's terms, benevolent 'social thought' that is synthetic to boot.

That is the real reason why the neo-liberals have feared my thinking: because it was thought of that kind. The fact that it was new Irish nationalist thought, not the traditional kind, not what they were caricaturing as Irish nationalism, but fresh thought of relevance to every man, woman and child in Ireland today, was irrelevant. When I was trying to convey that message, hoping I might thereby bypass the thought police, I was missing the point. No matter how I presented it, that set of values and ideas remained intellect directed benevolently, critically and correctively to the condition of the Irish nation, and that, whether it came from me, or from whomsoever, in whatever form, was out.

I became aware of this as I considered how the thought of Tom Barrington and Raymond Crotty was treated, and as I identified the common character of our thinking. 'Nationalism' was not a word that sprang to mind when Tom Barrington and his work were mentioned. If Crotty's thought, because of its critical opposition to the EC and its emphasis on our colonised history, had a whiff of the nationalist stereotype, it was the merest whiff; its largely economic reference and content put it clearly in a different category. But there could be no doubt that their thought, as mine, was benevolent social thought; was intellect directed benevolently, critically and correctively to the condition of the nation; was in the tradition and spirit of the Irish Revolution; and was, like my thought, excluded from public discussion.

Clearly Tom Barrington's central value is the nation, understood as a community of communities, families and persons. He has devoted much of his intellectual energy to arguing for an Irish state that would serve this nation better than the existing one does. (For practical reasons he deals only with the six-sevenths of the nation that is in the Republic, but open-endedly, in a manner applicable to the other seventh, and indeed to the Ulster British, should they wish.) He wants a multicentred administration, coherently organised, which would cater effectively for the citizens' practical needs and promote their human development. Their collective power, now concentrated in a few hands in Dublin, would be diffused throughout Dublin and the counties. Their democracy, now nominal, would be replaced by a real democracy of the multi-communal people, actually governing themselves. Barrington is the leading voice among the many voices which, since Charles McCarthy's *The Distasteful Challenge* in 1968, have called in vain for a decentralised Irish democracy in place of an imperial state that has the weakest local authorities in Europe and, apart from Britain, the fewest. We have 1 per 32,000 inhabitants, compared with 1 per 20,400 in the Netherlands, 1 per 17,600 in Denmark, 1 per 3,300 in Austria and 1 per 3,200 in Luxembourg. Our local authorities handle 13 per cent of total government expenditure, as against 70 per cent in Denmark. Barrington's writings and lectures, since his Addendum to the Devlin Commission Report in 1969, have been marked by the decorum of a former civil servant who was for many years Director of the Institute of Public Administration. Both for this reason, and because he has not urged his case noisily, in the media or otherwise, it has been possible to prevent the public discussion of his ideas without recourse to measures of the third degree, but simply by applying silence (of both kinds) and dismissal (as 'impractical').

For all the public attention that was paid to it, his first book, *From Big Government to Local Government* (1975), might not have appeared. In 1978, when he had retired from the Institute and I was lecturing in Politics at University College Galway, I prevailed on the college to invite him to give a year's lectures, which he did. He developed these lectures into his book *The Irish Administrative System*, which was published in March 1980 and followed by a month's silence. Because I did not want to see this second book go the way of the first, I wrote an article in the *Sunday Press* which the newspaper entitled 'The Great, Sad Silence'. It began:

> The two most important books published in Ireland in the last ten years are *From Big Government to Local Government* (1975) and *The Irish Administrative System* (March 1980). The first of them was, generally speaking, not reviewed and hardly talked about, and the second is suffering a similar fate.

It was a book, I wrote, which 'suggests what must be done to make [our administrative system] into an instrument serving our humanity, our practical needs, and our democratic will. I said "our humanity" and that may have shocked. But the central theme of this book is the high, humanistic purpose of public administration, properly understood.' To illustrate this, I quoted from Barrington's last chapter:

> Over the centuries, an objective of government has been the transition from personal rule, dynastic rule, class rule to, one may hope, rule in the general interest . . . One of the objectives of a Christian, democratic society is a wide sense of personal and group responsibility. On the other hand, the drift of our society is towards a concentration of responsibility in public offices. Is it possible to devise means by which, as new duties and responsibilities come in at one end of the governmental machine, at least a corresponding number are discharged to individuals, groupings and localities at the other?
>
> Is the professional task of public administration, in this sense, to accept readily new responsibilities, to intervene effectively, and to move on, leaving orderly, healthy and autonomous activities behind, just as a doctor intervenes temporarily to get his patient back on his feet, or to deliver a new child into the world? In this sense, the task of public administration may not be so much to do things, as to discover and release dynamics within the society that will lead to spontaneous creativity.

In other words: to set the Irish people free to realise themselves in action.

Six days later, in the *Irish Times*, James Downey, an assistant editor, reviewed *The Irish Administrative System:*

> This book crowns the career of T.J. Barrington . . . It is difficult to write about it except in superlatives. It is one of the most significant works ever published in Ireland on any topic. It is comprehensive, weighty, profound, authoritative and humane. It is, in the best sense, thought-provokingly political.

But to judge by the amount of public or academic discussion it subsequently generated, it might as well have been André Kehoe's *Christian Contradictions and the World Revolution,* published in Dublin in 1991. This 500-page book, an articulate, passionately critical survey of the present world system and of Ireland's place and role in it, by an Irishman who has worked for years in UNESCO, the World Bank and similar bodies, was not even reviewed, either in the national media or in any academic journal. (This defies language. How often does an Irishman write, or an Irish publisher publish, a book of such scope? In no other European country of Ireland's size is such treatment of such a book conceivable. Oh, I know: the present writer, Ray Crotty and the Sinn Féin president, Gerry Adams, are quoted favourably in a few pages!)

In 1991 Tom Barrington was called out of retirement to chair an official advisory committee on the structure of subnational government. Unwelcome political necessity had compelled the majority government party, Fianna Fáil, to accede to the demand of its small coalition partner, the Progressive Democrats, that something be done about the matter. The advisory committee recommended a watered-down version of Barrington's ideas and its proposals were adopted as policy by the government. They have survived, at Labour's urging, in the lengthy programme of the new Fianna Fáil-Labour administration. Both as proposals and as policy, the same absence of media discussion has attended them as attended Barrington's writings and ideas, that is, they are debarred from attaining public currency. Consequently, while a little, nothing decisive, has been done to implement them, it is unlikely that much more will be done. Certainly, in the lifetime of the present government, nothing approaching what Barrington and his school have recommended will be realised. Current, Dublin 4 ideas – about contraceptives, divorce, abortion, interpretative centres – will take precedence over the noncurrent idea of a decentralised Irish democracy. The vested interests opposing it are strong and, in the silence surrounding it, will prevail.

Raymond Crotty's central concern and motivation has been our inability, over a long period, to provide a satisfactory living in Ireland for more than half our people. Applying his mind to the Irish nation as an economic entity, he has diagnosed it as suffering, along with over a hundred other nations, from the enduring and maiming effects of capitalist colonial undevelopment. In *Ireland in Crisis* (1985), he sketches the economic history of the world in three erudite and intellectually thrilling essays – an enterprise unequalled in scope on the Irish intellectual scene since Yeats's *A Vision*. His analysis has led him to view the present holders of power and wealth in Ireland as beneficiaries and administrators of the Tudor Conquest, and the existing state, therefore, as the 'enemy of the nation'. To become the nation's friend and servant – to release us from the *karma* of undevelopment – the state must reorganise its finances so that the prices of labour, land and capital 'are made to reflect the economic realities [of Ireland] rather than the privilege created by capitalist colonialism'; so that the expenditure on bureaucracy is greatly reduced; and so that a weekly national dividend is paid to every resident citizen. Those are the merest bones of a detailed argument. Crotty, as Ireland and the EC know, has been a prominent activist. Consequently, to prevent his thought being taken seriously and publicly discussed, it has been necessary to take measures of the third degree – to brand him a 'crank', 'eccentric', 'lunatic' and, with a snobbish touch, 'culchie'.

In coming to the realisation that my own thought, and that of Barrington and Crotty, were essentially of the same genre, I was helped by an unusual article from an unexpected source. Appearing in *Magill* magazine in July 1987, it was unusual because it discussed contemporary Irish social thought, and unexpected because it came from Fintan O'Toole, a prominent neo-liberal journalist and intellectual. Under the heading 'Ploughing a Lonely Furrow', O'Toole reported on 'the increasing isolation of nationalist intellectuals' and summarised the thinking of those whom he so described. These included, besides Barrington, Crotty and myself, Anthony Coughlan, Mícheál Ó Loingsigh, Michael McKeown and Proinsias Mac Aonghusa.[4] Apart from the acuteness of the writer in identifying us as intellectuals of similar ilk, he was acute in the ambiguous manner in which he defined our kind of thinking. After listing books by Coughlan, McKeown, Barrington, Crotty and myself, he wrote that they had 'all attempted, in sometimes widely different ways, to prove that there is life beyond the death of nationalism'. In other words, for O'Toole, our thinking was both 'nationalist' and 'beyond nationalism'. For me it was intellect directed benevolently, critically and correctively to the condition of the Irish nation – as Irish nationalist thought had always been. I will call it 'national' thought. That qualifier provides a bridge between the thought of revolutionary nationalism and the kind of thinking which, whether explicitly or not, works in that tradition today.

I realised a second thing as the mists of obfuscation cleared. For me as for many, Dublin 4 ideology, that new and strange

4. In the matter of applying intellect to the welfare of Ireland during the mindless years, I have already mentioned some valued colleagues, and have now via Fintan O'Toole named others. My complete list would also include the late Dáithí Ó Conaill, Ruairí Ó Brádaigh, Conor Cruise O'Brien (for a time), John Hume (occasionally), Bernadette McAliskey, Gerry Adams, Robert Ballagh, Declan Kiberd, Seamus Deane, Ivor Browne and Mary Ellen Synon.

phenomenon, had appeared through the years now as consumerist liberalism, anti-nationalism, revisionism or secularism, now as anti-Catholicism, provincialism or absolutist individualism. According to the circumstances or the observer, one could imagine that one or other of these isms was the central or driving force. Now, as I grasped that 'national thought' was the kind of thought the media intellectuals did not want discussed – except, as in the unusual case of O'Toole's article, to point out its 'increasing isolation' and futility – I realised that the defining core of this neo-liberalism, which gave rise to all the rest as logical epiphenomena, was fundamentalist individualism – the polar opposite of national thought. Liberalism, individualism – I should have seen it earlier, but I had not.

Garret FitzGerald, and he is a good authority, sees it clearly. As I began writing this essay in the late summer of 1992, FitzGerald, in his weekly column in the *Irish Times*, was providing, with the help of the letters page and the paper's readership, a living illustration of much that I have been saying. To begin with, on 8 August, he put forward an idea, a 'moral dilemma', that is not publicly discussed in Ireland. A fortnight later, 22 August, under the heading 'Ignoring our Moral Dilemma will not Make it Disappear', he expressed extreme disappointment at the virtual absence of discussion of his idea, whether in the *Irish Times* or otherwise. Arising from his original piece, the newspaper had printed an article and a few letters to the editor; but only one letter – and another from a private correspondent – had dealt, he complained, with his proffered idea. Most of the correspondence had been about a reference he had made to contraception, and specifically about the meaning of 'natural' contraception. FitzGerald speculated on the reason why his main idea had been avoided.

His first explanation was that a reluctance to discuss ideas is an Irish characteristic. 'As a people', he writes, 'we are, I think, resistant to – indeed somewhat afraid of – ideas. Certainly, it has

been my experience over many years that attempts either in lectures or articles to put forward ideas evoke remarkably little
response.' There is 'a strong Irish preference for the concrete as
against the conceptual'. This explanation does not hold water.
It can hardly stand against the evidence of the first four decades
of this century in Ireland. In those years, not only were concepts
of various kinds publicly discussed and vigorously debated, but
many people took ideas about Ireland so seriously that they were
prepared to kill and die for them. Moreover, even today it is simply
not the case that 'ideas are not discussed'. Concepts, general ideas,
are rarely discussed. The new social ideas produced in the last
twenty-odd years have not been processed by the intellectual community. But if the idea which FitzGerald put forward were about
Irish Catholicism: harm it does, English Irish literature, the rewriting
of Irish history, the life of the unborn or feminism, it would stand
a good chance of being discussed, not only in the *Irish Times*,
but elsewhere in the media and perhaps in public seminars or
summer schools. And, in the event, his article did give rise, though
inadvertently, to some lively discussion of an idea: that of 'natural'
contraception!

At all events, further into the article, FitzGerald implicitly aban-
dons the 'national characteristic' argument by suggesting another
explanation. In common with the rest of the English-speaking
world, he believes, we are unconsciously influenced by Anglo-
American analytical philosophy, which 'abandoned the world of
ideas for the study of language'. This has particularly been the
case since the decline in influence, from the sixties onward, of
scholastic philosophy, which took ideas seriously. The trouble
here is that, even if, as FitzGerald believes, we have been influenced by analytical philosophy, that would still not explain why,
even when he had repeated his 'moral dilemma' idea in the second article and made a song and dance about it, he could raise
no discussion of it in a newspaper in which some ideas are certainly discussed. As if to illustrate this, over the following three

weeks his reference to analytical philosophy led to a stream of letters discussing the pros and cons of that philosophical method!

So what is this idea which, despite its sponsor's two efforts, raised no discussion in the pages of the *Irish Times*? In his first article FitzGerald wrote: 'In the media there is more often than not an uncritical acceptance of "liberal" positions, the sometimes dubious intellectual basis of which is seldom questioned.' Instead, he argued, we have an arid slagging match between a dogmatic 'liberal' individualism and ecclesiastical dogmatism. He continued:

> Behind this dialogue of the deaf there lies a deep division of intellectual approach that is rarely addressed directly by either side: the fundamental dichotomy between modern individualism and the whole concept of a social morality . . . Our community is at present deeply pervaded by the powerful influence of a modern individualism that is preaching, without effective intellectual challenge, both a superficially attractive hedonistic message and at another level a self-serving economic materialism. And unhappily the moral vacuum that has increasingly been left by a disorientated institutional Church is not being filled by any alternative force. Issues of fundamental importance to our society are consequently going largely by default because they are almost never seriously addressed in any forum. The situation does little credit to the intellectual vigour of our society and is certainly not conducive to its moral health.

That, the lack of a much-needed, persuasive social morality, and the question of what form it might take is the theme that FitzGerald put forward in his first article, reiterated in his second, and which was not discussed in the *Irish Times*, or anywhere else for that matter.

Its author failed to explain this refusal of discussion because he failed to take into account the particular nature of his idea and the circumstances in which he was asking for public response to it. Leave aside the numbed surprise of Dublin liberals at finding him, Garret FitzGerald, their one-time darling, uttering such strictures and such thoughts. The *Irish Times* has been the pioneer and *Pravda* of the 'hedonistic, economically self-serving individualism' that so alarms him. Now, in its pages, he invited discussion of a 'social morality for our community' that would fill the vacuum left by the Catholic Church and successfully challenge and restrain that individualism. Thus, he invited from his readers discussion of a subject which they had been trained, for more than twenty years, to regard as taboo. The very notion of social morality is associated in their minds not only with the Catholic Church and its 'common good', but also with Irish nationalism – its 'common good', 'your duty to Ireland', 'Ireland calls on her children', and all that. For more than twenty years they have seen these forces, and particularly the twin social moralities established by them, depicted as inimical to the values of right-thinking (liberal, individualist, secularist) people. They are aware that the moral community of both those moralities, the community in which they were established and for which they provided a moral consensus, was the Irish nation. Consequently, the notion of re-establishing a 'social morality for our community' which would have persuasive force – even the notion of publicly discussing this – conjures up a banished but haunting spectre. Taken seriously, it would mean directing intellect benevolently, critically and correctively to the condition of the nation in respect of its social morality. It would mean national thought.

One need not search further for the reason why FitzGerald failed to raise discussion of his idea. It is surely an illuminating instance of the state of affairs I have been discussing, and of how its discouragement of national thought, and its exclusion of such thought from public debate have become an in-built, self-operating feature of our public communications system.

Having begun with Joe Lee as historian, it remains to fit him into the picture as a national thinker whose radical thought, despite the fame of his book, has received the standard treatment. His book has been widely talked about as history, which it mainly is. More precisely, that part of its narrative that shows Irish economic performance since independence as a grave if relative failure has been widely referred to in the media and in Doheny & Nesbitt's public house. But in the book's final, summing-up chapter, the nationally thinking side of Lee comes to utterance as a critique of the intellectual habits of the state – in his words, the 'policy-makers'. He argues that the Irish state, in the collective person of these policy-makers, has been serving the nation badly by its ignorance of how to learn from foreign example or from history. It has chosen the wrong kind of example: England mainly, which is unlike Ireland in size and has been suffering a long decline, instead of small, successful European nations. It has also been unaware that learning from foreign example means, not duplication, but judicious adaptation to domestic circumstances. As to learning from history, Lee urges the Irish state, at least now and in this matter, to do so by literally changing its mind. Living in Dublin, the hub of the nation if not of the universe, I have noted the noisy silence that has entombed these observations and admonishments, the daily discourse of media and politicians proceeding as if Lee had never uttered that argued critique of the state's intellectual method over the past seventy years.

The national thought we have been sampling and examining is not only the polar opposite of absolutist individualism. Because of the changes and measures it calls for and implies, it is a very real threat to the power, privilege and agenda of the well-to-do adherents of that creed who are concentrated in Ireland's wealthiest district at the centre of a very centralised national communications system which they control, and a very centralised state which they are on the way to controlling. For these adherents of rootless, untrammelled individualism, the overriding priorities are the hegemony of their ideology in the public domain, the maintenance and expansion of their individual rights and, in aid of both, the continuing provincial dependency of the Irish state, economy and intellectual currency. The nation weak, as it is, the state precisely as it is, the national media as they are, suit them. A state sharing out governing power and media facilities among the nation's communities, decolonising the financial and economic system, and substituting conversation with, say, Austria and Denmark for its intellectual hotline to London would undermine their special position. The nation rendered strong and active by such measures, by a state under its intellectual and democratic control, by a functioning intellectual community, a satisfactory national identity, a renewed and persuasive social morality, a language of its own – the nation thus normalised and enabled would brush them aside, put them in their due place, pursue not their priorities but those the national thinkers say the nation should be pursuing: British recognition for our 600,000 nationally unrecognised, peace and the additional national strengthening that would entail, dignity and security for the 3 million Irish men, women and children marginalised by forced emigration or unemployment, and the enhanced national performance that would ensue; a multicentred Irish democracy. As Wolfe Tone said of an earlier sect that occupied a somewhat similar 'special position', it is 'not to be supposed they would ever concur in measures, the certain tendency of which must be to lessen their influence as a party, how much soever the nation might gain'. That being the case now as then, it was inevitable that the Dublin liberals, having won hegemony in the national media in the sixties and monopoly control in the seventies, should use this power, liberally, to prevent national thought gaining currency.

Understanding all this, both as history and as continuing fact, is valuable in itself; but it is valuable also because of what it explains. It must be obvious that the state of affairs I have been exposing explains the paralysis and drift of the Irish state and nation during the past twenty years. Our policy-makers, deprived of new national ideas in politically usable – processed, current – form, have been obliged to continue drawing on a currency of outworn notions and failed ideas, most of them made to fit a different and declining body politic. Our intellectuals, deprived of a functioning intellectual community by their failure to form one, have been unable to deliver to the nation, directly and through its policy-makers, the services that are a national intelligentsia's social role. National thinkers who tried to deliver individually were prevented by a breakaway section of anti-national ideologues who attained and held predominance, and by another section that was indoctrinated or intimidated by these. What else could come of this disorder but drift, paralysis and a national performance at home and abroad falling far beneath potential?

However, the most valuable thing to emerge from this exploration is neither our recent intellectual history nor the explanation of our paralysis that it provides. It is the concept 'national thought', defined as intellect directed benevolently, critically and correctively to the condition of the Irish nation. On the one hand, this designates the kind of thought that promotes, if it is allowed to, the nation's welfare. On the other, it enables us retrospectively to cut a swathe through Irish intellectual history and to clarify the line in which today's national thinkers stand, regardless of whether they are intentionally nationalist or neo-nationalist, or whether the national thinking that preceded theirs was done in an Ireland nominally independent or under British rule. Cutting that swathe, it emerges that national thought is the only continuous Irish intellectual tradition of the last two centuries and, as a way of tackling the world with thought, our particular inherited way of doing that. As such, it invites our curious attention.

It began when Irishmen contemplating the condition of the Irish nation saw radical disorder, analysed it, thought of actions by the nation or by part of it that would correct it, willed that these actions be taken, and urged accordingly. As a kind of thinking, it belongs to the category that Marx distinguished and advocated in his 'Theses on Feuerbach' when, criticising earlier philosophers, both idealist and materialist, he wrote, 'The philosophers have only *interpreted* the world differently; the point is, to change it.'

Perhaps, before the original or Gaelic Irish nation was destroyed in the seventeenth century, some national thought occurred with reference to that nation; but if it did, we have no record of it. In so far as it survives in prose or verse, the thought of the last, stricken generations of Gaelic intellectuals, in Ireland and on the Continent, was merely elegiac or historical, angry or messianic. Thought that had the qualities of national thought, except that its object was unrealistically perceived, was directed to the 'Irish nation' of the Protestant Ascendancy. It occurred along that well-known line stretching from Molyneux through Swift and Berkeley's *The Querist* to the 'patriots' and Volunteers of Grattan's time. In the 1770s and 1780s the notion that the majority of the Irish might conceivably some day belong to the Irish nation infiltrated a few colonial 'patriot' minds. But it was not until the 1790s and the bold intellectual breakthrough of the United Irishmen, and of Wolfe Tone in particular, that national thought, realistically grounded, was conceived and born. Naturally, then as later, perceptions of the nation's disordered condition varied somewhat from mind to mind, and even in the same mind at different times; but disorder, both moral and (in the broadest connotation) constitutional, was always there, and supplied the impetus. In Tone's pamphlet on behalf of the Catholics, at the points where he contemplates the condition of his nominally independent nation, we glimpse the new thinking in embryo:

> The present state of Ireland is such as is not to be paralleled in history or fable. Inferior to no country in Europe in the gifts of nature; blest with a temperate sky and a fruitful soil; intersected by many great rivers; indented round her whole coast with the noblest harbours; abounding with all the necessary materials for unlimited commerce; teeming with inexhaustible mines of the most useful metals; filled by 4,000,000 of an ingenious and a gallant people, with bold hearts and ardent spirits; posted right in the

track between Europe and America, within 50 miles of England,
300 of France; yet, with all these great advantages, unheard of
and unknown, without pride, or power, or name; without
ambassadors, army or navy; not of half the consequence in the
empire of which she has the honour to make a part, with the
single county of York, or the loyal and well regulated town of
Birmingham.

In the course of the 1790s Tone gave national thought its enduring
ground by representing the modern Irish nation realistically. Partly
he did this by identifying himself and the United Irishmen,
explicitly with 'the Irish people' during the 'six centuries of
oppression and slavery [that] have passed in melancholy succession over our fathers' heads and our own' so that 'our name has
been forgotten among the nations'. Effectively, the Irish nation
that he bequeathed was located throughout the island, was the
continuation and successor of the Gaelic Irish nation as the butter-
fly is of the caterpillar, was conscious of that and open to all who,
like Tone, shared that sense of it and chose it. This new nation
of the United Irishmen – which they saw as including most of,
and potentially all, the inhabitants of Ireland – was for O'Connell
and the Young Irelanders an assumed fact.

Since those beginnings, national thought has retained, besides
its defining characteristics – the United Irish concept of the nation, the perception of national disorder, and a general eye to
the nation's welfare – six other noteworthy characteristics:

1   It is critical of the existing state. If the state is Irish, as in Tone's
     day or the present Republic, it identifies the ways in which
     it is failing to belong fully to the nation and to serve its well-
     being and potential. If foreign, as in the North, it denies its
     right to rule the Irish nation or any part of it.
2   It denies the right of a privileged sect to possess the state and
     the best pulpits and thereby to lord it over the nation.
3   It highlights the needs of the most deprived sections
     (Catholics, tenant-farmers, slum-dwellers, or today, the

nationally unrecognised, the economically marginalised) and presses state and nation to make their needs the nation's priorities.

4   It has the freedom of all persons, within the context of the common good, as its ultimate aim.

5   It diagnoses the nation's disordered condition as a lack of normal, healthy being and action, caused by external and internal factors and offensive to nature and justice.

6   It perceives in self-government the means of overcoming the disorder.

What is the self-government of a nation? How is a self-governing Irish nation to be achieved? These have been the two questions at the core of Irish national thought. During most of its history it accepted, by and large, the successive answers of classical European nationalism. First, self-government is a political matter, and it is achieved by having a parliament and a state apparatus in Dublin, with jurisdiction over the entire island. Later, when a nation was perceived to be not merely a political but a human community, self-government was seen to have several interdependent aspects; consequently, political autonomy, to be really that, must be accompanied by other autonomies – intellectual sovereignty, cultural authenticity, economic self-maintenance; and the way to achieve the lot is by having a parliament and a state apparatus in Dublin, with jurisdiction over the entire national territory, and committed to pursuing the other prerequisites. There were a few dissenting voices. Connolly said yes to all that, except that the nation is its workers, and their organisations must replace the state and thus ensure the self-government of their class and nation. Hyde said, first, intellectual sovereignty. Yeats said: art can liberate the nation. Horace Plunkett and AE said, the spirit and practice of cooperation will make a free and prosperous people. Today's national thinkers, facing the same two questions, also dissent – having had seventy years to learn from. No longer accepting the stock nationalist answers, they offer fresh thoughts on what national self-government means and on how a reasonably self-governing Ireland can be brought about.

Viewed in this historical perspective, the frustration of the last twenty-odd years is not alarming. Irish national thought has passed through longer periods of frustration and been used in the end. Meanwhile the thinking has moral, practical and self-serving justification: moral, because it is a labour of love; practical, because it moves with the times so as to be always suitable for immediate use; self-serving, because the vitality and high performance of his country is in the thinker's own interest. There is also – as Raymond Crotty has shown and as I have hinted in this essay – something new to be done that does not depend for its efficacy on Dublin media intellectuals or policy-makers.

Consider that national thought is our inherited way of tackling the world with thought, and that it has been efficacious, through the action it has generated in Ireland and the influence of that action, in changing the world considerably. In the twentieth century – to go no further back – it has inspired Irish political and cultural action that gave heart to many stateless European nations, made most of Ireland independent, began the break-up of the second British Empire, restructured the British Commonwealth, and named a street in Teheran after Bobby Sands. It enabled English Irish literature to become a presence in world literature, and inspired the men and women who conducted the largest Christian missionary enterprise in Irish history – extending from west Africa to China and Peru. Beside this, set the following quotation from a Thomas Davis Lecture by Seán Ó Tuama broadcast in 1969; his subject was 'The Gaelic League in the Future'.

As a people, we have few ideas of our own; our model, in most cases, is still the English (or sometimes the American) model. In business, science, engineering, architecture, medicine, industry, law, home-making, agriculture, education, politics and administration – from economic planning to PAYE, from town planning to traffic laws – the vast bulk of our thinking is derivative. One doubts if we have added anything of real importance to sociological or theological, philosophic or aesthetic thought.

What that last sentence means, in effect, is that, while the action and literary creation generated by our national thought have impinged on the world at large, the thought itself – our characteristic, well-proven way of tackling the world intellectually – has not. That is almost as true today as it was in 1969, or in 1972 when the lecture was printed in *The Gaelic League Idea* edited by Ó Tuama. Even Irish music has achieved an outreach which our ideas (in so far as we have ideas that can be called ours) have not approached.

The reason is simple. Until recently, apart from a few thinkers in the revolutionary period (mainly Connolly, AE and Yeats), all our thinking and writing about the disordered condition of our nation – about the politics, economics, ethics, linguistics, psychology, ontology, sociology and theology of it – have been done exclusively in particular, Ireland-related terms; not in particular and general terms simultaneously, or in general terms primarily. We have not done with our contemporary Irish data what Fanon and Memmi did with their contemporary Algerian and Tunisian data when they used those immediate experiences of colonisation to contribute to the world's understanding of colonisation as such, especially its psychological aspects. To have done that, we would have needed to find a concept, or concepts, of our disordered condition that grasped and treated it as an instance – our local instance – of a widespread or general condition of man. During the past twenty years or so, something approaching this has been done with our history; for example, to remain with colonisation, the historical colonisation of Ireland has been viewed and presented as an instance of European colonisation generally, and some deductions about colonisation generally have been drawn from this. But I am talking about the conceptualisation in generic terms not of our history or its episodes, but of our present, still clearly disordered condition.

Obviously such a conceptualisation would enable us to contribute from our experience to the thought and self-awareness of the contemporary world. More, it would enable our national thinking to do what it has failed to do – generate world-changing action, not only as hitherto by Irish people, but by others also, both to their advantage and to ours. But these rewards, however valuable, are not the fundamental argument for generalising our perception of our particular condition. It is a matter, in the first place, of doing our national thinking well; better because more realistically than when we thought about the disordered condition of our nation in isolation from the condition of all other nations and of contemporary mankind – as if ours were a unique case. If it is not, as I believe it is not, then this has been a serious misapprehension which it is high time we corrected. That we will be rewarded for our truer grasp of the Irish condition by an increased influence and efficacy of our national thought is important; but it is no more than the reward that follows, from thinking realistically about a human reality.

How can we perceive our national condition as an instance of a more general disorder? What manner of seeing, what concept, fills the bill? Two candidates have appeared and they make the matter concrete. Ray Crotty identifies our disorder as the *economic and political* condition of 'undevelopment', resulting from the impact of individualist capitalist colonialism on a society that was communally organised; and he reckons that we share undevelopment with 137 other nations that have had the same, maiming experience. His elaborate theory manages to embrace the different forms of undevelopment that obtain in Ireland and, say, India. The capitalist colonialism that Crotty refers to is the external kind; he does not deal with the internal colonialism-imperialism that capitalist metropolises practised, and still practise, within their respective nation-states. With that and its collaborator, provincialism, in mind, I have identified our disorder as the many-faceted *human* condition of 'provinciality', caused by epistemological, psychological and material factors operating in Ireland and the world now, and making provinciality, in differing degrees, the typical or normal condition (radically abnormal condition!) of contemporary mankind (see pages 64–71). I recommend both conceptions to all who ponder creatively on the present condition of Ireland in the world.

'Undevelopment' is a more useful concept than 'postcolonial condition', if indeed the latter concept really exists. Crotty tells us exactly what undevelopment means, and we can see its occurrence in Ireland and many other nations, whereas those writers – and they are many – who discourse on 'postcolonialism' have not made clear whether there is a definable social condition that might be termed 'postcoloniality', and if so, what its characteristics are. Because Crotty's diagnosis provides startling illumination, I hope that he himself, and others with him, will pursue and develop it. However, for several reasons provinciality comes closer to what I think of as the lever by which our national thought might lift the world.

'Provinciality' (whose opposite is 'communality') designates, not just the material aspects of our present condition but its totality – its intellectual, cultural, psychological, economic, political, even theological dimensions, all at once. It designates the present condition of Ireland and of the majority of mankind as one which, regardless of how it was brought about in different histories, is being caused to continue in existence by present, contingent, and therefore superable factors. Thus 'provinciality' opens the way to a practical, contemporary humanism. Shortly after my book that first dealt with it (*Beyond Nationalism: The Struggle against Provinciality in the Modern World*) appeared, in 1985, I had some slight but impressive evidence of the concept's range of relevance. The book, I should explain, extracts its generalised account of provinciality mainly from contemporary Ireland. In Minneapolis a woman who was to interview me on radio remarked, after she had read a few pages, 'You are describing Minnesota in relation to New York.' Later, a friend in Zagreb to whom I had sent a copy rang to say, 'You know, this stuff you have about provinciality is our situation in Croatia', and invited me to a conference. But finally, I see it as a good key to open the world for us because we are provided in Ireland, in everything from high finance to aesthetics,[5] with such an extreme example of the genre. It is uncommon to find a politically independent country in which to 'escape from the provinces' to the capital is not to lessen one's involvement in provinciality but possibly – when one thinks of some lively, 'peripheral' parts of Ireland – to increase it!

Having said that, what I would most like is that Crotty's 138-nation undevelopment could somehow be fitted into provinciality as a species or variant of its economic and political dimension – perhaps as the specific, economically and politically provincial, condition that has been brought about, historically, by external capitalist colonialism, but is maintained in existence by the general provincialising factors that make our world a hierarchy of provinces. If that were possible, it would be neat; but Crotty may consider the condition that results from external capitalist colonialism too *sui generis* for inclusion in the broader concept.

One way or the other, my point is that, while the blockage persists in Dublin, we have this matter of the generic approach to our disorder to think about, discuss in private, and work on. It is not, as I hope I have shown, a matter of thought or theory for its own sake. For Ireland to be self-governing, we need a deprovincialised, deimperialised world, and it makes good sense that our thinking should contribute to that by helping to alienate

5. Patrick Kavanagh was making a comment on provincial aesthetics – as well as the provincial mentality generally – when he wrote that the provincial 'does not trust what his eye sees until he has heard what the metropolis – towards which his eyes are turned – has to say on the subject'. In some unpublished lectures, Ivor Browne has defined Ireland as a 'dependency culture', in its internal as well as its external aspects. This comes close to 'provinciality', except that Browne does not identify 'dependency culture' as a condition that, in varying degrees, is typical of contemporary mankind.

people everywhere from the world as it is structured now. Since the insights we will then be coming up with will be for discussion out there in the world, we can suitably publish them out there – or even in Belfast where it all began! Tiocfaidh ár lá.

DUBLIN, AUGUST 1992–JANUARY 1993

INDEX

state paternalism, 34–5
Station Island (Heaney), 133, 142, 147, 160–1, 166
Stephens, James, 25
Stevens, Wallace, 149, 161, 169, 170
  Heaney on, 172–3, 174
Studies, 235
summer schools, 222
Sunday Business Post, 193, 207
Sunday Press, 101, 104, 108, 109, 225, 227, 256
Sunningdale Agreement, 109
Sweden, 179
Sweeney Astray (Heaney), 133, 140
Swift, Jonathan, 267
Switzerland, 99, 244
syndicalism, 33, 43, 48
  synthetic, 30–1
Synon, Mary Ellen, 259n

Taylor, Alice, 152
technology
  small-scale use, 71
television, influence of, 5
Thatcher, Margaret, 110, 116, 119, 178–9, 196
Theosophical Society, 40
theosophy, 40–1, 43–5
  and Christianity, 46–7
Thomas Davis lectures, 217, 270–1
Thompson, William, 24, 27, 28, 31, 46, 182, 245
  influence of, 16–17
  socialism of, 9–15
  view of modern state, 47
  view of women, 49
tithe war, 16
Tone, Theobald Wolfe, 243n, 265, 267–8
Tovey, Hilary, 233
trade unionism, 16–17, 36, 63
  and cooperatives, 17
  Irish membership, 25–6
  lack of development, 50

'one big union', 30–1, 43
  and republicanism, 33–4
  and socialism, 13–14, 26–32, 48
Trades Union Congress (TUC), 17
Translations (Friel), 3

Ulster British, 82, 107–8, 112, 121
  decline in power, 142
  development of term, 102
  history of, 84–5, 93–4
  recognised as community, 243–4
  and Six-County Irish, 248–9
  in united Ireland, 128
Ulster Defence Association (UDA), 105, 143
Ulster Defence Regiment (UDR), 127
Ulster Volunteer Force (UVF), 143
'undevelopment', 272–3, 274
unemployment, 59, 204
unionism, 34, 85, 94, 201; *see also* Ulster British
  and Anglo-Irish Agreement, 122–3
  Britishness of, 106–9
  in New Ireland Forum Report, 113–16
united Ireland, 96, 107–8, 110, 248
  federation, 80, 104–5, 108, 124
  in New Ireland Forum Report, 115–16, 124
United Irishman, 106
United Irishmen, 267, 268
United Nations Organisation, 74, 82
United States, 19, 30–1, 47, 65, 66, 75, 82
  Fennell tour cancelled, 203
  Heaney's reputation in, 130–1, 147, 151, 154, 158–66
  influence on Ireland, 62
  Irish-Americans, 76, 197, 202, 211
  liberals in, 181
University College Dublin, 55, 224